Compliance & Conviction

Also from Curtis J. Crawford, *Corporate Rise: The X Principles of Extreme Personal Leadership*

Compliance & Conviction

The Evolution of Enlightened Corporate Governance

Curtis J. Crawford, Ph.D.

XCEO, INC., SANTA CLARA, CALIFORNIA

Published by XCEO, Inc.
2901 Tasman Drive, Suite 222
Santa Clara, CA 95054

Publisher's Cataloging-in-Publication Data
Crawford, Curtis J., Ph. D.

Compliance & Conviction : The Evolution of Enlightened Corporate Governance / Curtis J. Crawford. – Santa Clara, CA : XCEO, Inc., 2007.

p. ; cm.
Includes bibliography and index.

ISBN: 0-9769019-1-9
ISBN13: 978-0-9769019-1-4

1. Corporate governance. 2. Directors of corporations. I. Title.

HD2741 .C73 2007
658.4—dc22   2006932653

Project coordination by Jenkins Group, Inc • www.BookPublishing.com
Cover design by Christian Fuenfhausen

Printed in the United States of America
11 10 09 08 07 • 5 4 3 2 1

Dedication

Compliance and Conviction is dedicated to all corporate directors who demonstrate extreme personal leadership in their pursuit of excellence while serving their shareowners. Further, *Compliance and Conviction* is dedicated to all of the industry professionals and corporate leaders who have contributed to my personal development.

Again, Gina, a special thanks!

Acknowledgments

Very special thanks go to the XCEO, Inc. marketing, research and development, and administrative teams. Michelle Ronco, MBA; Fred Dalili, Ed.D., CEO of Productivity Plus; Richard Chen, Ph.D. student at The University of Washington; Nancy Geyer, BA; and Christina M. Pagkalinawan, AA; who keeps the organization on track! Your teamwork and superlative support are both the foundation and the very heart of this book. Thanks for all your hard work, valuable counsel, and personal commitment to excellence at XCEO, Inc.

Your experiences, from publishing our first book, *Corporate Rise: The X Principles of Extreme Personal Leadership*, were fundamental to the success of this project. As individuals, each of us continues to learn, grow and develop. However, as a team we are learning how to flourish at a much higher level.

Our team continues to grow because of your demonstrable passion for excellence and unquenchable thirst for knowledge. Your scholarly interest and personal insight provide me with added inspiration to do what I love to do! Again, thanks for the extreme personal leadership and extraordinary contributions that each of you made to this project. I will continue to be forever grateful to each of you!

Compliance and Conviction is a success because of your continued <u>*extreme personal leadership!*</u>

Michelle, you deserve special attention. *Compliance and Conviction* belongs to you, as much as it belongs to anyone. You have grown immensely throughout this project. You were the publisher, the lead marketer and the lead research and development partner on this project. Thanks for the exceptional job you have done for XCEO, Inc. This project would not have been completed without you. My heartfelt thanks! You have learned a lot and your extreme personal leadership is showing.

Many friends and colleagues contributed to this book by taking time to meet with me and discuss my views of enlightened corporate governance. Others, I have benefited from by mere association. Your collective support has given me the courage and confidence to write this book. Thanks for the wisdom, keen insight, and friendship throughout this entire process. Again, thank you very much for dedicating some of your valuable knowledge and time to the completion of *Compliance and Conviction*. Your continued support is very much appreciated.

Very special thanks go to Chad Holliday, Jr., Chairman of the Board and CEO of DuPont, Sydney Taurel, Chairman of the Board and CEO of Eli Lilly, Roger M. Kenny, Managing Partner of Boardroom Consultants and Anne Fisher, Senior Writer of *Fortune* Magazine. I very much appreciate the personal time each of you invested in reviewing this book. Your thoughtful perspectives will continue to help me improve the overall quality and focus of my work. I know how busy each of you is everyday, thus I am honored that you took personal time to assist me as I wrote this book. It clearly demonstrates how important corporate governance is to each of you.

My heartfelt thanks also go to all of the shareowners, board members, and consultants who shared their perspectives on corporate governance with me.

Once again, a special thanks goes to Judy Hardesty. Judy you are truly one of a kind. I continue to be thankful for your outstanding contributions to my work! As noted before, you are simply the absolute best editor on the planet! Thank you for your excellent support.

Contents

Preface

From the mid-1970s to the present moment, U.S. corporations have struggled to adapt to a globalizing economy, stunning technological improvements, and a reshaping of the corporate environment through mergers and acquisitions, downsizing, and re-engineering. With widespread political reforms afoot, the corporate boards charged with directing and overseeing America's public corporations faced dramatic changes in their functioning, governance processes, and composition. In the midst of this turmoil, the stakeholders of U.S. corporations—shareholders, employees, communities, and government—held corporate CEOs and directors increasingly responsible for corporate failures and successes.

Many traditional boards, filled with executives who served reciprocally on each other's boards, seemed so complacent in their fiduciary oversight of corporations that they were considered mere rubber stamps for the wishes of CEOs. When corporations performed poorly, pension and mutual funds blamed corporate directors for their reluctance to challenge poor management decisions that cost shareholders money. As these funds grew and held ever-larger blocks of shares, they forced corporate boards to hear their complaints and, in many cases, to act on them. Eventually, the business press and government stepped in to help change the way corporations were governed.

As will be discussed throughout *Compliance and Conviction*, the rules and customs by which large U.S. public corporations are organized, financed, and governed have undergone intense scrutiny and changed substantially since the late 1990s. The challenges facing most boards have become ideal launch pads for initiatives of a new, enlightened form of corporate governance in which corporate boards take increasing responsibility for making sure that corporations are accountable to their shareholders, employees, communities, customers, and suppliers.

Compliance and Conviction addresses some of the major issues facing corporate directors during the last 3 decades, a time of significant transition in corporate governance. Reading *Compliance and Conviction* will be useful to anyone who wants an insider view of some of the major issues facing today's corporate boards and directors. Equally important, reading this book will benefit business leaders interested in creating agendas aimed at reforming corporate governance to meet the challenges of the coming era.

Good corporate governance is no accident. It results from careful planning, implementation, coordination, and evaluation. Like any other endeavor, its success depends on extreme personal leadership. When boards leave governance structures to chance or complacently fail to change them, they risk becoming reactive bodies that do little except respond to situations as they arise. Effective governance procedures streamline board structures and eliminate processes that waste time, thus permitting the enlightened board to focus on monitoring trends and planning corporate strategy and executive succession, three activities central to keeping a company nimble in today's ever-changing market.

The corporate failures of the first decade of the 21st century and the repercussions of these failures, including the Sarbanes-Oxley Act of 2002, certainly have intensified focus on corporate governance. Unfortunately, like for most calls to action, fear was the primary driver, and both stakeholders and corporations sought compliance with the new regulations designed to restore confidence to shareholders. Now that the trepidation has subsided and the financial performances of Corporate America again have reached a reasonably steady state of appreciation, corporate stakeholders are likely to turn their attention to other, more pressing, issues.

Many great achievements have flowed from accidental breakthroughs, and many others have been motivated by some kind of fear. Good corporate governance, however, should not be left to chance. Serendipity is a poor surrogate for strategy and never should be considered a foundation for building long-term shareholder value. Nor should corporate governance be driven by fear. In *Compliance and Conviction,* I suggest that corporate boards use enlightened corporate governance as a touchstone for delivering sustainable long-term shareholder value.

Corporate directors must remain vigilant in the pursuit of increasing long-term shareholder value and stakeholder appreciation. As the heightened awareness of, and interest in, the Sarbanes-Oxley Act of 2002 begins to wane, corporate boards must strive to maintain a deliberate focus on compliance and demonstrate a strong conviction for business success. We all have a vested interest in the continued evolution of the governance of the American corporation.

Introduction

If no individual vote matters, why do people do it?

**The path to success lies in overcoming obstacles
that debilitate creativity and conceal opportunities.**

—Curtis J. Crawford, Ph.D.

The disastrous failures of responsibility at Enron, WorldCom, Global Crossing, American Insurance Group, TYCO, Fannie Mae, and a number of other U.S. corporations underscored the need for corporate compliance with the highest regulatory and ethical standards. More far reaching, I believe, was the reminder to corporate directors of the vital importance of acting on the conviction that the whole of society's fabric is strengthened by the long-term success of America's corporations.

A corporate board must keep a firm grip on the tiller of their company's future, and the great task facing today's corporate directors is that of creating agendas for their companies that will stand up to the tests of the coming era. This book, I hope, will help directors meet this

1

challenge by offering some desperately needed insight into the governance systems of publicly owned U.S. corporations. This subject now is understood only by a relative few, but it profoundly impacts the daily fortunes of just about every American.

Corporate governance, the unwieldy name given to the systems that guide the control and management of corporations, is a relatively recent term that came into being in the 1970s. Because corporate governance structures and processes specify the various roles and duties of corporate directors, senior executives, shareholders, and other stakeholders in the corporation, they play a large role in determining how responsible and accountable a corporation's leaders will be in exercising their authority. When properly designed, governance processes guide companies toward useful objectives and help them monitor and measure their progress in achieving those objectives; when poorly designed, these processes permit companies to drift toward painful losses for shareholders and everyone else with a stake in the company.

A company's corporate governance—whether good or bad—is established by its board of directors. Ideally, these directors will be energetic, experienced people deeply concerned about the company's welfare. Because the board's most pivotal responsibilities are to *hire* and *supervise* the company's chief executive officer (CEO), these directors should *not* be company employees who work under the CEO's direction; instead, they should be independent of the company's management. When *independent directors* know how to work effectively with the company's senior management team, they are likely to produce a corporate climate that accelerates the growth of long-term shareholder value. This is what I call *enlightened corporate governance*, and its cornerstone is what I call *extreme personal leadership,* which was the topic of my book, *Corporate Rise: The X Principles of Extreme Personal Leadership.*

As I detailed in that book, *X-Leaders* have high aspirations and very positive attitudes about their futures. They are highly motivated and academically well prepared. They believe in creating their own opportunities rather than waiting in line for the next big break. They inspire creativity and ever-higher levels of performance. They are responsible and accountable, and they expect to deliver outstanding results. They want to win with a passion.

In every corporation, extreme personal leadership should be omnipresent in the board of directors, which, after all, is (or should be) the company's topmost center of power. X-Leadership always generates a strong force of energy, but when it exists at the top of a company its positive effects are felt throughout the entire leadership team and flow through the entire company. One of the chief ways directors who are X-Leaders lead their companies to greatness is by identifying, selecting, and nurturing highly qualified company leaders. In fulfilling this responsibility, they consider anything less than the pursuit of excellence as unacceptable.

Because most of the people hurt by corporate disasters have limited knowledge of how corporations are governed, would like to know how their investments were lost, and want to protect their future investments, corporate governance has become a hot topic. The public's interest in keeping top corporate leaders honest may be at an all-time high, but their concerns certainly are not new. The corporate world never has been completely free of questionable leadership and greed for excessive compensation and lavish perks, examples of which have made headlines for many, many years. Sadly, despite widespread awareness of such problems, during our most prosperous times even the people most knowledgeable about the potential damage that can be done by poor leadership have accepted it as a marginal risk.

Although I am greatly disappointed by the scandalous behavior of some business leaders, I cannot claim to be entirely surprised by it. Like the rest of society, the corporate world has its own distribution of immoral and dishonest people. Yet, I do believe that, overall, the leadership of Corporate America is rock solid and in the hands of very qualified and dedicated men and women, people who are committed to maximizing the returns for their shareholders and working for the betterment of all their stakeholders.

For the past 200 years, U.S. corporations have been serving their shareholders effectively in many respects. Although the value generated for shareholders has not been shared equally among all investors, most investors have been quite pleased with their returns as measured against other investment opportunities, a fact made quite evident by the billions of dollars aggressively invested over the past 3 decades. For example, the NASDAQ Stock Market, which became synonymous with the technology sector during the 1990's high-tech boom, has approximately 3,300 listed companies. During the 1970s, the index performance of the NASDAQ grew from 100 to 151.14. The following decade, the index grew to 454.80, and, during the 1990s, it continued to accelerate. Even as all major stock indices sharply declined during the final years of the 20th century, the NASDAQ managed to finish the year 2000 at 2470.52. By the end of 2005, the NASDAQ index closed at 2205.32. These consistently significant long-term gains demonstrated substantial investor achievement.[1] Clearly, most corporations have generated tremendous returns for their investors and have substantially improved the quality of life for people around the world.

In general, then, Corporate America continues to be quite healthy! The fact is that most corporations have accomplished their results by being good corporate citizens. Not surprisingly, most examples of great leadership by directors and corporate management, no matter how appreciated by shareholders, go unnoticed by the general public. Although examples of the positive often are not presented in the media, my experience has been that good leaders disproportionately outnumber the bad ones.

Americans are not plagued by weak leadership at the top of most of our companies, but we do have some serious problems that are being addressed in earnest. What most deeply disturbs the majority of investors is an apparent increase of blatant corporate dishonesty and calculated fraud. Investors *do not* understand why a corporate leader who is doing a poor job gets paid a king's ransom, and they certainly *do not* excuse dishonesty, deceit, or unethical practices cooked up to mislead them. Although only a small number of business leaders have been convicted of illegal business practices, the whole of Corporate America has been blemished by the splatter, and U.S. corporations must work hard to regain their stakeholders' respect and confidence. I am confident that the strength of U.S. corporate leadership will succeed in weeding out most of the obvious bad seeds.

Corporate governance is a fundamental driver of shareholder value, and it is built on personal leadership. The key to outstanding corporate governance is extreme personal leadership in the boardroom. As indicated in figures I.1 through I.4, there are several examples of how leadership is deployed in the boardroom. In this book, I discuss some of the most significant

Chairman of the Board & CEO (Publicly Traded Company)

COMPANY A

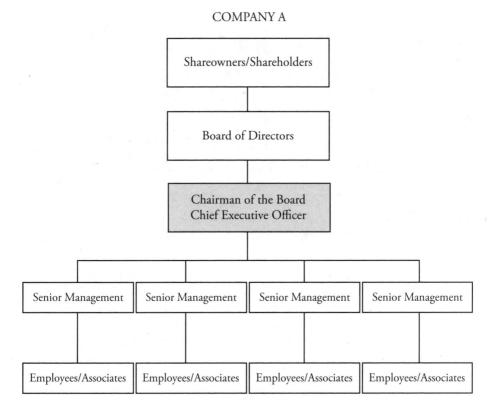

Figure I.1

Non-Executive Chairman (Publicly Traded Company)

COMPANY B

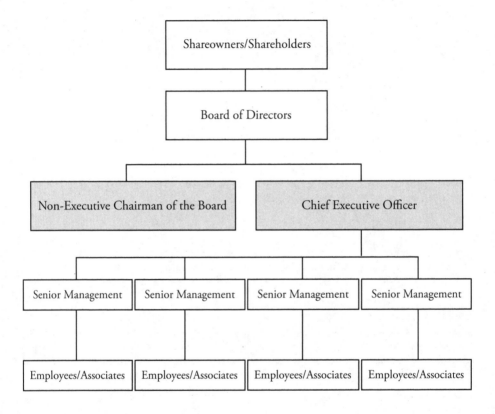

Figure I.2

Executive Chairman (Publicly Traded Company)

COMPANY C

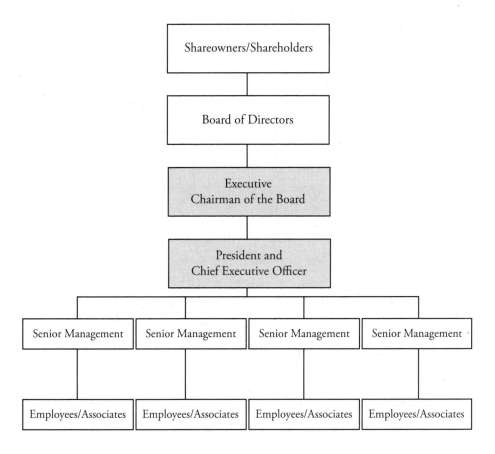

Figure I.3

Non-Executive Chairman (Majority Owned Company)

COMPANY D

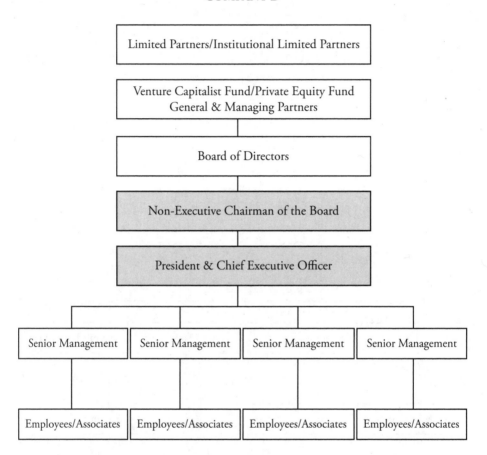

Figure I.4

issues corporate boards and individual directors are facing today. Chapter 1 explains how corporate governance in the United States has changed over the years and what brought it to the attention of American investors. Chapter 2 provides an overview of the formative issues that shaped today's corporate governance, with special focus on how the 1980's hostile-take-over era changed investors' views of the role of corporate management. In this chapter, the basic principles of contemporary corporate governance are examined. Chapter 3 presents a look at the strong effects on overall company value of the board's hiring, nurturance, and supervision of the CEO.

In Chapter 4, the concerns of a fully engaged and committed corporate board are outlined. These concerns include corporate strategy planning, CEO succession planning, CEO supervision, executive compensation, director independence, and board composition. In chapters 5 through 10, each of these issues is examined in detail.

Chapter 11 is an examination of three categories of boards, the traditional board of the recent past, the standard board of today, and the enlightened board at the cutting edge of corporate success. Chapter 12 is designed to help boards and individual directors evaluate their performances. To help boards focus on activities that lead to long-term shareholder value and to help committed directors do their best work, two new self-evaluation tools are available, the *Enlightened Corporate Governance Profile®* and the *Enlightened Individual Director Performance Profile®*. Both of these tools, which were developed by my team at XCEO, Inc., are modeled on enlightened corporate governance principles discussed throughout this book.

Chapter 13 presents the candid opinions of a diverse group of CEO's, corporate directors, and corporate governance experts about what works and what doesn't work in today's boardrooms. In interviews, this group revealed real-world boardroom responses to the pressures placed on them by large pension funds and other institutional shareholders. The beliefs of this group of mostly CEO's and directors are examined briefly in the larger context of the global corporate environment.

Finally, in Chapter 14, corporate governance is discussed as a work in progress. Good corporate governance inspires faith in our marketplace and earns premiums from investors because it focuses companies on solid efforts to gain long-term shareholder value. More work needs to be done to protect shareholders and companies, however, and the main patterns of future reform are outlined, together with some observations of the future of corporate governance in response to the Sarbanes-Oxley Act of 2002.

Notes

[1] Historical Prices for NASDAQ Composite. *Yahoo! Finance.* Retrieved September 26, 2006, from http://finance.yahoo.com/q/hp?s=%5EIXIC&a=01&b=5&c=1971&d=11&e=31&f=2005&g=d.

Chapter One

The Rise of U.S. Corporate Governance Reform

Why should you drive 65 miles per hour when everyone else is?

To understand the ongoing evolution of enlightened corporate governance, it is necessary to understand some of the history of corporations and the events that led to stakeholder activism.

A central tenet of the Western concept of ownership holds that those who own a property are motivated to manage it in a manner compatible with the interests of the larger society. Although the corporation was built on this concept, the development of corporations created a new set of challenges for the larger society.[i] Originally, corporate organization meant that the rules governing the way property was held transcended royal power. Corporate power was limited, but it countered what had been the unlimited authority of the king. By owning shares in corporations, people gained wealth that was not automatically available to the ruler. Although corporate power initially threatened government power, the corporate form of ownership eventually became an ally of government. The independence of the corporation made government authority more acceptable and ultimately, for protection of private property, more necessary. The Sarbanes-Oxley Act of 2002, which will be discussed at some length in this book, further personified this fundamental concept.

The struggle to hold private property without interference from the state was a theme of the Enlightenment, a European intellectual movement of the late 17th and 18th centuries emphasizing reason and individualism in contrast to tradition. This theme was written into the Declaration of Independence as "the pursuit of happiness," and guaranteed in the Constitutional protections of "life, liberty, and property" for citizens of the new nation.[ii] Over time, Constitutional protections such as freedom of speech and the right to due process were extended to corporations, which were legally viewed as persons, thus providing corporations with some of the same rights as citizens.

The first corporations to operate in the American colonies were two joint stock companies, the West Virginia Company of London and the Virginia Company of Plymouth (later the Massachusetts Bay Company), both of which operated under royal charter by the King of England. Two bodies governed these companies. The first was a local council of colonists who managed day-to-day operations, and the second was a supervisory board in London, answerable to the sovereign, that dealt with matters of policy and strategy.[iii] In today's parlance, these two governing bodies were none other than inside and outside directors.

After the American Revolution, the first U.S. Secretary of the Treasury, Alexander Hamilton, created the Society for Establishing Useful Manufactures. Hamilton's prospectus provided for a board of 13 directors and an early version of the audit committee called the Committee of Inspectors.[iv] Hamilton probably would have no trouble recognizing today's board of directors, which typically has between 9 and 13 members, down from a larger size of 11 to 15 members during the 1980s. From Hamilton's time until the present, the primary role of the board of directors has been monitoring management on behalf of shareholders. As in Hamilton's time and before, today's board of directors exists to oversee management and select company executives. Today, however, providing effective governance over company operations requires considerably more time than it did in Hamilton's day.

In theory and in law, company management serves at the pleasure of the board. In practice, however, directors traditionally have been nominated, compensated, and informed by company management. Today it requires significantly more time and effort to provide effective governance over company operations.

As corporations gained the rights of citizens, owners of corporations enjoyed their rights as individual shareholders as well as the benefits of the rights extended to their corporations. Unlike owners who enter into partnerships, the corporate shareholder's liability is limited to the amount of his or her investment, which makes it possible for corporations to take substantial risks and incur substantial liabilities without endangering the personal resources of their owners. Limited liability, however, does not mean that the risks of investment disappear. Business failures affect shareholders, employees, the community, and the government.[v] When corporate power is not used in the best interests of society, the true costs of criminality or failure generally are not borne by the perpetrators.

Kenneth N. Dayton, former chairman of Dayton Hudson Company (now the retailer Target), placed the blame for poor corporate governance squarely on the corporate board:

> My conviction is that the board of directors is the Achilles' heel of the American corporation . . . . [E]very time you find a business in trouble, you find a board of directors either unwilling or unable to fulfill its responsibilities.[vi]

In most cases, the failures of corporations to act responsibly can be traced to board membership and board composition. Today, under increasingly heavy public scrutiny, many boards are working to reconstruct themselves to overcome decades of apathy and inertia that were standard operating procedures during the 1940s, 1950s, and 1960s, when a company's directors held their seats at the discretion of the CEO and most boards consisted almost entirely of current and former CEO's selected from a relatively closed network. The typical American board of the mid-20th century was filled with CEO's who served reciprocally on each other's executive compensation committees and thus, not surprisingly, were less than eager to rock any boats. Moreover, because directors usually sat on several boards, most had little time to devote to any one of them.

Although a corporate board's chief responsibility always has been to oversee the profitability, management, and dispensation of shareholders' property, in reality, many boards were not actively engaged in executing these fiduciary responsibilities, as pointed out in 1997 by John A. Byrne, Executive Editor of *Business Week Magazine*:

> The corporate board long has borne the primary responsibility for corporate governance. Nevertheless, until quite recently serving on a corporate board was considered a none-too-stressful honor that required attending board meetings at which reports were heard, resolutions were approved, and a nice lunch was served.[vii]

This problem obviously has not been fully solved. In general, corporate boards were not highly motivated from within, and, unlike today, they certainly were not highly motivated from without; the fundamentals of corporation law had seemed settled, at least in practice, since the Great Depression, along with most of the other legal, cultural, and institutional arrangements that determined how corporations were controlled and how they related to their shareholders, customers, employees, suppliers, creditors, and the communities in which they operated.[viii] However, beginning in the mid-1970s, domestic and global changes began to spur investors, the media, and academicians to scrutinize how corporations were being governed.

The first of these developments was the failure of many U.S. companies to hold their own against foreign competitors in the manufacture of autos, consumer electronics, machine tools, semiconductors, computers, copiers, steel, and textiles.[ix,x] The growth of U.S. productivity lagged behind that of other countries and, in the mid-1970s, wages and living standards for most working people in the United States virtually stopped growing. Many accused U.S. corporations of abandoning markets to their Japanese, German, and

U.K. rivals rather than committing themselves to compete more efficiently and effectively for market share,[xi] but some scholars and policy-makers began asking whether these outcomes were a consequence, at least in part, of the way corporations were owned and controlled, and how they were influenced by financial markets.[xii,xiii,xiv,xv,xvi]

In the 1970s, the typical CEO of a U.S. corporation held almost exclusive power over that company by controlling corporate operations as the chief executive and also chairing the board of directors, in effect leading his (or, rarely, her) in-name-only supervisors. When more than 400 top companies were accused of illegalities, particularly bribery,[xvii] investors and scholars asked why their boards had failed to prevent these illegalities. Many of the concerned parties, including the U.S. Securities and Exchange Commission (SEC), began to call for the presence of more outside directors on boards, even though many of the transgressor companies had boards dominated by outsiders.[xviii]

By the early 1980s, massive layoffs in smaller companies and rust-belt industries began working their way through almost every sector of the economy. During the 13 years between the start of 1980 and the end of 1993, more than a million jobs were lost at just nine of the nation's largest corporations: Exxon, Ford, GE, GM, IBM, Mobil, Sears, USX, and Westinghouse.[ixx] The ability of U.S. corporations to maintain workers' standards of living seemed doubtful.

U.S. companies fell behind their Japanese and German counterparts in the introduction of new products and pursuit of new markets, and they also lagged worryingly behind corporations in other industrialized nations in rates of investment in plants, equipment, and research and development. For example, from 1976 to 1987, Japan invested twice as much of its gross national product into machinery and equipment than did the United States (14.9-20.6% of Japanese GNP compared to 7.5-9% of U.S. GNP, according to the National Science Foundation and the Council on Competitiveness).[xx] Corporations in other nations were increasingly competitive by other measures as well, such as output per worker hour, which grew more than twice as fast in Japan as in the U.S. between 1973 and 1989.[xxi]

In this climate of sharply increased competition from Japanese, German, and U.K. corporations, the United States' post-war dominance of the global economy ended. The growth of multinational and transnational corporations was accelerating, accompanied by an international movement toward free trade unhindered by protective regulations or tariffs. Significant improvements in telecommunications technologies also were driving the world's regional economies into one big global economy, and pundits correctly forecasted that the Internet, often called the *information superhighway*, would radically change the ways in which commerce would be conducted in the 21st century. Geopolitical transformations were creating major new markets and bold, imaginative, new competitors like Sun Microsystems, Qualcomm, and Oracle. In the United States, the crossover from the Industrial Age to the new Information Age would dominate the last quarter of the 20th century and was to be extremely painful for many Americans.

In ongoing public-policy debates over the ability of U.S. firms to provide a growing standard of living for U.S. citizens and to compete effectively in international markets,[xxii] corporate governance issues were scrutinized. Throughout the 1980s, the pages of the business press were dominated by examinations of corporate governance issues, particularly the power and responsibilities of corporate boards, the role and influence of institutional investors who controlled large consolidated blocks of shares, the rules governing corporate takeovers, and the compensation packages of CEO's.[xxiii,xxiv,xxv,xxvi]

Political reforms accelerated by strong economic growth in China, Brazil, and India opened new markets and powered new competitors. During this time of exceptional market growth and retraction, an unending procession of large and small mergers, acquisitions, and restructurings reshaped the global corporate environment. The evolution of AT&T during this period provides one example of the convoluted change being experienced by many corporations. In 1984, AT&T was ordered to divest itself of its local telephone service operations, and its progeny included seven regional corporations called Baby Bells. In the early 1990s, as most boats were rising with the robust U.S. economy, AT&T acquired McCaw Cellular Communications and NCR Corporation. In 2005, the tables of AT&T's good fortune turned, and it was acquired by SBC Corporation, one of its seven Baby Bells. Almost in parallel, another of AT&T's progeny, Verizon Communications, acquired MCI, a remnant of bankrupt WorldCom that had for 3 decades been AT&T's number one nemesis.

Throughout the 1980s, Corporate America was pounded by wave upon wave of hostile takeovers and leveraged buyouts. Hostile takeovers had first become common in the 1960s, when they often were regarded as instruments for sharpening or replacing ineffective management. Advocates of hostile takeovers, such as Michael Jensen of the Harvard Business School, argued that hostile takeovers were the means by which financial markets disciplined lazy or unsuccessful corporate leadership.[xxvii] In the late 1970s and early 1980s, however, hostile takeovers were focused mainly on empire building;[xxviii] the hostile takeover targets often were as well managed as their unwelcome suitors. Critics of hostile takeovers, such as the California Public Employees' Retirement System, the giant pension fund known as CalPERS, insisted that hostile takeovers provided evidence that short-term pressures by financial markets were making corporate executives afraid to maximize long-term performance at the cost of short-term returns.[xxix] For both sides of the argument, it was clear, poor corporate management was at the heart of the hostile takeover trend.

Corporate managers quickly developed numerous defenses against hostile takeovers, but these defenses raised many legal and policy questions concerning their appropriateness, the rights of shareholders, and the roles and responsibilities of directors. Hostile takeovers and leveraged buyouts became less frequent after 1989, but another serious wave of them hit in 1993 and 1994.[xxx] In the face of not only another wave of hostile takeovers but also a series of widely publicized corporate excesses, investors and governmental agencies finally began to articulate serious questions about board leadership and duties.

In 1990, however, surveyed members of the Industrial Research Institute did not blame boards for the deterioration of U.S. competitiveness in technology; they were placing blame on the "short-term horizons" of U.S. corporate management.[xxxi] Nearly all of 2000 surveyed members of the Financial Executives Institute attributed the nation's lost competitiveness in technology to high cost of capital, poor or misleading internal measurements systems, compensation systems that provided the wrong incentives, and financial market pressures that compelled corporate executives to focus on the next quarter's earnings at the expense of long-term performance.[xxxii]

Amid all the turmoil of the 1980s and 1990s, CEO compensation packages skyrocketed. In the 10 years between 1983 and 1993, a decade in which real-term median compensation for nearly all categories of workers and professionals remained, at best, flat, median annual pay for CEO's grew 70%, from $1.06 million to $1.82 million (calculated in 1993 dollars), according to annual surveys conducted by *Business Week*.[xxxiii,xxxiv,xxxv,xxxvi] In 1992, the board of HCA-Hospital Corp. of America awarded a compensation package worth a stunning $125 million to the company's CEO, Thomas F. Frist, Jr.[xxxvii] Public outrage was not assuaged by the fact that the largest pay packages were rewarding executives who presided over firms that were slashing payrolls, laying off unprecedented numbers of workers, and slipping badly in their returns to investors.[xxxviii]

Inside most boardrooms, directors were unfazed by shareholders' concerns about excessive executive pay. Between 1995 and 1996, according to *Business Week*, the median pay package for the top CEO's gained 39%, settling at $2.3 million.[xxxix] Between 2003 and 2004, compensation for a typical CEO of one of the largest U.S. companies rose 30.2% to $5.7 million, and, astoundingly, the average CEO at a company in the Standard & Poor's 500 index received more than twice that, $11.71 million.[xl] CEO pay packages of $10 million per year had become almost commonplace.

Lavish executive compensation packages combined with poor returns on investments, lagging profits, employee layoffs, and instances of fraudulent behavior—all were prompting shareholders to ask, "Where was the Board?"[xli, xlii] Throughout the 1980s, some boards succeeded in quietly steering toward more active monitoring of corporate affairs. By 1990, Compaq Computer's board members, chaired by Ben Rosen, who was not a Compaq executive but a venture capitalist with a significant stake in the company, were ready to conduct an historic assertion of power. After the company's first-ever quarterly loss and the subsequent plummeting of its stock price, the board took issue with the strategy of Rod Canion, Compaq's founder and CEO, and forced him to resign. Compaq's earnings increased rapidly and its stock price doubled in just one year.[xliii] (The independence of Compaq's board ended when Hewlett-Packard Corporation acquired Compaq in 2002.) Canion was one of the first CEO's to be displaced in the trend toward greater director independence, but many more were to follow. In 1993, called the "Year of the Sharp Knives," the CEO's of IBM, GM, American Express, Kodak, Westinghouse, Apple Computer, and other blue-chip corporations were pushed out.[xliv] Others were to follow.

Prodding boards toward increased director independence were the large pension funds that increasingly viewed active monitoring of corporate governance as a prudent exercise of their right to promote increases in the values of the shares they owned.[xlv] Their power to do so was new. In 1950, institutional investors held only 6% of publicly traded U.S. equities; during the 1980s, that figure rose to 50%.[xlvi,xlvii] But something else was happening as well: large pension funds were losing their ability to vote with their feet. As large institutional investors grew even larger, their holdings became so enormous that it was unrealistic for them to unload their shares in a major corporation;[xlviii] selling one block of shares lowered the price of the following block, and so on, eventually creating a financial crisis. The more money an institutional investor had invested in a company, the more difficult it was for the investor to unload that company's shares, and the more necessary it became for the investor to take an active role in the way that company was managed.[xlix] As the flexibility of institutional investors diminished, they needed to exert greater pressure on corporate boards to protect the value of their holdings.

Institutional investors had at hand important tools for promoting good corporate governance: the *proxy vote*, by which stockholders not present at a stockholder's meeting can authorize another party to cast their votes, and the *shareholder proposal*. The way had been paved by two well-informed activist shareholders of a previous generation. In 1932, Lewis Gilbert attended a meeting of Consolidated Gas and left unhappy that the chair would not take questions from the floor. In retaliation, he and his brother began buying stock in the company and attending meetings. Ultimately Gilbert's actions resulted in a 1942 ruling by the U.S. Securities and Exchange Commission that shareholders had the right to have their proposals included in company proxy statements.[1] This ruling opened the way for numerous shareholder resolutions on executive compensation, cumulative voting, and annual meeting location.

One of the first institutional investors to push for better share performance was LENS Inc., a Washington, D.C. investment fund. In 1992, Robert Monks, a principal of LENS, submitted an Exxon shareholder proposal to create a shareholder advisory committee comprised and elected by shareholders and funded by Exxon.[li] The following year, the Teachers Insurance and Annuity Association-College Retirement Equities Fund (TIAA-CREF), broke ground by issuing their all-inclusive *Policy Statement on Corporate Governance* to "encourage portfolio companies to improve their governance policies and practices so as to produce better long-term returns and enhanced accountability to shareholders."[lii] CalPERS, the California pension fund, set the terms of the debate by establishing a high-level commission to consider corporate governance reforms and numerous new laws.[liii,liv,lv,lvi]

More and more, as part of their efforts to evaluate how well corporate leaders were doing their jobs, institutional investors scrutinized the systems by which boards directed and controlled their corporations. Dozens of new journals and newsletters reported on developments in corporate governance, including *Directorship*, *Directors and Boards*, *Corporate Board Member*, *The Corporate Board*, and *Leader to Leader*. America's largest investment funds and money managers were rating corporations according to the independence and responsibility shown by their boards. The popular magazine *Business Week* began asking their annual survey respondents to rate the boards of U.S. corporations according to their delivery of corporate results to shareholders; in 1996, the highest ratings for superior board performance went the boards of Campbell Soup, General Electric, Compaq Computer, Microsoft, and IBM.[lvii]

Starting in the 1990s, when a corporation's stakeholder community believed that the rules no longer represented their best interests or that an exception was warranted, they often attempted to get the rules changed. Such was the case for shareholders in General Motors in 1997, when John G. Smale announced his intention to stand for re-election to GM's board, despite the fact that at the time of the election (May of 1998) he would be past the board's required retirement age of 70 years. Smale was a force to be reckoned with. Five years earlier, he had led a 1992 General Motors board coup that ousted GM's CEO and chairman, Robert Stemple. Smale went on to help overhaul the way American corporate boards operate, and his work and example emboldened other directors to take charge when management teams were steering their companies into trouble. Soon, directors were asserting their authority over blue-chip corporations such as Eastman Kodak, International Business Machines, Apple Computer,[lviii] and, later, over Hewlett Packard, Lucent Technologies, and Merck. Ira Millstein, the attorney who had represented GM's outside directors during the board coup argued that, "No rule was meant to be unyielding."[lix] GM's board agreed and waived the retirement requirement,[lx] allowing Smale to continue until May of 2000, when he finally retired from the board.

Institutional investors went on to use the power of the proxy vote against lavish CEO pay, anti-takeover measures (such as golden parachutes) and staggered boards, in support of succession planning. More and more, institutional shareholders held directors accountable for corporate performance, usually measured by increasing stock price. The power of institutional investors was growing. By 1996, institutional investors held as much as 85% of some publicly traded companies, notably Coca Cola, as estimated by Richard Koppes of the pension fund, CalPERS.[lxi]

Social activists were pressuring U.S. corporations to look beyond profit-making toward fulfilling social roles not related to corporate profit-making, although these activists did not yet seriously question, as institutional shareholders had done, the soundness of the fundamental rules and customs governing U.S. corporations. In the vigorous debate about the social responsibilities of business, Nobel laureate in economics Milton Friedman argued that, in a free society:

There is one and only one social responsibility of a business: to use its resources and engage in activities designed to increase its profits so long as it stays within the rules of the game, which is to say, engages in open and free competition without deception or fraud.[lxii]

Social activists countered that corporate social responsibility extended far beyond a company's financial performance to encompass causes considered equally important by environmentalists, human rights activists, and labor unions. Although some social problems, like those associated with job security and health care, had long been woven into the traditional business fabric, other problems, like those associated with day care provision and sexual harassment,[lxiii] seemed almost independent of business as it was traditionally defined.[lxiv] For corporations, dealing with some of these social problems often proved even more perplexing than managing business growth. In the face of great health concerns associated with the Dalkon Shield intrauterine device, its manufacturer A. H. Robins was ordered to set aside $2.4 billion to compensate those who were injured by that product; later, A. H. Robins agreed to pay nearly $17 million to its shareholders.[lxv] Eventually, the company was forced into bankruptcy by 14,000 product liability suits. Johns Manville Corporation, manufacturer of asbestos products, also took flight in a Chapter 11 bankruptcy.

In the last years of the 20th century, corporations still were coming to terms with increasingly familiar demands that board composition reflect the cultural diversity existing among consumers and workers. In 1996, few of the nation's largest companies gave more than nominal representation to women in their boards and senior management teams,[lxvi] a situation that caused John Hamill, then president of Fleet Financial Group, to comment, "As the workplace becomes more diverse, particularly as more women advance to higher and higher levels in their organizations, there is a need for different role models and people with different backgrounds in the corporate governance structure."[lxvii] In 1999, Linda Tarr-Whelan, President and CEO of the Center for Policy Alternatives observed:

> The increasing proportion of consumer dollars spent by African-Americans and Hispanics is a powerful, potential driver that I do not think is being used—at least it does not look like it when I look at the statistics of who is in the boardroom.[lxviii]

As the 21st century loomed on the horizon, U.S. corporations faced continuing dramatic change. Directors were finding it more and more difficult to ignore the public fears of consumer advocates, labor leaders, scholars, environmentalists, and policymakers that corporations in some industries were banding together to form oligopolies to control most of their market. [lxix,lxx] Corporate downsizing and restructuring were by now routinely accepted business strategies, and the latest trend was toward colossal business mergers such as the 1998 merger of Citicorp (banking) and Travelers Property Casualty Corp. (insurance underwriting) into the most profitable financial services firm in the U.S. and reportedly the biggest company in the world, with 300,000 employees and over 200 million customer accounts in more than 100 countries.[lxxi] By the dawn of the 21st century, colossal mergers were regularly reshaping the corporate landscape and influencing global economies. Strategic acquisitions became more creative; for example, in 2001, AOL acquired Time Warner through an unusual merger structure in which each of the two original companies merged into a newly created entity.[lxxii]

In 2002, nearly a quarter century of active pursuit of corporate reform took root in public policy with the passage of the Sarbanes-Oxley Act and the establishment of President Bush's Corporate Fraud Task Force. SOX, as the Sarbanes-Oxley Act often is called, changed federal securities law by requiring all publicly traded U.S. companies (and non-U.S. companies with a U.S. presence) to increase their financial disclosure by submitting to the U.S. Securities and Exchange Commission an annual report of the effectiveness of their internal accounting controls. The Corporate Fraud Task Force brought together the Department of Justice and eight U.S. federal agencies to help restore, in the words of former Deputy Attorney General Thompson, "the integrity of the market and the confidence of the nation" by establishing "with ever-increasing certainty the prospect that corporate criminals will lose both their fortunes and their liberty."[lxxiii] In the first two years following the formation of the Task Force, the Department of Justice charged more than 700 individuals and convicted or obtained guilty pleas from more than 300.[lxxiv]

Among the corporate leaders who faced legal action was Frank Quattrone, the former investment banking star of Credit Suisse First Boston, who was found guilty of endorsing a suggestion to "clean out" files to avoid litigation and then was ordered to serve 18 months in prison plus 2 years' probation and also was fined $90,000.[lxxv] On March 20, 2006 Frank Quattrone was granted a new trial when the 2nd U.S. Circuit Court of Appeals in Manhattan said that the evidence was sufficient to sustain a conviction but that the May 2004 verdict must be thrown out because the jury was improperly instructed on how to interpret the law. On June 2, 2006, the securities industry regulators dropped all charges against Quattrone. John Rigas, founder of cable giant Adelphia Communications Corp., was sentenced to 15 years in prison for concealing $2.3 billion of company debt;[lxxvi] his son, Timothy, was sentenced to 20 years.[lxxvii]

Both L. Dennis Kozlowski, former chairman and CEO of TYCO International Corporation, and Mark Swartz, Tyco's former chief financial officer (CFO), were convicted of stealing $600 million from their company and then sentenced to up to 25 years.[lxxviii] Kozlowski also paid $21.2 million to settle charges of avoiding millions of dollars of New York sales tax.[lxxix] Bernard J. Ebbers, once the chairman and CEO of WorldCom (formerly MCI, now Verizon), was sentenced to 25 years in prison for masterminding an $11 billion accounting fraud—the largest accounting fraud in U.S. history that also led to the largest (at that time) bankruptcy in U.S. history—and then lying about it to securities regulators.[lxxx,lxxxi,lxxxii] Scott Sullivan, Worldcom's former CFO, was sentenced to 5 years in prison—despite being the government's star witness against his former boss.[lxxxiii] Sanjay Kumar, chairman and CEO of the software maker, Computer Associates International, Inc., pled guilty to securities fraud and obstruction of justice for manipulating over $2 billion in revenue to prop up his company's stock price.[lxxxiv] Xerox, HealthSouth Corp., Qwest Communications International, and Cendant also faced accounting fraud charges.

After 5 years of effort, the U.S. government's Enron task force won guilty verdicts for Enron's founder, former chairman and CEO, Kenneth Lay, and former CEO, Jeffrey Skilling, the two men considered most responsible for "the most infamous business collapse in corporate history." The central allegations were that the pair hid company debt, inflated profits, and sold stock in a process that defrauded Enron's investors, employees, and a bank that accepted Enron stock as collateral.[lxxxv] Lay, who together with Skilling faced 25 to 40 years behind bars, died suddenly some months before his sentencing date in the summer of 2006.[lxxxvi] Enron's former CFO, Andrew Fastow, pled guilty to two criminal charges and agreed to serve a 10-year sentence, pay more than $27 million, and cooperate with the government's investigation.[lxxxvii,lxxxviii] His wife, Lea Fastow, former assistant treasurer of the company, served 11 months in a federal detention center for helping her husband hide money allegedly ill-gotten from Enron. [lxxxix,xc,xci]

At this writing in October of 2006, other corporate scandals are making headlines. Fannie Mae, the giant mortgage purchaser, recently agreed to pay more than $400 million as part of a settlement with federal agencies against a variety of claims. One of these was that Franklin D. Raines and James A. Johnson, both former Fannie Mae chairmen/CEO's, manipulated earnings so that they could receive bigger bonuses. Another was that Fannie Mae's management repeatedly presented directors with incomplete and sometimes misleading information.[xcii]

As the federal government went after corporate executives for illegal activities, the AFL-CIO, with nearly $400 billion of pension funds investments, determined to remove directors sitting on the compensation committees of certain targeted companies that included American Airlines, Cisco Systems, and Apple Computer.[xciii] "Directors," said Brandon Rees, a research analyst in the AFL-CIO's Office of Investment, "need to be held accountable for their judgment when they approve paying excessive amounts of shareholders' money to executives."[xciv]

Corporate scandals and rising CEO pay have dimmed many investors' hopes that decades of activism have really improved corporate governance. However, painful lessons have been learned. Corporations with apathetic boards have suffered through the learning process, but enlightened boards with high expectations have managed to reform their governance into competitive assets and are leading the way for Corporate America in the 21st century.

Who Is Most Affected by Corporate Leadership?

Corporate decisions affect people's pocketbooks, political situations, and commercial interests. Good decisions by a huge corporation lead to prosperity for the company's many stakeholders and exert enormous positive impacts across society. Bad decisions by a major company, however, cause major disruptions for all of the company's stakeholders. The Enron disaster, as one example, certainly had devastating impacts on the lives of most of Enron employees (including the middle managers and professionals who invested in the company-sponsored Enron 401[k] plans) and also caused suffering for many individual investors who purchased Enron stock on the open market. Thousands of other Enron stakeholders, including Enron's suppliers and customers, also suffered.[xcv]

So did Enron's physical community. In Enron's hometown, Houston, property values tumbled.[xcvi] Occupancy in downtown buildings dropped by 20%, and Enron's own buildings sold for 60 cents on the dollar. Opportunities for employment and promotion in Houston evaporated. Just when lengthening unemployment lines signaled that many Houston residents needed help,[xcvii] their city's charities lost not only the millions of dollars that formerly had been provided by its generous corporate citizen but also the combined giving of the thousands of Enron workers who had been laid off.[xcviii]

Corporate stakeholders who feel the financial impacts of decisions made in boardrooms can be viewed as belonging to the following four distinct groups, each having different degrees of interest and knowledge about corporate governance issues.

#1: Institutional shareholders and day traders. These savvy professional investors in financial markets have enormous financial stakes in the companies in which they invest, and they are likely to keep well informed about those companies and become deeply involved in their corporate governance.

#2: Individual investors and holders of 401[k] retirements. Investors who purchase stocks and bonds in the open market or through some structured investment relationship with a brokerage firm usually are well informed about the direction and management of the companies in which they hold shares, but generally they are only marginally involved in those activities. Like one accountant whose decision to purchase Enron stock was strongly influenced by Ken Lay's upbeat comments about Enron, many members of this group of investors succumbed to encouragement to purchase shares

in companies so poorly governed that some company leaders were able to engage in massive fraud.

#3: Mutual fund investors. Although many investors in mutual funds tie up much of their total net worth in 401[k] retirement plans, they generally are only marginally informed about their investments. This group includes people like the laid-off Enron administrative assistant who bounced from job to job for 4 years before landing a secretarial position with no health or retirement benefits, the former Enron employee who lost $50,000 of annual salary and almost lost her home as a result, the former Enron mechanic whose 2 years of unemployment wiped out his savings, and the worker at Enron's Duncan, Oklahoma facility whose monthly income dropped from $3,000 to zero and whose $50,000 401[k] account became worthless.[xcix,c]

#4: Non-investors. People with no 401[k] plan or other type of savings plan and very little time, interest, or capacity to invest in stocks and bonds generally have little interest in how corporations are run. Although people in this group have the least knowledge about corporate governance (and the least belief that they can influence corporate decisions), they have the greatest exposure to the effects of ineffective or irresponsible corporate governance because they are likely to suffer most profoundly during a faltering economy. Slowdowns in capital investing, employment, and housing construction more severely punish those with the fewest financial resources to help them function during—and recover from—an economic downturn.

After several years of careful consideration and introspection, I have concluded that the people who have the greatest capacity to invest also carry the least relative financial risk. Their lowered risk protects them from personal exposure to the effects of poor corporate governance. This seemingly counterintuitive conclusion is quite logical. Affluent, well-informed investors have much greater capacity to absorb the short-term impacts of a financial loss and have the greatest chance of bouncing back from a bleak economic situation. Ironically, the people least able to profit from exceptionally good corporate governance are precisely those most subject to the negative implications of exceptionally poor corporate governance. Figures 1.1 and 1.2. illustrate this in more detail.

The Need for Investor Confidence

According to an article published by *Business Week,* between 1992 and 2002 about half of all adult Americans—some 100 million investors—emerged as the new investor class.[ci] These were predominantly suburban, middle-class baby boomers who bought into the idea that stocks would make them rich.[cii,ciii] During the long bull-market run of the 1990s they exalted, but between 2000 and 2002 they lost 30% of their stock wealth ($5 trillion). [civ] During one extremely painful episode of corporate governance failure, Enron stock selling for over $90 per share only months earlier sold for less than 50 cents per share.[cv]

When the Enron debacle and some other scandalous failures of major U.S. corporations plunged investor confidence in corporate leadership to an all-time low, affluent investors were less willing to maintain their investment patterns in the equities markets. This initiated a vicious downturn in the investment cycle resulting in an overall economic slowdown that substantially affected corporate capital investing, employment, and housing.

Although the Sarbanes-Oxley Act of 2002 succeeded in reassuring many economically advantaged people that it was safe to invest in the market again, this legislation was not introduced primarily to encourage skittish investors to attempt to return to the capital gains heydays of the 1990s. Instead, it was crafted to introduce more direct positive effects on the average consumer by stimulating capital investment, employment, and housing construction. This kind of macroeconomic growth raises the economic tide, lifting the boats of average citizens even if they do not invest in financial markets. The loss of even one major corporation creates a chain of negative impacts that affect a surprisingly large number of people. Thus, the quality of the rules that govern U.S. corporations matter a great deal to the lives of most Americans.

Intuitive Stakeholder Impact

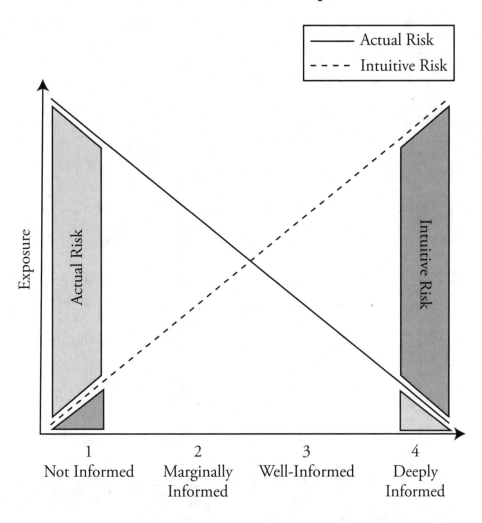

Figure 1.1

Actual Stakeholder Analysis

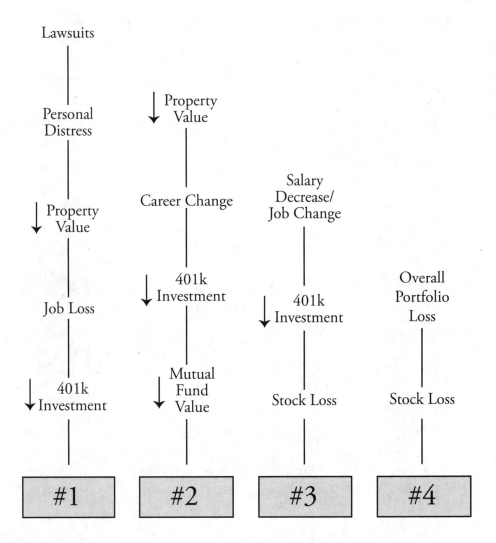

Figure 1.2

Accepting Responsibility for Compliance . . . and Beyond

Claudia Deutsch of the *New York Times* regretfully observed that since 1993, the "Year of the Knives," boards had become "quicker to punish incompetence—but no more apt to spot criminality."[cvi]

> [Boards] will howl when quarterly numbers are depressed, yet shut their eyes when the numbers are squishy or even fraudulent. They will use stock grants and options to align management's interest with that of shareholders, yet ignore the temptation the options create for management to drive up stock prices with false promises, take the money and run.
>
> "It now seems that what we had in 1993 was sporadic and random action by high-profile directors at high-profile companies, but no country-wide improvement in corporate governance," said Peter C. Clapman, the chief counsel of TIAA-CREF, the huge pension and mutual fund manager that has long fought for better boardroom vigilance.[cvii]

Although the experiences played out on the front pages of most major business publications depict an obvious breakdown in corporate leadership at some corporations, I do not believe these are typical of American corporate leadership. Ample opportunities for improvement of the overall corporate governance process certainly exist, but the situation is far from grim. Improving the performance of American corporations depends on improving the effectiveness of their directors. I see tremendous opportunities for enlightened directors to demonstrate bold leadership.

In my experience, corporate directors have accepted full responsibility for oversight of their shareholders' investments. The directors that I have been privileged to work with have demonstrated a commitment to taking on bold initiatives to increase value for long-term shareholders. Most boards and senior corporate leaders play by the rules and represent their investors in an ethical, legal, and moral manner. These enlightened leaders go far beyond compliance. These are the extreme personal leaders who demonstrate conviction in their pursuit of long-term shareholder value.

In the following chapters, I will review some of the most significant issues brought before corporate directors during the last 3 decades and highlight the new trends in corporate governance that have evolved as a result.

Notes

[i] Smith, A. (1937). *The wealth of nations,* p. 423. New York: Random House.

[ii] Norton, T. J. (1942). *The Constitution of the United States: Its sources and its applications.* New York: World Press.

[iii] Vance, S. (1983). *Corporate leadership, boards, directors, and strategy,* p. 1. New York: McGraw Hill.

[iv] Ibid., pp. 3-6.

[v] Downing, P. (1997). Governing for stakeholders. *The Corporate Board, 18*(107), 13. (Infotrac Article No. A20163325).

[vi] Beavers, J. T. (2003, October) Are boards control-literate? *Internal Auditor.* Retrieved May 27, 2006, from *LookSmart,* http://www. findarticles.com/

[vii] Byrne, J. (1997, December 8). The best and worst boards: Our special report on corporate governance. *Business Week,* 90.

[viii] Beavers, 2003.

[ix] Chew, D. H. (Ed.). (1997). *Studies in international corporate finance and governance systems: A comparison of the U.S., Japan & Europe.* New York: Oxford University Press.

[x] Kaufman, D. H. (Ed.). (1995). *Japanese corporate governance: A comparative study of systems in Japan and the United States.* New York: The Pacific Institute/The Asia Institute.

[xi] Blair, M. M. (1995). *Ownership and control: Rethinking corporate governance for the twenty-first century.* Washington, DC: The Brookings Institution.

[xii] Chew, 1997.

[xiii] Dimsdale, N., & Prevezer, M. (Eds.). (1994). *Capital markets and corporate governance.* New York: Oxford University Press.

[xiv] Guy, J. W. (1994). *How to invest someone else's money.* New York: Irwin Professional.

[xv] Jacobs, M. T. (1991). *Short-term America: The causes and cures of our business myopia.* Boston: Harvard Business School Press.

[xvi] Kaufman, 1995.

[xvii] Vance, 1983.

[xix] Blair, 1995.

[xx] Jacobs, M. T. (1991). *Short-term America: The causes and cures of our business myopia.* Boston: Harvard Business School Press.

[xxi] Ibid.

[xxii] Ibid.

[xxiii] Crystal, G. S. (1991, October 29). The compensation 500. *Financial World, 145,* 34-42.

xxiv Kay, I. T. (1998). *CEO pay and shareholder value: Helping the U.S. win the global economic war.* New York: St. Lucie Press.

xxv Kay, I. T. (1992). *Value at the top: Solution to the executive compensation crisis.* New York: HarperBusiness.

xxvi National Association of Corporate Directors. (1993). *Report of the NACD blue ribbon commission on executive compensation guidelines for corporate directors.* Washington, DC: Author.

xxvii Jensen, M. C. (1991). Corporate control and the politics of finance. *Journal of Applied Corporate Finance, 4*(2), 22-30.

xxviii Charkham, J. (1994). *Keeping good company: A study of corporate governance in five countries,* p. 16. New York: Oxford University Press.

xxix Jacobs, 1991.

xxx Blair, 1995.

xxxi Jacobs, 1991.

xxxii Ibid.

xxxiii Reingold, J., Melcher, R., & McWilliams, G. (1998, April 20). Executive pay: Stock options plus a bull market made a mockery of many attempts to link pay to performance. *Business Week, 3574,* 2.

xxxiv Blair, M. M. (1994, Winter). CEO pay: Why it has become so controversial. *Brookings Review 12,* 22-27.

xxxv Byrne, J. A. (1994, April 25). That eye-popping executive pay: Is anybody worth this much? *Business Week, 3368,* 52.

xxxvi Byrne, J. A. (1996, April 22). How high can CEO pay go? *Business Week, 3472,* 100.

xxxvii Blair, 1994, Winter.

xxxviii Reingold, J., Borrus, A., & Hammonds, K. H. (1997, May 12). Even executives are wincing at executive pay: Many say it's too high, though they're not as mad as the public. *Business Week, 3526;* 40.

xxxix Survey: CEO compensation jumps 30% in 2004. (2005, October 31). *USATODAY.com.* Retrieved May 26, 2006, from http://www.usatoday.com/

xl Ibid.

xli Lorsch, J. W., & MacIver, E. A. (1989). *Pawns and potentates: The reality of America's corporate boards.* Boston: Harvard Business School Press.

xlii Ward, R. D. (1997). *21st century corporate board.* New York: John Wiley.

xliii Monks, R., & Minow, N. (1996). *Watching the watchers: Corporate governance for the 21st century.* Cambridge, MA: Blackwell.

xliv Deutsch, C. (2003, January 26). The revolution that wasn't. *New York Times.* Retrieved May 26, 2006, from *Newsbank* Inc., http://infoweb .newsbank.com.

xlv Hawley, J. P., Williams, A. T., & Miller, J. U. (1994, Fall). Getting the herd to run: Shareholder activism at the California Employees' Retirement System. *Business and the Contemporary World, 11,* 12.

xlvi Freidheim, C. F. (1996). New world order in the boardroom. *Directors & Boards, 20*(4), 6-12.

[xlvii] Monks, 1996.

[xlviii] Fleming, R. W. (1998). Shareholder vs. stakeholder value: A view from Toronto. *Directorship, 24*(8), 1-3.

[xlix] Ibid.

[l] Vance, 1983.

[li] Monks & Minow, 1996.

[lii] TIAA-CREF. (2003, January 1). TIAA-CREF supports SEC proxy disclosure proposal: Introduction and background. *TIAA-CREF Web Center/Siteline*. Retrieved May 25, 2006, from http://www.tiaa-cref.org/siteline/

[liii] Cadbury, A. (1997). Summing up the governance reports. *The Corporate Board, 18*(107), 6. (Infotrac Article No. A20163324).

[liv] Cadbury Committee. (1992). *Cadbury Committee report: Financial aspects of corporate governance*. Basingstoke, England: Burgess Science.

[lv] Gordon, L. A., & Pound, J. (1993, January 11). Active investing in the U.S. equity market: Past performance and future prospects. Paper presented to the Board. Retrieved January 13, 2004, from http://www.governancematters.com.

[lvi] Monks, 1996.

[lvii] Byrne, 1996.

[lviii] Smale will stay on GM board beyond age 70. (1997, December 22). *The Wall Street Journal*, pp. B1, B11.

[lix] Ibid.

[lx] Smale to leave GM after turnaround. (1999, November 3). *The Cincinnati Post*. Retrieved from http://news.cincypost.com/

[lxi] Gembrowski, S. (1996, April 12). Institutional investors take larger control of companies. *San Diego Daily Transcript*.

[lxii] Friedman, M. (1970, September 13). The social responsibility of business is to increase its profits. *New York Times Magazine*.

[lxiii] Quinn, R., & Lees, P. (1984). Attraction and harassment: Dynamics of sexual politics. *Organizational Dynamics, 13*(3), 13-46.

[lxiv] Whiting, B. G. (1990). *Knights and knaves of corporate boardrooms*. Buffalo, NY: Bearly.

[lxv] Coffee, J. (1981). No soul to damn, no body to kick: An un-scandalized inquiry into the problem of corporate punishment. *Michigan Law Review, 79*, 386.

[lxvi] Women at the top: A scorecard. (1998, November 23). *Business Week, 3605*, 83.

[lxvii] Hamill, John. (1996). In pursuit of boardroom diversity. *Boston Business Journal, 16*, 18, p. 26.

[lxviii] The Conference Board. (1999). *Board diversity in U.S. corporations*. New York: Author. (1230-99-RR).

[lxix] Carson, T. L. (2003). Self–interest and business ethics: Some lessons of the recent corporate scandals. *Journal of Business Ethics, 43*(4), 389-394.

[lxx] Freeman, R. E. (1999). Divergent stakeholder theory. *Academy of Management Review, 24*(2), 233-236.

lxxi Citigroup, Inc. (2000, April 20). Citigroup successfully completes subsequent merger for Travelers Property Casualty Corp. *Citigroup Press Room*. Retrieved August 1, 2006, from http://citigroup.com/

lxxii McCullagh, D. (2000, January 10). AOL, Time Warner to merge. *Lycos Wired News*. Retrieved August 1, 2006, from http://www.wired.com/

lxxiii The President's Corporate Fraud Task Force. (2002). United States Department of Justice, Office of the Deputy Attorney General – Corporate Fraud Task Force. Retrieved May 20, 2006, from http://www.usdoj.gov/dag/cftf/

lxxiv Ibid.

lxxv Ackman, D. (2004, September 8). Judge throws the book at Quattrone. *Forbes.com*. Retrieved May 27, 2006, from http://www.forbes.com/

lxxvi Levine, G. (2005, June 20). Adelphia founder John Rigas sentenced to 15 years. *Forbes.com*. Retrieved May 27, 2006, from http://www.forbes.com/

lxxvii Fink, J. (2005, June 21). John Rigas sentenced to 15 years in prison. *Buffalo Business First*. Retrieved May 27, 2006, from http://www.bizjournals.com/buffalo/

lxxviii Hartocollis, A. (2006, May 13). Ex-Tyco chief to settle tax evasion charges. *New York Times*. Retrieved May 17, 2006, from http://www.nytimes.com/

lxxix Ibid.

lxxx Crawford, K. (2005, March 15). Ex-WorldCom CEO Ebbers guilty. *CNNMoney.com*. Retrieved May 17, 2006, from http://money.cnn.com/

lxxxi Johnson, C. (2005, July 13). Ebbers gets 25-year sentence for role in WorldCom fraud. *Washingtonpost.com*. Retrieved May 17, 2006, from http://www.washingtonpost.com/

lxxxii Crawford, K., March 15, 2005.

lxxxiii Ex-WorldCom CFO Scott Sullivan gets 5 years. (2005, August 11). *FoxNews.com*. Retrieved May 17, 2006, from http://www.foxnews.com/

lxxxiv Eltman, F. (2006, April 28). Guilty plea marks stunning fall for Kumar. *Examiner.com*. Retrieved May 26, 2006, from http://www.examiner.com/

lxxxv U.S. Department of Justice. (2004, July 8). Former Enron chairman and chief executive officer Kenneth L. Lay charged with conspiracy, fraud, false statements. [Press Release]. Washington, DC: Author. Retrieved August 17, 2006, from http://www.usdoj.gov/

lxxxvi Pasha, S. (2006, July 5). Enron founder Ken Lay dies. *CNNMoney.com*. Retrieved August 1, 2006, from http://money.cnn.com/

lxxxvii U.S. Securities and Exchange Commission. (2004, January 14). SEC settles civil fraud charges filed against Andrew S. Fastow, former Enron chief financial officer. Litigation Release No. 18543.

lxxxviii Fastow and his wife plead guilty. (2004, January 14). *CNNMoney.com*. Retrieved November 10, 2005, from http://money.cnn.com/

lxxxix Crawford, K. (2005, June 6). Lea Fastow ends prison term. *CNNMoney.com*. Retrieved May 26, 2006, from http://money.

xc Key witnesses in the Enron trial. (2006, May 17). *Washingtonpost.com*. Retrieved May 17, 2006, from http://www.washingtonpost.com/

xci Wray, C. (2005, February). Prosecuting corporate crimes. *eJournal USA*. Retrieved May 26, 2006, from http://usinfo.state.gov/journals/ites/0205/ijee/wray.htm.

xcii Dash, E., & Labaton, S. (2006, May 23). A Fannie Mae settlement is reported. *New York Times*. Retrieved May 24, 2006, from http://www.nytimes.com/

xciii Big labor goes to bat in boardrooms. (2004, April 15). *BusinessWeekonline*. Retrieved May 17, 2006, from www.businessweek.com/

xciv Ibid.

xcv Winners and losers in Enron's demise. (2001, November 29). *Fox News* Retrieved August 18, 2006, from http://www.foxnews.com/

xcvi Sarnoff, N. (2003, August 22). Granite soliciting bidders for now-famous Enron building. *Houston Business Journal*. Retrieved August 17, 2006, from http://www.bizjoiurnals.com/houston/

xcvii County Information Project. (n.d.). Houston county profile. Texas Association of Counties. Retrieved August 17, 2006, from http://www.txcip.org/tac/census/profile.php?FIPS=48225.

xcviii Nobles, M. E. (2006, March 27). Houston, we have a comeback: Nonprofits crawling out of Enron hole. *NonProfit Times*. Retrieved August 18, 2006, from http://www.nptimes.com/

xcix Romero, S. (2006, January 25). Hard times haunt Enron's ex-workers: Few find jobs of equal stature years after company's collapse. *New York Times* (Late Edition), p. C1.

c Armour, S. (2006, January 26). Enron woes reverberate through lives: Many saw retirement plans evaporate with stock price. *USA Today*, pp. 1B-2B.

ci Pew Research Center for the People & the Press. (2002, February 25). The new investor class. [Table.] *Business Week*. Retrieved August 18, 2002, from http://www.businessweek.com/

cii Ibid.

ciii Vickers, M., McNamee, M., Coy, P. Henry, D., Thornton, E., & Der Hovanesian, M. (2002, February 25). The betrayed investor. *Business Week*. Retrieved August 18, 2006, from http://www.businessweek.com/

civ Ibid.

cv Enron fights for life after bid collapse. (2001, November 29). *BBC News*. Retrieved August 17, 2006, from http://news.bbc.co.uk/

cvi Deutsch, C. H. (2003, February 23). Revolt of the shareholders: At annual meetings, anger will ratchet up a notch. *New York Times,* Sec. 3, p. 1.

cvii Deutsch, C. H. (2003, January 26). The revolution that wasn't. *New York Times,* Sec. 3, p. 1.

Chapter 2

The Intricacies of Corporate Governance

Understanding what has happened will help determine what will happen.

Today's efforts to reform and restructure boards are the result of a powerful surge of interest in corporate governance that took place in the last quarter of the 20th century. As described by Professor Jay Lorsch of the Harvard Business School and his research associate Elizabeth MacIver, the functions of a corporate board of directors are overseeing management, reviewing company performance, and ensuring that the various activities of the company are socially responsible and in compliance with the law.[i] Thus, corporate governance issues go far beyond the rules and regulations that give an organization legal standing. Governance involves authority, control, responsibility, and accountability.[ii,iii,iv] Although often poorly defined, these areas are extremely important to a company's day-to-day performance and crucial to its capacity to respond to changing conditions in the marketplace. E. W. Davenport, Jr., former CEO of Eastman Chemical, once pointed out that society is the ultimate stakeholder. CEO's and boards of directors have begun to recognize that the definition of customer can be broad enough to include employees, investors, suppliers, communities, and government agencies.[v,vi,vii,viii,ix]

As described in Chapter 1, the 1980s saw a worldwide surge of interest in improving corporate governance.[x] Globalization, hostile takeovers, and shareholder activism all pushed boards to increase their oversight of CEO's, strategic planning, executive succession planning, and accountability. The demand for improved corporate governance reached both the public and private sectors. In the public sector, a tighter economy and heightened economic uncertainty meant that people were less willing to support government programs at a time when the help of those programs was most needed. In the not-for-profit sector, fewer and smaller charitable contributions and lower rates of return on endowments forced institutions to restructure their operations.[xi]

The technological advances in communications and information processing of the 1990s multiplied the complexity of issues faced by corporations. Technologies that had been nonexistent or exorbitantly costly a few years before rapidly arrived on the market and then quickly dropped in cost as their next generations were anticipated. For corporations this meant a competitively risky tradeoff between being the first to invest in new technologies or waiting for costs to drop, neither of which could guarantee competitive success.[xii,xiii]

An onslaught of environmental and technological changes continuously challenged conventional notions of corporate structure. In times gone by, the companies that succeeded in turbulent times were those able to react quickly to external forces. However, under conditions of a globalizing economy, unprecedented technological complexity, imaginative financing methods, and opportunism, even nimble companies were at risk of hostile takeovers. During any single year of the 1980s, the value of corporate takeovers exceeded one quarter trillion dollars, an increase of 200% over a single comparable year in the 1970s.[xiv]

Some corporate governance luminaries believe that a major byproduct of the 1980s era of corporate takeovers was corporate neglect of shareholders' interests. In their view, corporate boards and senior management teams, facing hostile takeovers and struggling to maintain control of their companies to keep their jobs, often ignored the interests of shareholders. Although senior management teams and boards often were able to band together to protect their companies and their own positions from hostile raids, the takeover-defense measures they used, popularly known by such names as greenmail, the poison pill, and Pac Man, distanced them from shareholders.[xv]

Of these defenses against hostile bids, perhaps the most egregious was *greenmail*, the buying out of a large shareholder at a bonus over the market price. The greenmail defense was employed when the purchaser of a large stake in a company indicated an interest in taking over the company but management perceived that interest as undesirable. Greenmail made it possible for corporate raiders to make huge profits without even placing a real bid on a company. Although the corporation's managers and directors got to keep their jobs, shareholders bore the cost of the falling stock price.[xvi] Shareholders objected that directors should not allow management to keep control of companies by paying out large sums of shareholder money; they complained that boards neglected shareholder interests when they permitted management to employ the greenmail defense.

Another common takeover defense tactic was the *poison pill*, which usually came in the form of certain rights granted to shareholders; those rights were worthless unless triggered by a takeover attempt. In the event of a takeover attempt, shareholders could purchase shares from the target company, sell shares back to the target company, or buy shares from the potential acquirer at a steep discount.[xvii] Armed with this discount, many of the target company's shareholders would purchase shares of the potential acquiring company. Because shareholders of the potential acquiring company were not included in the poison pill plan, their equities were diluted once the plan was activated. Although the poison pill defense was useful in entrenching the management of the target company, it also protected the target company's shareholders from two-tier offers that gave some shareholders less money than other shareholders for their shares.

Of course, from a corporate governance perspective, the main problem with the poison pill defense is that it can be created without shareholder approval. In effect, it gives the board the authority to reject any bid for the company, no matter how beneficial it might be to the shareholders. This is problematic for short-term investors trying to make a sizeable return on a quick flip of the company's stock. Today's enlightened boards act in ways consistent with the interests of most long-term shareholders.

To make the poison pill more acceptable to institutional shareholders, some companies customized them to create a *chewable* pill. This new twist was based on a set of guidelines that placed conditions on an unsolicited bid. If the unsolicited bid was made for all shares and was fully financed, the defense mechanism would not be triggered.[xviii] Although the chewable pill gave the company's leadership team considerable authority, it did provide more assurance that any bid made for the company would be fair to all shareholders.

Other popular anti-takeover measures included the white knight, crown jewel, and the Pack-man strategies. In the *white knight strategy*, a friendly third party would agree to buy a large enough portion of the target company's stock to keep the company out of the hostile bidder's hands. However, in the *crown jewel strategy*, the target company would sell or otherwise freeze its most valuable assets as a protection against the uninvited bidder, thus making itself a less valuable—and therefore less attractive—target. Companies resorting to the crown jewel strategy, of course, risked destruction. The *Pack-man strategy* was even riskier because it involved the target company in bidding for shares of the hostile company, creating the potential for destruction of the target company. Eventually, the resulting explosive growth was followed by unprecedented high expectations from short-term oriented investors and egregious pay packages for some unsavory senior executive officers.

Today, these actions, which helped launch ambitious and often unreasonable corporate growth expectations, are viewed by many as the chief factors contributing to the ultimate demise of a number of industrial giants, including Enron, WorldCom, and Arthur Andersen. Although most institutional shareholders do not support anti-takeover measures, at times these measures have protected the interests of long-term shareholders. Nevertheless, institutional shareholders' victory in the raging debate over hostile-takeover defenses are justifiable, and very few companies now include the measures discussed above in their anti-takeover arsenals. In many cases, it is appropriate for corporations to implement anti-takeover measures when it is deemed by the board of directors to be in the best interest of long-term shareowners. However, today, the best anti-takeover strategy is consistent delivery of outstanding long-term shareholder value resulting in high multiples and high total enterprise value. In other words, the best defense against an unsolicited takeover bid is a great offense: high performance.

Throughout the years, when a director demonstrated loyalty and care in making business decisions, courts generally deferred to that director's judgment. Shareholders' early court challenges to takeovers and takeover defenses usually produced case law that reaffirmed the traditional notions of board duties. However, that has not always been the case. For example, in the infamous Smith v. Van Gorkum, a 1985 case concerning the sale of Trans Union Corporation, a holding company, the Delaware Supreme Court found that the directors who had approved the sale violated their duty to gain the best price for their shareholders.

In a wave of takeover litigation in the mid-1980s, the Delaware Supreme Court attempted to determine whether there was a limit to the legal actions a board could take to defend a company from takeover. In two cases (Unocal Corp. v. Mesa Petroleum Company; Revlon, Inc. v. MacAndrews & Forbes Holdings, Inc.), the Delaware Court criticized the boards facing takeovers for protecting their own interests rather than those of shareholders.[xix] As lawsuits brought by shareholders wound through the courts, activists sought to improve corporate governance structures.

Reflecting the general view of the activist shareholder community, the late management guru and prolific author, Peter Drucker, commented that an institution that has failed as often as the board of directors probably is not structurally sound.[xx] A flourishing new cottage industry of corporate governance gurus and management consultants attempted to come to the rescue. Today, shareholders, journalists, academics, and government agencies continue to examine the structures that support (or fail to support) boards in their duty to supervise CEO's in the interests of shareholders.

Those interested in board structure would like to know how board committees work and who serves on them. The first required board committee was the audit committee. In the initial years following the stock market crash of 1929, new business incorporation laws required publicly owned companies to publish annual financial statements audited by third-party accountants.[xxi] In 1978, the New York Stock Exchange expanded on the board's fiduciary accountability by making the formation of audit committees a precondition for listing on the Exchange.

Although many corporate leaders thought that audit committees would not prove useful, a decade later that attitude had changed.[xxii,xxiii,xiv] By 1988, audit committees had acquired expanded duties and had been credited with improving external and internal auditing, financial controls, financial reporting, and auditing effectiveness.[xxv] They had increased in size, and many were composed entirely of directors from outside the company.[xxvi,xxvii,xxviii,xxix,xxx]

Then, a wave of infamous frauds at WorldCom, Enron, Quest Communications, Impath, and other corporations convinced Congress that shareholders needed more protection, and Congress passed the Sarbanes-Oxley Act of 2002, which required auditor independence and imposed a number of new rules, standards, and penalties for non-compliance, all designed to restore investor confidence. The *audit committee* has become one of three committees required for boards of directors of publicly held U.S. corporations; its members are independent directors and its primary function is to reassure the board and shareholders of the integrity of the company's financial systems while providing auditors with a private forum in which to express any concerns they may have about company management.

Over the years, corporate boards also came to rely on *compensation committees* to oversee pay for directors and the senior management team. As discussed in Chapter 1, starting in the 1980s, corporate compensation committees began designing lavish CEO payment packages that drew public attention to their activities. Shareholder scrutiny has not caused CEO pay to decrease, but shareholders have not given up on their efforts to convince boards to establish meaningful linkages between share value and CEO pay. Shareholders are asking fundamental questions: *Is the CEO's compensation based on a correlation with returns generated for shareholders? Why does the CEO warrant huge compensation when the company is not performing well? How much pay is too much?*

Federal regulators have joined with institutional shareholders and other non-governmental shareholder organizations in insisting that compensation committees clearly and completely articulate their policies and strategies, in writing, for proxy disclosure to stockholders. Compensation committees generally are composed of independent directors, although the CEO often is invited to attend the committee's meetings to discuss the performances of other members of the executive team.

Corporate governance and nominating committees, required for publicly held companies, have also become a major focus of institutional investors. In theory, nominating committees screen potential board nominees and prevent CEO's from packing boards with rubber-stamp directors. In practice, however, even into the 1980s, many boards simply endorsed nominations by the CEO, prompting the CEO of California's pension fund, CalPERS, to suggest that many nominating committees were a "sham."[xxxi] Today, a high percentage of nominating committees hire executive search firms to assist them in their recruiting efforts. A number of factors beyond sound judgment feed into such a decision, including pressure from institutional shareholders and difficulty finding qualified candidates willing to serve as directors.

The 1990s was a decade in which seemingly strong corporations stumbled in their financial performances. Notable among these were General Motors, American Express, Sears Roebuck, and Archer Daniels Midland. Health care companies like Columbia/HCA also experienced problems. Although some have recovered, others have morphed into completely different entities (Sears, for example, was acquired by Kmart). In response, corporate governance activists began focusing on stopping corporate problems before they happened. Even in the 1990s, considerable evidence pointed to the idea that good corporate governance could make a difference in long-term company performance.

Most experts agreed that, although no set of guidelines could guarantee prevention of a corporate disaster, a proactive board of independent directors was more likely to identify and head-off potential problems than a passive board of inside directors.[xxxii] Today corporate governance practitioners realize that being independent is important but that it is not enough. Corporate America has witnessed the demise of companies with strong independent directors; only a highly enlightened board of directors, including a highly enlightened CEO, can effectively lead corporations in the 21st century!

The key to company success may be the preventive maintenance accomplished by an active board engaged in strategic planning and monitoring. Good practices of corporate governance are not mere academic fluff, as some executives believe. William Crist, president of the board of CalPERS, compared good governance to basic preventative hygiene. "If you brush your teeth all along," he said, "you'll probably have fewer cavities."[xxxiii] Too many boards, Crist warned, ignore good governance practices until prices fall or they encounter a crisis.

In a 1993 article in *Harvard Business Review*, veteran corporate director Walter Salmon listed the kinds of information an active, informed board needs to prevent crises.[xxxiv] On his list, Salmon included the company's operating statements, balance sheets, and cash-flow statements for the current period and year to date. Salmon suggested that the board compare these actual results with the plans previously made for the current period and then have management explain any deviations from the plan as well as provide the board with revised forecasts for the remaining year. Salmon also advised directors to acquire pertinent market information, minutes of management committee meetings, key articles on the company and its competition, consumer surveys, and employee-attitude surveys.

As reported by Bernard Marcus, former CEO of Home Depot, that company's board took director attentiveness directly into Home Depot stores by requiring directors to spend one full day at a Home Depot store each month, and visit 8 to 10 stores per quarter, both within and outside of the areas in which they live. Directors are expected to enter the store as customers and later identify themselves and make themselves available to talk with employees.[xxxv] It is unlikely that a director who fulfills these duties would need to read an employee-attitude survey.

Although this direct contact approach works well for consumer-oriented corporations such as Home Depot and McDonalds, different strategies are needed for most industrial manufacturing companies. Directors can hardly assume the identity of a customer and anonymously peruse the functioning of a DuPont Tio2 chemical plant or an ITT night-vision defense research center. Each company must design company-specific and situation-dependent requirements to keep their directors alert to company needs.

Corporate governance experts agree that the most important feature of a good board is active engagement of directors in the development of company strategy.[xxxvi] Without actually setting strategy, directors ensure that planning processes are in place, used, and produce sound choices. Enlightened directors, however, do more than inspect; they insist on adding value to the company's strategic planning process. In the enlightened boardroom, directors, the CEO, and the senior leadership team share in the development and ownership of the overall corporate strategy.

The goal of corporate governance generally is to help companies create wealth over time in ways that do not impose inappropriate costs on third parties or on society as a whole. Inappropriate costs to shareholders can take the form of excessive payouts; inappropriate costs to society can take the form of price fixing, pollution, or criminal behavior.[xxxvii] An effective corporate governance system imposes a set of checks and balances on corporate decision-makers by ensuring that the right questions are asked at the right times and that people with appropriate knowledge are available to answer those questions.

As discussed previously, the takeover era focused attention on the value of corporate governance as a tool for redefining the roles of the corporation and the corporate board. Stakeholders learned that corporate governance in theory had little relationship to corporate governance in actual practice. In many corporations, the interdependent relationships of directors and senior executives inhibited effective oversight and disenfranchised shareholders.[xxxviii] For all practical purposes, many corporations no longer operated under a system of checks and balances.

However, in today's corporation, the driving force is not tradition but dynamic change. Indeed, a new paradigm has developed in which the corporate board no longer functions as a legal formality but has become a competitive necessity. Today's corporations face a bewildering mosaic of fast-paced change, uncertainty, and stiff competition in a world of unprecedented opportunity for growth.[xxxix] For the company to respond, its board must be aware that changes are afoot and must monitor situations so that the company can develop appropriate responses and syntheses. An enlightened board reaches beyond its traditional watchdog role to drive organizational change and influence the CEO's decisions through the counsel and coaching that every CEO needs.[xl]

Traditional boards monitored past events by reacting to present events. Today's enlightened board must closely monitor current events while creating the future through active planning.[xli] To do so, the board must streamline decision-making processes to produce quick responses. The board must examine past events (of last month, last quarter, or last year) within the context of whether they helped the company meet goals, adapt, or learn lessons applicable to strategic plans. For example, a highly enlightened board led by a highly enlightened chairperson will work well with the current CEO, even as they simultaneously consider several successors to that CEO as part of succession planning.

One challenge of corporate decision-making is to find the right level of delegation. Executives must make some decisions immediately. Other decisions should be reviewed by various departments in the company. Still others should be considered by the board of directors. Some decisions must be brought to the attention of shareholders. A board must not interfere in the company's day-to-day business operations but should work closely with the CEO and monitor company operations in such a way that decisions are properly delegated.

Principles of Corporate Governance

To support company stakeholders while maximizing long-term financial returns to shareholders, corporate governance must be focused on company performance and competitiveness. Corporate governance should align, as closely as possible, the often-diverging interests of the company's leaders and shareholders while providing efficiencies and profits. Regulatory changes can strengthen the relationship between institutional shareholders and senior corporate leaders by reinforcing shareholder influence and board control in the interests of efficacy and accountability.[xlii]

The most universal principle flowing from the shared concerns of shareholders and corporate directors is that of disclosure.[xliii,xliv,xlv,xlvi] To monitor their corporations' activities, boards need relevant and timely information on which to base judgments. Openness and transparency, of course, are the basis for long-term support for corporations from the investment community and the public.

Another important principle threaded through the corporate governance debates is checks and balances. At the heart of many international corporate scandals is an undue concentration of power in one individual.[xlvii] The enlightened board insists that all board members become heavily engaged in all critical issues facing the company. Well-argued, healthy debates lead to better-informed decisions.

These generally accepted broad principles are incorporated into corporate governance codes that define the structural changes boards need to carry out their duties. To be effective, a board must be able to identify its job. Thus, the starting point for all corporate governance codes is clarification of the duties, powers, and responsibilities of the board of directors. A clear line must be drawn between the board's task of directing and the CEO's task of managing. Directors must have a shared understanding of their roles, responsibilities, and relationship to management.[xlviii] Boards reduce their effectiveness when they fail to think through the distinction between directing and managing.[xlix]

Board Selection and Composition

Corporate governance experts generally agree that boards should consist mostly of independent directors.[l,li,lii] Independence helps directors resolve conflicts and remain objective. Companies need their boards of directors to be collegial teams whose members are capable of working effectively with the CEO and who have been selected on the basis of merit and possession of diverse skills needed by the company.

Directors should be appointed to serve the company and not any particular constituency or interest. Corporate governance expert Jamie Orlikoff pointed out that boards comprised by directors who believe that their role is to represent a particular interest often are unable to focus consistently on what is best for the company and all of its shareholders and thus cannot govern effectively. Lack of board focus can be prevented, Orlikoff observed, by ensuring that directors understand the board's mission and by instituting a careful director selection process. In turbulent times, a board without a clear sense of its own mission might work on short-term strategies instead of examining trends and planning for the future, thus contributing to organizational drift. For this reason, Orlikoff recommended, the whole board should provide guidance during changes to its membership, leadership, and structure.[liii]

Fine-tuning Governance Structure

Whenever a board changes its strategic direction, alters the scope of its responsibilities, or adds or eliminates a function, it should follow through by fine-tuning its governance structures to facilitate governance rather than dictate the decision-making mode.[lix,lv,lvi,lvii] An effective board also appraises its own performance to clarify individual directors' roles and responsibilities and give directors a more complete understanding of what is expected of them. A properly designed board appraisal system will ensure a healthier balance of power between the board and CEO and actually improve the working relationships between them by improving board functioning and making it possible for the board and CEO to hold each other accountable to defined performance expectations.

In 1996, 69% of Fortune 1000 companies evaluated their CEO, but only 25% evaluated their complete board, and a mere 10% evaluated their CEO, complete board, and individual directors.[lviii] Today, all boards are required to conduct annual evaluations of the entire board and the CEO.

Summary

Implementing sound structures, clarifying board duties, and paying attention to board composition and selection should put a board well on its way to effective performance. The firm conclusion activists drew from events of the corporate takeover era was that the great freedom granted to CEO's must be balanced by accountability. A strong, active board of directors and vigilant shareholders can go a long way toward moderating the actions of a strong, dynamic CEO. If, however, the board does not work properly and most of the shareholders seldom work at all, CEO's and their teams will tend to entrench, as they did during the takeover era.[lix] When complacent boards leave governance structures to chance and tradition, they become reactive bodies that simply respond to situations as they arise.

Good corporate governance is no accident. It results from careful planning, implementation, coordination, and evaluation. Effective governance procedures streamline board structures and eliminate processes that waste time, thus permitting the board to focus on the trend monitoring, strategic planning, and succession planning that keep a company nimble in today's ever-changing market. Corporate governance certainly is not perfect, but it has improved immensely in the past 3 decades.[lx,lxi,lxii]

Notes

[i] Lorsch, J. W., & MacIver, E. A. (1989). *Pawns and potentates: The reality of America's corporate boards.* Boston: Harvard Business School Press.

[ii] Whiting, B. G. (1990). *Knights and knaves of corporate boardrooms.* Buffalo, NY: Bearly.

[iii] Ward, R. D. (1997). *21st century corporate board.* New York: John Wiley.

[iv] Shiller, R. J. (1992). *Who's minding the store? The report of the Twentieth Century Fund Task Force on market speculation and corporate governance.* New York: Twentieth Century Fund Press.

[v] Downing, P. (1997). Governing for stakeholders. *The Corporate Board, 18*(107), 13. (Infotrac Article No. A20163325).

[vi] Blair, M. M., & Uppal, G. (1993). *The deal decade handbook.* Washington, DC: The Brookings Institution.

[vii] Lorsch & MacIver, 1989.

[viii] Millstein, I. (1993a, November). Advising a CEO on boardroom relations. *American Lawyer, 87.*

[ix] Monks, R. A. G. (1996). The American corporation at the end of the twentieth century: An outline of ownership based governance. A speech given at Cambridge University, July, 1996. Retrieved May 27, 2006, from http://www.lens-library.com/info/cambridge.html.

[x] Bearle, A. A., Jr., & Means, G. C. (1932). *The modern corporation and private property.* New York: Macmillan.

[xi] Sifonis, J. G., & Goldberg, B. (1996). *Corporation on a tightrope balancing leadership, governance, and technology in an age of complexity.* Oxford, England: Oxford University Press.

[xii] Carver, J. (1997). *Boards that make a difference: A new design for leadership in nonprofit and public organizations* (2nd ed.). San Francisco: Jossey-Bass.

[xiii] Ward, 1997.

[xiv] Charkham, J. (1994). *Keeping good company: A study of corporate governance in five countries,* p. 215. New York: Oxford University Press.

[xv] Monks, R., & Minow, N. (1996). *Watching the watchers: Corporate governance for the 21st century.* Cambridge, MA: Blackwell.

[xvi] Ibid., p. 204.

[xvii] Ibid.

[xviii] Ibid.

[xix] Ibid., p. 203.

[xx] Drucker, P. (1981). *Toward the next economics and other essays,* p. 110. New York: Harper & Row.

[xxi] Downing, 1997.

[xxii] Bacon, J. (1981). *Corporate directorship practices: The nominating committee and the director selection process.* New York: *The Conference Board.*

[xxiii] Bacon, J., & Brown, J. K. (1975). *Corporate directorship practices.* New York: *The Conference Board.*

[xxiv] Charkham, 1994, p. 191.

[xxv] See Ward, 1997.

[xxvi] Korn/Ferry International. (1996). *23rd annual board of directors study. Board meeting in session.* New York: Author.

[xxvii] Korn/Ferry International. (1997). *24th annual board of directors study. Board meeting in session.* New York: Author.

[xxviii] Spencer Stuart Executive Search Consultants. (1994). *Board trends and practices at major American corporations. 1994 Board Index.* San Francisco: Author.

[xxix] Spencer Stuart Executive Search Consultants. (1996). *Board trends and practices at major American corporations. 1996 Board Index.* San Francisco: Author.

[xxx] Spencer Stuart Executive Search Consultants. (1997). *Board trends and practices at S&P 500 corporations. 1997 Board Index.* San Francisco: Author.

[xxxi] Monks & Minow, 1996, p. 182.

[xxxii] Byrne, J. (1997a, December 8). Directors in the hot seat: Activists are singling out individual board members who don't measure up. *Business Week*, 100.

[xxxiii] The best and worst boards: Our special report on corporate governance. *Business Week,* 90. (1997b, December 8).

[xxxiv] Marcus, B. (1992, October). How directors mind the store at Home Depot. *Directorship, 42*(10), 1.

[xxxv] Marcus, 1992.

[xxxvi] Byrne, 1997b, p. 91.

xxxvii Blair, M. M. (1995). *Ownership and control: Rethinking corporate governance for the twenty-first century.* Washington, DC: The Brookings Institution.

xxxviii Charkham, 1994, pp. 215-225.

xxxix Charan, R. (1998). *Boards at work: How corporate boards create competitive advantage.* San Francisco: Jossey-Bass.

xl Charan, 1998.

xli Orlikoff, J. (1998, January). Seven practices of super boards. *Association Management, 50*(1), 52.

xlii Cadbury, 1997, p. 6.

xliii Boros, E. (1995). *Minority shareholders' remedies.* New York: Oxford University Press.

xliv Cadbury, 1997.

xlv deGruyter, W. (1994). *Institutional investors and corporate governance.* Berlin, Germany: WB-Druck Gmbh, Rieden.

xlvi Dimsdale, N., & Prevezer, M. (Eds.). (1994). *Capital markets and corporate governance.* New York: Oxford University Press.

xlvii Cadbury, A. (1997). Summing up the governance reports. *The Corporate Board, 18*(107), 6. (Infotrac Article No. A20163324).

xlviii Orlikoff, 1998.

xlix Coulson-Thomas, C. (1993). *Creating excellence in the boardroom: A guide to shaping directorial competence and board effectiveness.* New York: McGraw-Hill.

l Blair, 1995.

li Monks & Minow, 1996.

lii Ward, 1997.

liii Orlikoff, 1998.

liv Carver, 1997.

lv Charan, 1998.

lvi Coulson-Thomas, 1993.

lvii Ward, 1997.

lviii Conger, J., Finegold, D., & Lawler, E., III. (1998). Appraising boardroom performance. *Harvard Business Review,* 98102, 136-140.

lix Charkham, 1994, p. 225.

lx Verstegen Ryan, L., & Buchholtz, A. K. (2001). Trust, risk, and shareholder decision-making: An investor perspective on corporate governance. *Business Ethics Quarterly. 11*: 177-193.

lxi Schroeder, M. (2003, July). Corporate reform: The first year: Cleaner living, no easy riches; Critics say Sarbanes-Oxley law hobbles stocks, chills risk taking, but upshot is far less dramatic. *Wall Street Journal,* Eastern edition.

lxii Byrnes, N., Henry, D., Thornton, E., and Dwyer, P. (2003, September 22). Reform: Who's making the grade. *Business Week Online.* Retrieved August 2, 2006, from http://www.businessweek.com/

Chapter 3

Correlations between Corporate Governance and Share Value

Does daily exercise make you live longer, or just feel better?

A fundamental question about corporate governance is whether its quality correlates directly with overall value creation by a company. In other words, does good corporate governance increase shareholder value? Over and over again, the evidence says *yes*. Good corporate governance is the result of careful planning, implementation, coordination, and evaluation. Effective governance procedures streamline board structures, thus eliminating time-wasting processes that hamper the trend monitoring, strategic planning, and succession planning needed to keep a company nimble in today's ever-changing market.

The tidal wave of activism for improved corporate board performance sustained over a quarter century certainly indicates that financial investors and other corporate stakeholders firmly believe that the outcomes created by corporate governance are important. A key finding of a 2002 global investor opinion survey of 200 institutional investors "put corporate governance on par with financial indicators when evaluating investment decisions."[i] According to the report of those findings, prepared by McKinsey and Company in cooperation with the Global Corporate Governance Forum:

> An overwhelming majority of investors are prepared to pay a premium for companies exhibiting high governance standards. Premiums averaged 12-14% in North America and Western Europe; 20-25% in Asia and Latin America; and over 30% in Eastern Europe and Africa.

Institutional investors have put huge sums of money behind good corporate governance and, the more money they control, the more they clamor for corporate governance improvements. In the 3 decades from 1965 to 1994, institutional investors' aggregate ownership stakes in U.S. equity markets grew from 16% to 57%.[iii] In the next decade, they grew even more. By 2004, institutional investors controlled 59.2% of outstanding equities in the U.S. (7.974 trillion).[iii]

Shareholders have plenty of motivation for wanting corporate directors to actively lead their companies' general affairs rather than passively participating in them. Active boards honor their on-going responsibility to appropriately monitor the CEO's performance. Boards having a majority of independent directors with a real diversity of skills and meaningful experience are more likely to supervise and appropriately reward CEO's for building long-term shareowner value. How well the board members integrate the fruits of their experience into the ethos of the corporation profoundly impacts the corporation's overall performance. Together with employees and communities, shareholders want to know that boards are actively protecting their interests and providing for more corporate accountability. These demands translate into a need for boards to reform the way they govern corporations.

Linking CEO Performance to Company Performance

Long before shareholders concluded that corporate leadership by directors is critical to corporate success, they admired the contributions of highly quali-

54

fied CEO's. The mention of General Electric, for example, evokes an immediate association with Jack Welch, their most recently retired CEO, and the string of successful CEO's groomed in the GE culture, including Welch's successor Jeff Immelt. IBM is another corporation considered to be an incubator of great leaders such as John W. Thompson (CEO of Symantec), George Conrades (former CEO of Akamai Technologies), Michael Armstrong (former Chairman and CEO of AT&T), and Sam Palmisano (Chairman and CEO of IBM).

To shed light on the effect of CEO leadership on company value, my team at XCEO Inc. conducted a study in which we looked at what happens to shareholder value when a company experiences a change in CEO. Figures 3.1 through 3.13, later in this chapter, highlight our findings. For this study, we chose to measure shareholder value as stock price (including dividends). We looked at CEO transitions in 18 corporations selected from a field of 50 listed on the Yahoo Finance database. These were Alcoa, Alcan, American Express, AMD, AMR, AT&T, Ford, HP, IBM, Intel, 3M, Lucent, Maytag, Merrill Lynch, Microsoft, Pfizer, Starbucks, and Xerox. We selected only well-branded global companies with locations throughout the Americas, Europe, and Asia. All were viewed by Wall Street analysts as top-tier companies in their respective industries, which included consumer services, finance, hardware/software technologies, manufacturing, pharmaceuticals, telecommunications, and transportation. These corporations all had large market caps with annual revenues ranging from $10 to $200 billion. Some, such as Starbucks and Intel, were considered revenue-growth investments and others, such as AT&T and Xerox, were thought to hold opportunities for continued consistent earning potential.

We studied each company over a period of 5 years: the 2.5 years before a new CEO assumed his or her position and the 2.5 years during which the company transitioned from the residual effect of the outgoing CEO to the subsequent impact of the new CEO. In this study, we did not consider the reasons for the change of CEO.

To measure each company's financial performance, we compared its share values to Dow Jones and NASDAQ averages, two of the best-recognized indices for measuring individual corporate performance. Of the

18 companies we studied, nearly 72% demonstrated an improvement in relative performance (based solely on financial results) compared to the Dow Jones average during their leadership transition; 89% of the companies outperformed NASDAQ averages. Representative of the companies with improved share value were American Express (Ken Chanult), Intel (Craig Barrett), Starbucks (Orin Smith), and 3M (Jim McNerney). Obviously, the companies that improved following their leadership transition were doing something right. Conversely, AT&T (David Dorman), Ford (Bill Ford), Kodak (Daniel A. Carp), and Microsoft (Steve Ballmer) were representative of companies that experienced decreases in relative shareholder value following their leadership transition. For a view of the relative monthly share prices of these corporations during the 5-year time window again, please see figures 3.1 through 3.13.

By the way, our decision to compare solely financial indicators in no way implies that we believe only one factor influences corporate value. Obviously, many variables influence the creation of shareholder value, including industry trends, macroeconomic issues, and the global environment. Moreover, a short-term reduction of a company's share price does not necessarily indicate poor leadership; on the contrary, it might result from a wise strategic move by strong leaders to build long-term sustainable value at the cost of a temporarily stagnant share price. Courageous CEO's are capable of accepting the wrath of short-term investors when audacious moves are necessary to build long-term shareholder value.

The results of our study invite some interesting questions. On the positive side, did Intel's carefully calculated and thoughtful succession planning process, which resulted in a well-groomed internal CEO successor, favorably impact the actual (or perceived) performance of the company? How does the Intel success compare with that of another company, 3M, whose board had to go outside their company ranks to take quick advantage of the CEO runoff at GE? Did Starbucks' director independence positively impact its performance, or did a cup of java from Starbucks just taste better than one from McDonald's? How about American Express—was their success driven by better leadership or better products?

Company List

Company	CEO	Announcement Date
Lucent	Patricia F. Russo	January, 2002
AMR	Gerald J. Arpey	April, 2003
Xerox	Anne M. Mulcahy	August, 2001
AT&T	David W. Dorman	December, 2000
AMD	Hector de J. Ruiz, Ph.D.	January, 2000
Intel	Craig R. Barrett, Ph.D.	May, 1998
Microsoft	Steven A. Ballmer	January, 2000
IBM	Samuel J. Palmisano	March, 2002
HP	Carleton S. Fiorina	July, 1999
Ford	William Clay Ford, Jr.	October, 2001
American Express	Kenneth I. Chenault	January, 2001
Alcoa	Alain Belda	January, 2001
3M	W. James McNerney, Jr.	January, 2001
Starbucks	Orin Smith	June, 2000
Pfizer	Henry A. McKinnell, Ph.D.	January, 2001
Alcan	Travis D. Engen	March, 2001
Merrill Lynch	E. Stanley O'Neal	December, 2002
Maytag	Ralph F. Hake	June, 2001

Figure 3.1

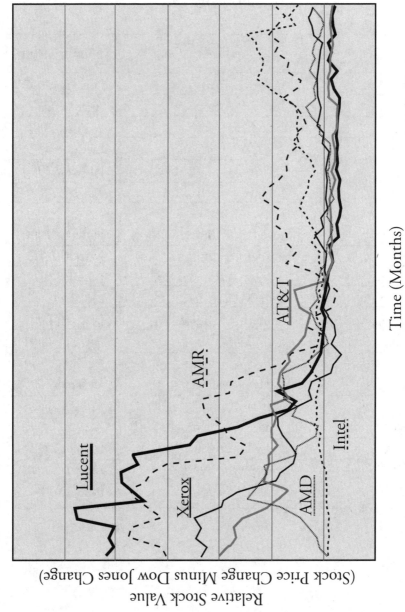

Figure 3.2

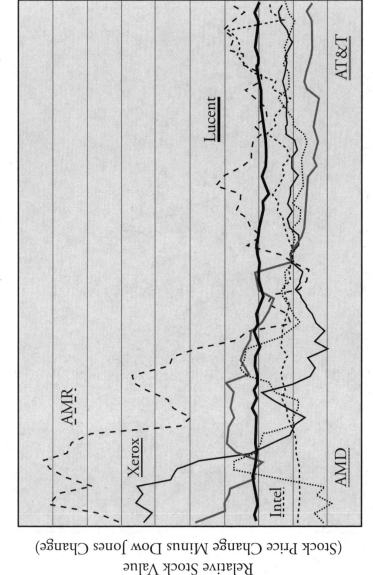

Company Stock Price Correlated with CEO Change (NASDAQ)

Data from Yahoo! Finance

Figure 3.3

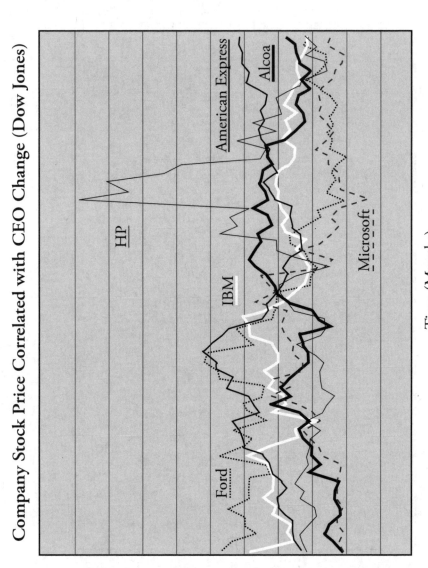

Company Stock Price Correlated with CEO Change (Dow Jones)

Relative Stock Value
(Stock Price Change Minus Dow Jones Change)

Time (Months)

Data from Yahoo! Finance

Figure 3.4

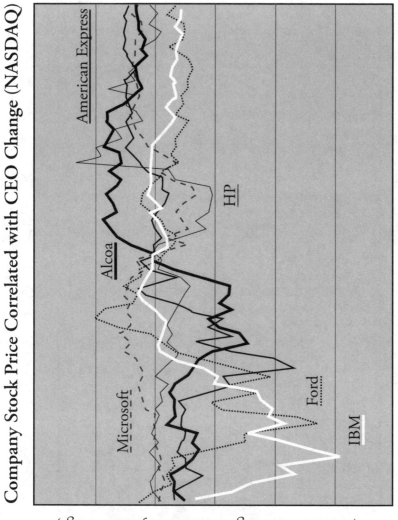

Company Stock Price Correlated with CEO Change (NASDAQ)

American Express

HP

Alcoa

Microsoft

Ford

IBM

Relative Stock Value
(Stock Price Change Minus Dow Jones Change)

Time (Months)

Data from Yahoo! Finance

Figure 3.5

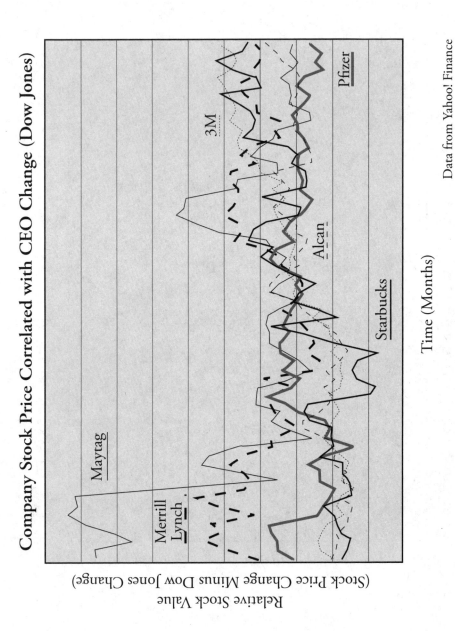

Figure 3.6

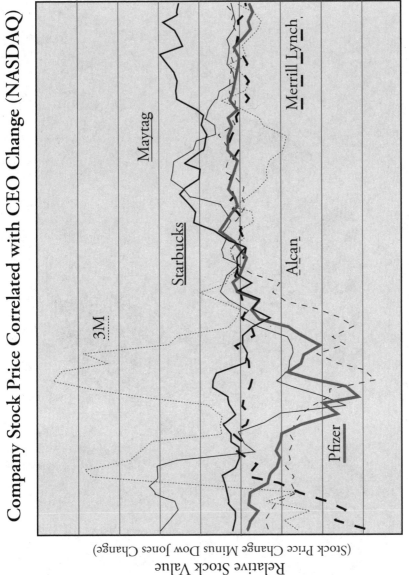

Company Stock Price Correlated with CEO Change (NASDAQ)

Relative Stock Value
(Stock Price Change Minus Dow Jones Change)

Time (Months)

Data from Yahoo! Finance

3M

Starbucks

Maytag

Alcan

Merrill Lynch

Pfizer

Figure 3.7

Dow Jones Index (DJI) Trend Comparisons

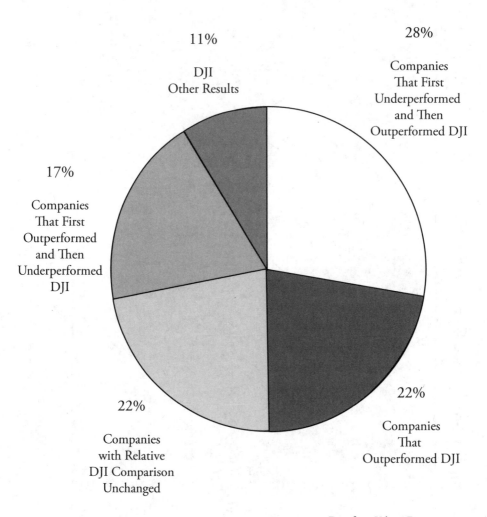

11%

DJI
Other Results

28%

Companies
That First
Underperformed
and Then
Outperformed DJI

17%

Companies
That First
Outperformed
and Then
Underperformed
DJI

22%

Companies
with Relative
DJI Comparison
Unchanged

22%

Companies
That
Outperformed DJI

Data from Yahoo! Finance

Figure 3.8

Dow Jones Index (DJI) Performance Comparisons

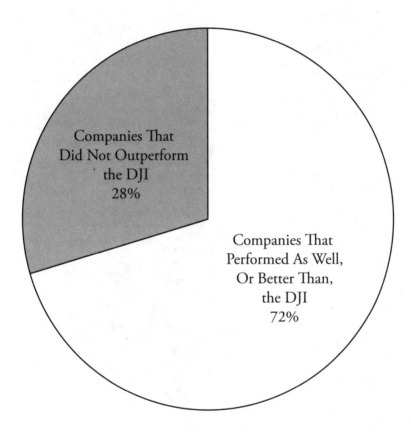

Companies That
Did Not Outperform
the DJI
28%

Companies That
Performed As Well,
Or Better Than,
the DJI
72%

Data from Yahoo! Finance

Figure 3.9

NASDAQ Trend Comparisons

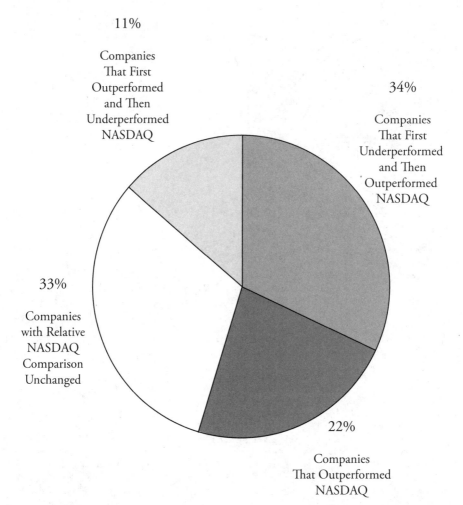

11%

Companies
That First
Outperformed
and Then
Underperformed
NASDAQ

34%

Companies
That First
Underperformed
and Then
Outperformed
NASDAQ

33%

Companies
with Relative
NASDAQ
Comparison
Unchanged

22%

Companies
That Outperformed
NASDAQ

Data from Yahoo! Finance

Figure 3.10

NASDAQ Performance Comparisons

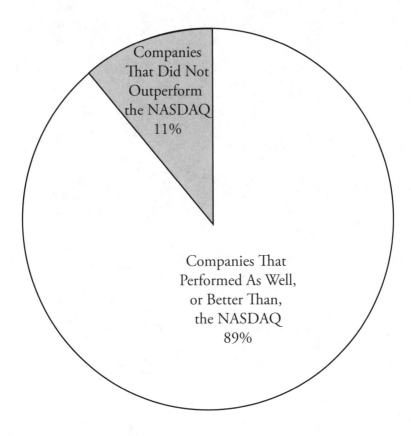

Companies
That Did Not
Outperform
the NASDAQ
11%

Companies That
Performed As Well,
or Better Than,
the NASDAQ
89%

Data from Yahoo! Finance

Figure 3.11

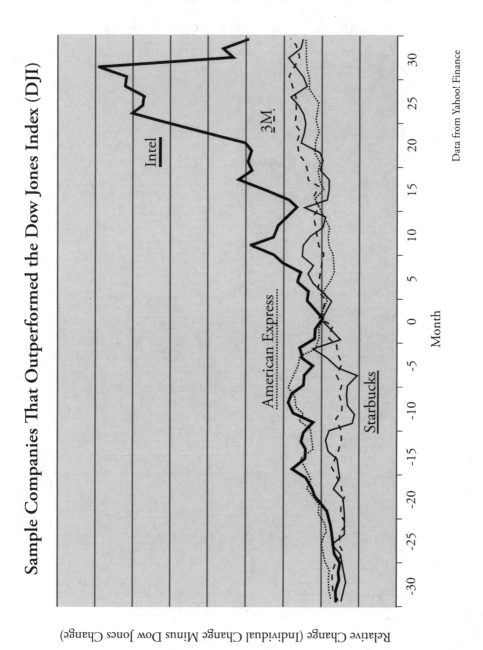

Sample Companies That Outperformed the Dow Jones Index (DJI)

Intel

3M.

American Express

Starbucks

Relative Change (Individual Change Minus Dow Jones Change)

Month

-30 -25 -20 -15 -10 -5 0 5 10 15 20 25 30

Data from Yahoo! Finance

Figure 3.12

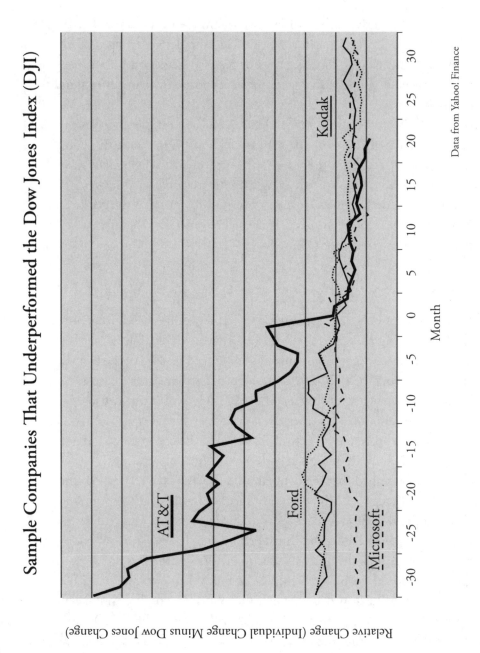

Sample Companies That Underperformed the Dow Jones Index (DJI)

Relative Change (Individual Change Minus Dow Jones Change)

AT&T

Ford

Microsoft

Kodak

Month

Data from Yahoo! Finance

Figure 3.13

On the negative side, did excessive family influence on Ford's CEO adversely impact Ford's performance? Were the deteriorating performances of AT&T and Kodak consequences of hazy strategies and poorly executed plans, or were these industry monarchs dethroned by stronger or fraudulent competitors?

What about the effects of CEO compensation on success? Was the CEO of American Express, who operated under short-term executive compensation, just hungrier than the CEO of Microsoft, whose pay plan was a continuation of his process of amassing extreme personal wealth?

Although the variables are many, it seems obvious that the qualities of the company's head of operations, the CEO, are central to the success or lack of success of those operations.

Linking Board Performance to CEO Performance

Clearly, a corporation's board must be extremely diligent in hiring, nurturing, and monitoring the CEO and ensuring that he or she selects a senior team capable of delivering great organizational leadership. Part of the board experience is replacing the CEO. In fact, one process that sends a clear message of board confidence in and support of the CEO is a robust succession planning process that lays the groundwork for an orderly future transition. When the CEO and the board are collectively engaged in the corporate succession planning process, they are more likely to have shared expectations.

It is to be hoped that the company's leadership is so strong that the CEO retires in accordance with an orderly succession plan. This, of course, is not always the case. CEO's sometimes voluntarily leave companies to accept other positions, and sometimes they must be forced to leave because of poor performance. Unfortunately, CEO's occasionally die in office, as did Texas Instruments' Jerry Junkins in 1995 and McDonalds' Jim Cantalupo in 2005.

It also is to be hoped that, when the board has conducted the transition from one CEO to the next, the results will be favorable to the company's stakeholders. Whether the incoming CEO has accepted his or her new position to pursue the challenge of leading the company from poor performance to the heights, to try something new and different, or to build more personal wealth, the board must remember that in nearly all situations investor confidence in the CEO is a very strong leading indicator of long-term stock performance.

For example, when John Akers, CEO of IBM, left the company, its stock was trading at approximately $45 a share. Some believe IBM had lost its way under a complacent board blindly basking in decades of well-earned success. Shareholder confidence in Akers was low, and the board boldly moved to recruit Lou Gerstner to replace Akers in 1993; the board then supported and nurtured Gerstner in his new role. When Gerstner retired from IBM in December of 2002, IBM's stock was selling on a pre-split basis at $180 per share.

Without bold action by IBM's board, Gerstner would not have set foot in IBM's headquarters in Armonk, New York, except perhaps to demand better support from his information systems supplier. Such strong leadership deserves recognition.

A board's hiring, nurturing, and supervisory actions can impair or optimize company performance. If a weak or apathetic board does a poor job of selecting, grooming, and developing a CEO who leads company operations into poor performance, that board must share responsibility for the company's failure to generate increased shareowner value. Conversely, if an active board successfully hires, nurtures, and monitors a good CEO who produces good results, that board should be recognized for its contribution to overall company performance. Constructive nurturing of the CEO includes insisting that he or she seek continued training and developmental opportunities.

Beyond their basic obligations to select, guide, and monitor the CEO's performance, directors also have many opportunities to act as enlightened role models for excellence. The board processes on which the company's future success depends are those that will optimize CEO transitions, facilitate collaboration between the board and the CEO, and streamline decision-making.

The board of directors has a responsibility to work in collaboration with the CEO and his or her leadership team. In today's intensely competitive global markets, teamwork can make a big difference. Extreme personal leaders in the boardroom should act on the logical connection between their leadership skills and the company's future success by pursuing maximum shareholder value in partnership with the CEO. When the board and the CEO work together, they empower each other to make bold, calculated moves that earn the company opportunities to serve shareholders, possibly for hundreds of years into the future. Companies in which the board and CEO work in close collaboration, like DuPont, IBM, and General Electric, are able to risk reinventing themselves to deliver sustainable value over the long term. The issues boards face as they reinvent themselves in the interests of long-term shareholders is the subject of the next chapter.

Notes

[i] McKinsey & Company. (2002). *Global Investor Opinion Survey: Key Findings.* New York: Author. Retrieved July 27, 2006, from http://www.mckinsey.com/clientservice/organizationleadership/service/corpgovernance/pdf/GlobalInvestorOpinionSurvey2002.pdf.

[ii] David, P., Kochhar, R., & Levitas, E. (1998). The effect of institutional investors on the level and mix of CEO compensation. *Academy of Management Journal, 41*(2): 200-208.

[iii] The Conference Board. (2005, October 10). U.S. institutional investors boost control of U.S. equity market assets. *The Conference Board: News.* Retrieved August 2, 2006, from http://www.conference-board.org/

Chapter 4

Concerns of the Fully Engaged Corporate Board

While there are many steps to solving a puzzle, some are more important than others.

The corporate board's primary responsibility traditionally has been fiduciary oversight, with due diligence and care, of the profitability, management, and dispensation of the corporation's property. Although the duty of fiduciary responsibility remains of utmost importance in corporate governance, over the years directors have been forced to ponder to whom that duty is owed[i] as the voices demanding better corporate performance and accountability included new constituencies of customers, suppliers, partners, employees, minority groups, and environmental activists. Today, these groups are better informed, more vocal, and more demanding of accurate disclosure. [ii] This is an obvious and very appropriate realignment between the interests of stakeholders and those of directors and CEO's.

Over the past 3 decades, boards have faced many demands of accountability for corporate citizenship. Outspoken advocates of corporate governance reform, such as Robert A. G. Monks, the pioneering shareholder activist and chairman of the activist advisory firm LENS, have argued that because corporations are legally treated as persons they must endeavor to act under the laws of the land, just as ordinary citizens must do. Consumer advocates like Monks, Ralph Nader, and Richard Koppes helped draw media attention to unethical and illegal behaviors of some of the country's largest corporate citizens.[iii] Well-publicized charges of price-fixing, poor labor practices, and environmental offenses plagued many leading corporations. Community advocacy groups criticized corporations for meeting their bottom lines at the expense of the communities in which they operated, and community activists pressured boards to address training, unemployment, medical, and disability issues.

A decade ago, Monks argued that companies must realize that their decisions have wide impacts across society, and that they must incorporate that awareness into their decision-making processes. To do so, Monks said, corporate boards and CEO's must envision the future effects on society of their present actions or inactions.[iv] In response to community activists' efforts, by 1990, nearly half of the states had adopted multi-constituency laws that redefined the corporate director's fiduciary duty such that this duty is owed not only to the company's shareholders but also to many other constituencies.[v] As today's directors practice due diligence, they are compelled to ask difficult questions about the company's core functions in terms of safety, morality, and ethics.

Today, just as for the last 2 decades, boards face the arduous task of finding a balance between the two competing demands, responsible community citizenship on the one hand and shareholder profitability on the other.[vi,vii] Boards must lead their corporations into an equilibrium between support of vested interests of various corporate stakeholders and optimization of long-term shareholder value. They must determine the extent to which their decisions ought to address public priorities versus commercial priorities. For example, a 1990 Pennsylvania anti-takeover law permits management in the process of weighing takeover bids to give first consideration to employees, customers, suppliers, or the community rather than to shareholders.[viii] Of course, enlightened directors and boards understand that leveraging a positive position with all stakeholders is the best long-term strategy for generating sustainable shareholder value.

The Fully Engaged Board

After all viewpoints are considered, and no matter where stakeholders think a company should be headed, the best way the board can meet stakeholder demands is to address the challenges facing the company. The better the board meets those challenges, the more stakeholder interests will be served.

Fully engaged directors do the homework necessary to understand their corporation and its industry. They participate in all board activities, including meetings, conference calls, and site visits. When an issue arouses their concern, they become hair-shirt directors who convey to the CEO that they do not sit in the boardroom to watch things happen but to make things happen in the best interests of the corporation's stakeholders.

Inside enlightened 21st-century boardrooms, a tremendous amount of exciting hard work is taking place as fully engaged directors assert their passionate commitment to the success of their corporations. Today's directors enjoy many opportunities to participate in optimizing shareholder value and meet the demands of other stakeholders, but the following topics seem to be getting the most attention:

1. strategic planning,
2. succession planning,
3. CEO supervision,
4. executive compensation,
5. independence, and
6. board composition.

This chapter provides a brief overview of each of these important topics, which will be discussed in greater detail in later chapters.

Strategic Planning

Planning the company's strategy is one of the best ways to positively impact all of the company's stakeholders. For this reason, directors should ensure that the company develops and then implements a well-considered strategic plan. As Jonathan Charkham, an international authority on corporate governance, has pointed out, "In theory, information flows from shareholders to the board to the management team and back again, and should result in plans and decisions that favor the long-term interests of shareholders." Because strategic planning is the key to corporate survival, the board should make sure that strategic plans are executed as soon as they are devised.

Preventing the board from drifting aimlessly is every director's job, and one of the most rewarding aspects of board service is the opportunity to help set the company's direction. Each director should be intimately involved in developing the corporation's strategy and in the follow-through for full implementation of that strategy, even if these responsibilities demand stepping into hair-shirt director mode to be aggressive with the senior leadership team. Truly enlightened directors seize opportunities to aggressively support the company's pursuit of strategic goals designed to maximize stakeholder value. One way to exercise this leadership is to promote a plan to proactively seek improvements to the governing process, an important part of which is developing better awareness of corporate governance.

Succession Planning

Another key duty of the board is to ensure that the company has a preeminent CEO to lead its overall operations and an executive team who successfully supports the CEO's company operations program. Ensuring stellar executive leadership for the company requires focused planning of succession for the CEO and the senior executives from among whose ranks the next CEO is likely to be selected. The enlightened board understands that succession planning is an ongoing process, not a one-time program or an annual review of the corporation's best talent.

The first major challenge in the succession planning process is developing a CEO profile of the projected qualifications of the company's next CEO. Which characteristics are required? Which are desired? In this profile, the board should include specific skills, experiences, personal leadership skills, and individual personal attributes.

CEO Supervision

For at least 2 decades, concern among investors, employees, and regulators over who—if anyone—actually supervises the CEO, has steadily intensified. A great many corporate stakeholders have been made wary by the historical lack of management oversight in numerous corporations. The crux of the problem was well described by the late Jonathan Charkham, one of the founding figures of corporate governance reform:

> Corporate governance exists to protect shareowners by providing for an elected board of directors, accountable to the shareowners, to monitor management activities and decisions. . . . In practice, however, corporate governance may fall so dismally short . . . that effective oversight fails to occur and shareowners are disenfranchised.[ix]

The question has been whether many CEO's are in fact accountable to a higher level of authority. The very least that shareholders expect of their company's board of directors is that they will prevent the CEO and his team from engaging in illegal activities that could capsize shareholder interests.

To prevent the CEO from having undue influence on directors who traditionally were members of a closed, interlocking network of CEO's who served on each other's boards, institutional investors rallied behind the idea of increasing the number of independent directors on boards in the hopes that their distance from the company's influence would increase their level of oversight. In theory this plan seemed workable, but, as pointed out in 1997 by John A. Byrne, Executive Editor of *Business Week Magazine,* many directors who were considered independent instead were quite dependent on the corporations they served:

Many so-called outsider board members were not really independent of the company: among them might be the firm's bankers, lawyers, suppliers, or key customers—the very type of interdependent hand-picked directors for which Michael Eisner, CEO of Walt Disney, was recently criticized for selecting.[x]

Whether or not directors are independent, they can do significantly more in their supervisory capacity than merely safeguarding shareholders' interests from disaster. It is far better for everyone's interests if directors step up to the plate to work in close collaboration with the CEO in an atmosphere of mutual support aimed at maximizing company and shareholder value.

Executive Compensation

As enlightened boards proactively link executive pay to long-term shareholder value, the federal government and its agency, the U.S. Securities and Exchange Commission, will be exercising their prerogative as corporate stakeholders to mandate certain corporate activities with regard to executive compensation.

One SEC intervention in corporate compensation is the so-called *million dollar rule* of the Internal Revenue Code, which limits the tax deductibility of executive compensation to $1 million unless that compensation is tied to performance objectives established at the beginning of each annual performance period. As explained by Securities and Exchange Commissioner Paul S. Atkins, "Thus, in effect, it costs companies 35% more to pay their top executives more than $1 million per year because of the corporate tax rate."[xi]

Although the million dollar rule was designed to keep boards focused on the pay-for-performance principle, it failed to motivate boards to decrease total executive compensation, according to the findings of a study conducted in 2000 by Brian J. Hall and Jeffrey B. Liebman of Harvard University. Instead, firms made only minor substitutions to adjust the composition of CEO pay packages away from salary and toward "performance related pay."[xii]

The SEC has continued to weigh in on executive compensation policies by establishing various blue-ribbon reports on guidelines for audit committees and by demanding reports from compensation committees. These efforts to ensure disclosure and transparency concerning the company's true financial performance and governance practices have been thoughtfully designed to assist boards in executing their responsibilities. In late July of 2006, the SEC announced that publicly owned corporations will be required to tell shareholders how much the five most-senior executives, including the CEO and CFO, earn from salary, stock options, and other benefits. The SEC also will demand detailed information about corporate director pay and the timing of stock option grants to prevent companies from backdating stock options to give executives guaranteed profit.[xiii] This gesture may expose a few irresponsible boards that shower their executives and directors with excessive pay, but it will not address the fundamental need to link executive compensation to long-term shareholder value, which is the job of the shareholder's representative, the enlightened board.

Director Independence

The significant pressure on corporations to be more transparent when reporting financial results to shareholders is responsible for today's greater need for independence in the boardroom. Most directors understand and generally accept this need. To demonstrate more effective oversight and a renewed focus on the fundamentals of protecting stakeholders' interests, corporations must ensure unquestionable director independence.

How is unquestionable independence being defined? Substantial debate has clouded the process of developing an appropriate definition. The chief justice of the Delaware Supreme Court approved one basic definition of an independent director in the bylaws of General Motors:

> One who is not, and has not been, employed by the corporation, or its subsidiaries, for the past five years; is not a significant advisor, lawyer, consultant, customer or supplier of the corporation, or its subsidiaries; does not have personal services contracts with the corporation or its subsidiaries; is

not affiliated with a tax exempt entity or its subsidiaries; and is not a spouse, parent, sibling, or child of any inside director.[xiv]

The Sarbanes-Oxley Act of 2002 caused further debate around the definition of independent directors, as will be discussed in greater detail later in this book.

It is intuitively logical that independent directors are more likely to represent the best interests of the shareholders if these collide with the interests of management. However, whether a director supports the status quo or drives for change, he or she must understand the ethos of the company. At the very least, a director should co-exist within the corporation's culture and strive to develop constructive working relationships with other members of the board.

In his book, *A Theory of the Firm,* Harvard professor Michael Jensen wrote:

> A well-functioning board should be capable of providing the organizational culture and support for the organizations they serve! Board culture is an important component of board failure. The emphasis on politeness and courtesy at the expense of truth and frankness in boardrooms is both a symptom and cause of failure in the control system. CEO's have the same insecurities and defense mechanisms as other human beings; few will accept, much less seek, the monitoring and criticism of an active and attentive board.[xv]

To illustrate the hidebound attitudes often found in traditional board environments, Jensen related an experience of John Hanley, the retired CEO of Monsanto, after he accepted an invitation from another CEO to join his board.[xvi] As Hanley recounted:

> At the first board dinner, the CEO got up and said, "I think Jack was a little bit confused whether we wanted him to be a director or the chief executive officer." I should have known right there that he wasn't going to pay a bit of attention to anything I said.[xvii]

So it turned out and, after a year, Hanley quit the board in disgust.

Jensen believed that this type of restrictive boardroom environment would produce a continuing cycle of board ineffectiveness. By rewarding consent and discouraging conflicts, the CEO controls the board, ultimately reducing his or her own performance and that of the company. The difficulties created in this downward spiral are likely to manifest as a crisis instead of a series of small problems met by a continuously self-correcting mechanism.[xviii] Like Jensen, I believe that ineffective corporate board cultures will not be reformed in response to mere calls for change from policymakers, the press, or the academic community. Changing a board's culture requires extreme personal leadership by the CEO and an enlightened board of directors intent on leading themselves to the higher levels of performance expected by their shareholders.

However they are defined, truly independent directors bring value to the board because better ideas generally flow from a group of independent thinkers. This probably is the best reason for a highly motivated board to insist on director independence.

Of course, it is to be expected that independent directors will vote differently than their trusted colleagues from time to time. However, independence does not suggest that the director's positions on issues must always differ from those of his or her colleagues. The board as a whole and each individual director should stay attuned for signs of misalignment among their ranks and consider what this misalignment indicates. For example, a director whose views usually oppose those of fellow board members might not be the right person to serve on a particular board. On the other hand, the misalignment may be a warning signal that the board is heading for great difficulty. Broad misalignment of a director with the collective board signals a time for introspection on the part of the director whose views are misaligned as well as a time for thoughtful consideration by the rest of the board.

Director independence is important, but it is not a surrogate for leadership. Directors should not use their independent status solely to get things done according to their own terms; the board must operate in a collegial environment to be effective. Teamwork is what makes the dream work.

Board Composition

In 2004, more than 10,000 directors served on the boards of publicly owned corporations listed on the major stock exchanges: NYSE, NASDAQ and AMEX. According to Spencer Stuart, in 2005, 85% of all directors of the Fortune 500 firms were white, non-Hispanic men.[xix] Although directors' education levels, socioeconomic status, gender, race, age, and other characteristics put them in a more-or-less homogeneous group, they certainly are not all equal!

Most corporate directors are highly successful and quite experienced business people. However, some have no business experience at all and bring to the boardroom valuable political or community perspectives. Although corporate directors usually hold enormous responsibilities as a result of their talent and hard work, they are very much real people who are, in many respects, much like most middle class Americans, with many of the same concerns about their personal lives, compensation, recognition, and workload. Although they probably are less likely to admit having worries about their working lives, they are just as prone as most people to complain about trivial problems.

As in the larger world, directors bring with them a diversity of personalities and approaches. Predictably, some directors have tremendous corporate operations experience and approach everything with a logical and dispassionate view. Some of these directors may even believe that most situations are binary: on or off, black or white, good or bad. Surprisingly, though, other directors with equal operating experience lead with their emotions. Others are guided by political considerations, hidden agendas, or passionate concern about their areas of specific interest.

Enlightened directors bring balance to the boardroom. They know the difference between logic and emotion and recognize the need for both. They know how and when to use one or the other and tend to lead with logic and avoid becoming overly influenced by emotion. Of course, boards can take many actions to improve the quality and diversity of talent in their boardrooms. Ways for boards to tap into the talent that companies need will be discussed later in this book.

Summary

In 1989, Jay Lorsch and Elizabeth MacIver aptly defined the corporate board's responsibility as overseeing management, reviewing performance, and ensuring that the various activities of the company are socially responsible and in compliance with the law.[xx] Today these duties are more important than ever. However, the board's responsibilities must be extended to encompass all of the new areas of focus for the 21st-century board, such as independent thinking and inquisitive action. The strong convictions of enlightened directors will drive the board's need to focus beyond full compliance with all laws, rules, and regulations to embrace strategic planning, succession management, linking executive compensation to long-term shareholder value, and achieving greater financial transparency for shareholders. Every great company needs a great CEO, however, and the focus of the next chapter is on how boards can help CEO's attain great long-term company performance.

Notes

[i] Blair, M. M. (1995). *Ownership and control: Rethinking corporate governance for the twenty-first century*. Washington, DC: The Brookings Institution.

[ii] Ibid.

[iii] Markoff, J. (1997, October 6). Microsoft is the latest target of Nader's consumer crusade. *The New York Times*, pp. D1, D10.

[iv] Monks, R. A. G. (1996). The American corporation at the end of the twentieth century: An outline of ownership based governance. A speech given at Cambridge University, July, 1996. Retrieved May 27, 2006, from http://www.lens-library.com/info/cambridge.html.

[v] Longstreth, B. (1990). Takeovers, corporate governance, and stock ownership: Some disquieting trends. *Journal of Portfolio Management*, 54-59.

[vi] Jacobs, M. T. (1991). *Short-term America: The causes and cures of our business myopia*. Boston: Harvard Business School Press.

[vii] For a similar idea, see Jones, T. M., & Wicks, A. C. (1999). Convergent stakeholder theory. *Academy of Management Review*, 24(2) 206-221.

[viii] Shiller, R. J. (1992). *Who's minding the store? The report of the Twentieth Century Fund Task Force on market speculation and corporate governance*. New York: Twentieth Century Fund Press.

[ix] Charkham, J. (1994). *Keeping good company: A study of corporate governance in five countries*, pp. 215-225. New York: Oxford University Press.

[x] Byrne, J. (1997, December 8). The best and worst boards: Our special report on corporate governance. *Business Week,* 90.

[xi] Atkins, P. S. (2006). *Remarks before the Securities Regulation Institute. Speech by the Securities and Exchange Commissioner,* San Diego, California, January 19, 2006. Retrieved July 5, 2006, from http://www.sec.gov/news/speech/spch011906psa.htm.

[xii] Hall, B. J., & Liebman, J. B. (2000). The taxation of executive compensation (NBER Research Working Papers 7596). Cambridge, MA: National Bureau of Economic Research, Inc.

[xiii] O'Hara, T. (2006, July 27). SEC rules tightened on pay disclosure. *WashingtonPost.com.* Retrieved August 5, 2006, from http://washingtonpost.com/

[xiv] Sorensen, O. (1997). Board size, composition, and maintenance. *The Corporate Board, 18*(107), 32.

[xv] Jensen, M. C. (2000). *A theory of the firm: Governance, residual claims, and organizational forms.* Cambridge, MA: Harvard University Press.

[xvi] Ibid.

[xvii] Magnet, M. (1992, June 15). Directors, wake up! *Fortune,* 85-92, as cited by Jensen, 2000.

[xviii] Jensen, 2000.

[xix] Spencer Stuart. (2006). 2006 board diversity report. New York: Author. Retrieved August 2, 2006, from http://content.spencerstuart.com/sswebsite/pdf/lib/Board_Diversity_Report_2006.pdf.

[xx] Lorsch, J. W., & MacIver, E. A. (1989). *Pawns and potentates: The reality of America's corporate boards.* Boston: Harvard Business School Press.

Chapter 5

Corporate Strategic Planning

People who brought you candles will never bring you electricity.

With regional boundaries essentially eliminated by global competition, corporations need their boards to be vigilant strategic planners who can handle diversity in every aspect of the corporation's operations, including the company's workforce, customer base, and global opportunities. Clearly, shifting demographics will be driving economic and social changes. These changes may seem small from year to year, but their cumulative impact will be far-reaching. Boards must understand and embrace these changes and recognize the opportunities and challenges they present.

Some researchers have pointed out that ingrained habits and rigid systems keep companies stuck in low gear.[i] When a CEO decides to shape the company's opportunities, corporate governance shifts into high gear, and the board starts removing cost-regulation policies and procedures that might obstruct change. The board reorganizes itself around issues, thus creating a lighter, more flexible, and more responsive governance structure that makes it much easier to channel strategic information and focus decision-making. This high-velocity corporate governance approach, researchers P. G. Leemputte and P. Benda have argued, enables corporations to initiate new business opportunities with "no-holds-barred" enthusiasm.[ii]

A corporation's strategy is its roadmap, and all its decisions are founded on its guidance. A hotly argued debate in corporate governance is whether boards are responsible for developing corporate strategy or merely for ensuring that the CEO and senior management team develop one. No doubt any company would gain considerable competitive advantage if its board had the time and competency to develop effective strategic plans for the company, but that is hardly the reality. Most directors are selected for their strong general management skills and experiences and not for specific industry knowledge. Instead of attempting to develop corporate strategy, corporate directors should work with the senior management team to ensure that a comprehensive strategic plan is developed, approved, and effectively implemented. To carry out this role, the board should select some directors with industry-specific experiences and encourage all board members to acquire a good working knowledge of the industry. Directors also should develop an appreciation for the company's culture and challenges.

In light of the critical importance of developing and maintaining a competitive corporate strategy, the board should consider authorizing the creation of a standing committee for strategic planning, thus authorizing a subset of the full board to allocate more time to this concern. This should be considered when there is a need for a more focused effort beyond regular board meetings. The board chair or CEO should chair this committee. Like all other board committees, the strategic planning committee works on behalf of the full board and must not be considered its surrogate. This committee should regularly brief the board on its activities and hold discussions with the full board as required.

Strategic planning is a process by which corporate leadership can plan, organize, and deploy the company's assets. The strategic plan should be the baseline for allocating all corporate resources. Because all corporate resources are fundamentally fungible, they must be distributed based on some priority established by the corporate leadership. Therefore, it is appropriate that the board be actively involved in some decisions regarding the use of shareholder resources, such as cash, capital equipment, and human resources. The corporate strategy should help the corporate leadership team focus their energy on ensuring that the company's employees are working toward a common set of objectives.[iii] In essence, strategic planning should produce essential decisions and actions that shape and guide what an organization is, what it does, and why it does it, with a focus on the future.

As stewards of the corporation, directors must endeavor to protect the assets of the company's investors. In their pursuit of maximum long-term shareholder value, directors are responsible for considering all reasonable strategies available to the corporations they serve. In an extreme situation, these strategies might include merger with another firm to bolster the corporation's position in its market, sale of the corporation to the highest qualified bidder, or even sales of assets that, based on the realities of the market, will lead to closing of the corporation. In some circumstances, it is in the best interests of some stakeholders and investors for a corporation to be dissolved, but dissolution of a corporation is an atypical outcome, normally not desired. To fulfill its long-term responsibilities to stakeholders and shareholders, a corporation generally must continue to exist.

Building a corporation that generates consistent long-term value for its shareholders is a much more difficult task than splitting the company apart, selling it, or closing its operations. To help ensure sustainable corporate success, the board must be involved in the development and implementation of the company's overall strategic direction. However, it is important to reiterate that directors are not corporate managers. Nonetheless, as a general rule, although directors should not interfere in the day-to-day operations of the corporation, it is quite valuable and very appropriate for them to challenge the CEO's operation of the company when the CEO is failing to deliver the desired results. The board's most important role in company operations is to support the CEO and senior management team by insisting on excellence, maintaining high expectations, and providing assistance when required.

The Corporate Board's New Role in Strategic Planning

Many publications, including *Business Week*, *Forbes*, and *Fortune*, conduct annual surveys to discover the best managed and best governed companies. *Business Week* conducted its first such survey in 1996. The results showed that, with few exceptions, the most successful U.S. companies encouraged the participation of knowledgeable, independent boards. Importantly, these boards either contributed to shaping corporate strategy or carefully questioned CEO's on corporate strategy.[iv]

Based on the survey results, Campbell Soup Company received *Business Week's* highest ranking in light of its board's active role in shaping Campbell's turn-around. Over a 6-month period, Campbell's board had met eight times to design the corporation's strategic goals, question the decisions of CEO David W. Johnson, and lay out long-range strategic plans for the corporation. To evaluate the impact of the newly devised strategy, the board had commissioned its own outside investment banker and legal counsel.[v] Although this level of board engagement was an exception to the rule a decade ago, it has become typical of highly enlightened boards of the 21st century. Informed shareholders expect corporate directors to be constructively engaged in the strategic development process. Competent and confident CEO's welcome board participation and support.

Involving the board in corporate strategic development is desirable, but it is not easy to accomplish. Board guidance of strategic decision-making is a formidable task that involves the brokering of power between directors and the CEO and his or her team. To establish a board process of corporate strategy involvement, the board and CEO must first establish a relationship based on mutual respect and trust. Constructive engagement is the baseline for success.

Traditionally, corporate boards reviewed and gave final approval to corporate strategies devised by the senior management team. Often, directors felt obliged to approve, unquestioningly, the CEO's goals and plans for the company because they lacked the industry-specific perspectives needed to contribute meaningfully to the company's strategy and they recognized that the corporation's senior executives had invested significant effort, research, and planning into developing the company's strategies and goals.

Although the corporate board has a fiduciary responsibility to provide oversight of the company and its senior leadership team, it nonetheless must earn the right to be actively engaged in the corporate strategic planning process. The board earns opportunities to help lead this fundamental effort by providing on-going constructive counsel and guidance to the CEO and his or her team. Of course, their level of engagement in strategy planning always will be guided by the degree of support proffered by the board chair, a situation that could influence the board's decision to combine or separate the roles of CEO and board chair. Furthermore, the number of insiders on the board certainly affects the senior management team's level of acceptance of board engagement in the strategic planning process.[vi] As pointed out by Kenneth R. Andrews, the Harvard business professor who became known as the Father of Corporate Strategy, senior executives might feel threatened by the board's evaluations of their motives and decision-making processes even when the board is satisfied with their performance. Traditional CEO's often view board participation as intrusions on their managerial roles. They also might be unaccustomed to articulating and analyzing unstated or incremental strategy decisions.[vii]

At many of the nation's top corporations in the 1980s and 1990s, the inclusion of more outside directors on boards and the creation of auditing, compensation, and strategic planning committees empowered those directors at least to question corporate strategies and to participate in their development. Often, the board and senior managers would work together to complete strategy audits that provided the corporation with an assessment of where it stood in the new business environment and where it should be in that environment, thus, as Harvard professor Gordon Donaldson suggested, using the strategic audit as a tool for recognizing successes and anticipating problems.[viii]

However, in today's globally competitive environment, corporations no longer have the leisure to sit back and wait to audit the appropriateness of their corporate strategies. Enlightened directors want to be constructively engaged in assisting the CEO in developing macro-level company strategy.

CEO's with good insight and personal confidence not only welcome board involvement in strategy development but also insist on it!

According to management consultant John E. Balkcom, boards most often are tempted to concern themselves with corporate strategies that address discontinuous change.[ix] Discontinuity surrounds reorganizations such as mergers, acquisitions, takeovers, and downsizing. Deregulation also can dramatically transform ordinary business practices, as can legislation such as the Administration for Disabilities Act (ADA) and regulations enforced by the Occupational Safety and Health Administration (OSHA) and the Environmental Protection Agency (EPA). Political and economic changes in foreign countries can affect competitive markets, foreign subsidiaries, and joint ventures. Changes in manufacturing and communications technologies can negatively affect a corporation's financial standing. To maintain or increase profits amid this flurry of discontinuity, boards are realizing that they must shape and guide corporate strategic decisions.[x] Today the highly enlightened board wants to be engaged in assisting new growth initiatives as much as they are involved in assuring the status quo.

As discussed earlier, active participation in corporate strategic planning does not imply that directors should micro-manage the corporation's operations. Operational decisions must be left to management. However, as directors assume more active roles in the corporations they direct, the distinction between corporate planning and corporate management can become blurred if not managed effectively. For example, deciding to enter a new line of business and establishing the goals for its success are part of the planning process. However, deciding how to implement and achieve the new line's objectives is a management responsibility. The board has to remain cognizant of the potential distortion. Directors must distinguish the differences and govern accordingly.

The idea that boards are expected to actively involve themselves in designing the architecture of corporate strategy is the reason why succession planning, CEO supervision, executive compensation, director independence and board composition have become so vitally important and controversial. Shareholders expect directors to light the way, not stumble around in the dark hoping not to trip over any significant problems.

When directors actively engage with the CEO in developing corporate strategy, they must do so with a conceptual understanding of how these areas of importance are inextricably linked together. The strategic plan must reflect the implications of the CEO succession plan, for example. The board must be populated with directors committed to overseeing implementation of the corporate strategy. Moreover, CEO compensation must be tightly linked to the overall strategic plan and resulting shareholder value. And finally, equally important, independent directors who exercise good judgment in the interests of long-term shareholders must comprise the board.

The next chapter deals with another critical board planning process, succession planning.

Notes

[i] Leemputte, P. G., & Benda, P. (1998). High-velocity approach places a premium on opportunities. *Executive Agenda*, 27.

[ii] Leemputte & Benda, 1998.

[iii] Alliance for Nonprofit Management. (n.d.). What is strategic planning? *Overview.* Retrieved August 7, 2006, from http://www.allianceonline.org/FAQ/strategic_planning/what_is_strategic_planning.faq.

[iv] Byrne, J. A. (1996, April 22). How high can CEO pay go? *Business Week*, 3472.

[v] Byrne, 1996.

[vi] Balkcom, J. E. (1994). The new board: Redrawing the lines. *Directors & Boards, 18*(3). 25-27.

[vii] Andrews, K. R. (1980). Directors' responsibility for corporate strategy. *Harvard Business Review*, 58(6), 30-42.

[viii] Donaldson, G. (1995). A new tool for boards: The strategic audit. *Harvard Business Review, 73*(4). 99-107.

[ix] Balkcom, 1994.

[x] Ibid.

Chapter 6

Effective Succession Planning and Implementation

The first decision in getting somewhere is determining who is going to drive.

The job of corporate CEO comes with many extraordinary benefits. CEO's soar around the world in corporate jets or, at the very least, when they travel on commercial airlines, they fly first class. At theaters, political and sports events, and the world's finest dining establishments, they sit in the best seats in the house.

Such perks might seem like superfluous luxuries to most people outside the corporate world, but they often are the foundation on which the corporation's successes are built. In the business world, corporate customers want to engage with suppliers and partners who demonstrate extraordinary leadership within their industries and reek of success. Most corporate customers do not want to build a long-term business relationship with a supplier who travels coach or standby, even if that company has an incredibly unique set of products and services. Corporate customers expect their suppliers to be highly successful.

Although CEO's enjoy *very* comfortable incomes and build substantial foundations of wealth, I believe that they take equal pleasure in the other trappings associated with their positions. The perks afforded to the people fortunate enough to reach the pinnacle of corporate success are plentiful, and being a CEO is a fantastic job that offers significant opportunities to wield power and influence.

However, the trappings of corporate success and power have their downsides, too. Greed and abuse of power have made the names of some formerly celebrated CEOs infamous. A more likely consequence of lavish corporate benefits, however, is that CEOs become so wedded to their positions that they fail to develop and implement effective CEO succession plans.

In many ways, this is understandable. Being a CEO in Corporate America is a very rewarding job, but it also is a very demanding one, and only a relatively few people are both qualified and willing to do what is necessary to pursue it. Once a person has earned the right of passage to this leadership position, he or she naturally wants to enjoy it as long as possible. Given the rewards and excitement of the CEO position, it is not surprising that many CEO's do not find the task of developing a successor an appealing one. Especially when the CEO is performing well and is consistently delivering outstanding shareholder value, he or she isn't likely to think that developing a successor is a high-priority (or even necessary) task. Robert Stobaugh, retired Harvard business professor and director of the chemical company, Ashland Inc., summed up the situation when he said, "A lot of people enjoy the power and perks of being a CEO. When the time comes, they don't want to go."[i]

Nevertheless, a CEO should stay in the job no longer than he or she can generate value for long-term shareholders. Any CEO who fails to do so and does not enjoy his or her job should not be the CEO. A CEO has to show up for work every day ready to kick down the door! Unfortunately, some boards allow their CEOs to stay longer than they should.

The directors of an enlightened board, however, who do everything in their power to support the CEO in his or her efforts to build long-term shareholder value, also recognize the need for an executive succession planning process that protects the company as much as possible from the uncertainty and upset of transition from one leader to another. This endeavor is important no matter what the age, tenure, or performance of the incumbent CEO may be.

Understanding the Succession Planning Process

Developing a succession plan is merely identifying what to do when there is a need to select a new CEO. However, to develop an effective succession plan, the board needs guidance. That's where the succession planning *process* comes in. Succession planning processes exist to guide the board of directors through the steps needed to ensure that the board identifies the best qualified candidates for the CEO position and then makes sure that they are properly developed and positioned for succession when the time comes. Therefore, before developing an executive succession plan, the board first must develop and implement a comprehensive succession planning process.

During the past 2 decades, I have participated in nearly a dozen CEO successions. For all of them, the basic process was the same. First, the board assessed the readiness of all appropriate candidates within the company. Next (in most of these cases), the directors discussed whether it was appropriate and necessary to pursue candidates from outside the company. Usually the incumbent CEO played an active role in supporting the board throughout the process.

Succession planning should be conducted in a methodical manner. For an experienced executive, establishing the process, identifying the obvious candidates, and completing the replacement tables, that is, are very basic steps of thoughtful planning.

However, identifying and developing the CEO's potential successors inside the corporation are much more difficult tasks. Like athletic coaches, business leaders must master the art of talent identification and development. Because talent is the key to success, some boards attempt to identify potential CEO candidates very early in their careers and watch them throughout their development. Other boards wait until talented people reach a certain level in the company and then put them on a track for accelerated development. Some boards wait until a small pool of qualified people emerges inside the company and then choose from among them.

IBM, General Electric, and DuPont are among the companies that start the process very, very early by identifying high-potential individuals and then grooming them throughout their career. For example, early in my career at IBM, Sam Palmisano, now IBM's chairman and CEO, and I both were executive assistants to senior officers of the company at the same time. Sam and I, along with a small cadre of others, had been placed on the "special list" to be groomed as future senior officers of the company. Placement on IBM's high-potential list is considered a highly coveted privilege, and IBM's fast-track process is a rigorous one! With few exceptions, notably Lou Gerstner (who moved to IBM's CEO position from RJR Nabisco), all IBM senior executives have gone through this basic process.

Such programs develop executive talents throughout a company, ultimately creating intense competition for the company's top jobs. When a company develops people to do great things, that company must provide opportunities to do great things or lose many of them to the competition, an unfortunate risk many corporations face. Of course, it is better to lose some great people than never develop great people at all.

Early in its history, Intel's board established a very orderly methodology for moving people into increasingly responsible assignments until the board is able to identify and develop the CEO's future successor. As part of the successor's development, this individual assumes some of the CEO's responsibilities, an approach that gives the future successor an opportunity to refine his skills in an environment safe from public scrutiny. Intel's very orderly succession process reduces internal bickering about who should be CEO and ensures an uneventful transition. Intel's succession planning process works so well because Intel's board prioritizes succession planning as its number-one job. Intel directors work in earnest to identify and groom successors to the CEO years in advance.

The job of succession planning is becoming more challenging—and more vital to the company's success—as the average tenure of CEO's shrinks. In a series of studies of the 2,500 largest publicly traded corporations in the world by Booze Allen Hamilton, researchers discovered that, from 1995 to 2001, the rate of turnover of the CEO's of major corporations increased by 53%, from 6% percent in 1995 to 9.2% in 2001. Nearly half of the CEO changes were caused by company mergers or by the CEO's failure to perform at the level expected by the board.[ii]

Average tenure for a CEO has shrunk to about 5 years, down from a much longer term a decade ago, according to Leslie Gaines-Ross, chief knowledge and research officer at the public relations firm, Burson-Marstellar.[iii] In the 1980s, CEOs called all the shots in the game of "Pass the Baton," but today's more assertive boards and influential investors play much bigger roles in the timing of the CEO's exit.[iv] Boards are giving CEOs only about 20 months to deliver the results shareholders expect.[v] This is a major imperative, and enlightened boards always should have a plan ready to deal with any of the situations that ultimately can lead to the need to replace the CEO, especially considering that the circumstances of the CEO's departure might not be anticipated.

The Board's Responsibility in Planning Successor Selection

Because the board's responsibility is to select the best possible CEO for the company, planning the CEO's succession is one of the board's most important responsibilities. The compensation and personnel committee should help the board in this responsibility by leading the succession planning process.

Nevertheless, it is imperative that the entire board approve the process and be fully engaged in it. Like most things in business, outstanding preparation and flawless execution constitute the foundation for consistent delivery of increased shareholder value. Therefore, directors must vigilantly pursue an effective succession plan. Succession planning should become part of every director's DNA!

Once the succession plan has been established, the board must regularly review and modify it. Succession planning sets the stage for the entire company's focus on people development. Because an effective succession planning process conveys an attitude throughout the company, the succession plan must be viewed as a dynamic, fluid, living document that changes with the company's needs.

Although developing the succession plan is a somewhat methodical process, it is usually an intense—and sometimes quite emotional—experience. Each director brings to the process his or her own set of experiences that influence the way the succession planning process works. There are no proven right or wrong ways to implement a succession planning process. However, a great deal of dialog and evaluation should take place in the boardroom to gradually align the board to whatever approach is best for the company at the given time. The board must invest time in understanding the succession planning process.

Directors should resist the urge to gain alignment too early in the process, but instead should focus on selecting the candidate most likely to be effective in leading the company and maximizing shareholder value. They should not be too eager to close the discussion of possible candidates. Each director should take the time to really understand the strengths of each candidate and measure those strengths against the director's own set of criteria. Building a comprehensive succession plan is not a one-time program, and it is not an annual review of the corporation's best talent! Successful succession planning is an ongoing process.

Succession planning should go far beyond regulatory compliance and structural requirements. Although directors refer to replacement tables to help them in their selection, they should focus on their judgment, not on statistical measurements!

Steps in the Succession Planning Process

A number of critical decisions make up the succession planning process. By perseveringly and methodically following a series of steps, the board can be guided through this process. An overview of the main decision-making steps follows.

Develop a CEO profile. The first major challenge for the board engaged in developing a succession plan is to define the competencies and characteristics the board believes are required for the next CEO. The board should develop a profile that specifically identifies the skills, experiences, and attributes the directors believe will be necessary for the next CEO to have. The board also should define the desired personal leadership skills and individual personal attributes. While developing this profile, the board should use the incumbent

CEO as a benchmark for comparison. The board should ask: *Does the current CEO have the skills needed to fill the job if it were open today?* It might be quite evident that the current CEO would not meet the current requirements. This often is the case because many company requirements are situation driven and change over time.

Prepare for both an insider and an outsider. The next step in the process is to prepare for the eventuality that, when the time comes, the board probably will have to decide whether an insider or outsider CEO will best serve the long-term interests of shareholders.

The answer to this question usually is a function of preparedness and necessity. The succession plan should include a comprehensive evaluation of the talent within the company and also include candidates from outside the company. When the board considers outside candidates, their effort should not be merely perfunctory but an honest and objective assessment of extremely qualified individuals that might be available to fill the CEO position now or in the future. In any case, it is never a good idea for the board to make major comprises to justify the selection of an insider over an outsider or vice versa.

The board's preferred strategy usually is to select a successor from within the company. Barring unusual circumstances, if the company has been diligent in developing leadership talent, several internal candidates should be available for consideration.

Boards are most likely to pursue an outside successor when the company has not groomed an internal successor or when the company's internal candidates are being groomed and are not quite ready for the next step in their career. Sometimes the board has little time to make the final decision, as in the case of the incumbent CEO's severe illness or death. At other times, the board has considerable time to make the final decision because the resigning CEO has given plenty of notice.

Generally speaking, internal candidates are preferable to external candidates. A number of studies and several articles have suggested that selecting an inside successor is a better answer than choosing someone from outside of the company. For a host of reasons, many externally sourced CEOs have failed to deliver as shareholders expected, meaning, of course, a failure to maintain significant improvements in the company's share price. Some of the many examples of disappointing performances by outsider CEOs were John Walters at AT&T, Carleton S. Fiorina at Hewlett Packard, and more recently, Michael Lawrie at Siebel Systems.

Not surprisingly, there also are many examples of highly successful outside CEOs, such as Lou Gerstner at IBM and John W. Thompson at Symantec. External candidates should not be excluded for policy reasons, and the board should maintain a relationship with an external consulting firm to keep abreast of possible candidates who are qualified, available, and interested in being considered. If the board decides to conduct a search for external candidates, the corporate governance committee may lead this effort or the board may designate a special committee to do so. Sometimes a board selects an external candidate because the market reacts more favorably to the announcement of an external candidate than to the announcement of an internal one,[vi,vii,viii] particularly when the new CEO comes from an industry-related firm.[ix] Smaller boards, which generally are more independent than larger boards, are more likely to hire outsiders, including outsiders from industry-unrelated companies.[x]

The most relevant question to be addressed by the board of directors in the succession planning processes is not whether to choose an insider or an outsider, but whether the company is, at this moment, aggressively developing the best candidates to compete for the job of CEO and effectively lead the company in the future.

Plan the successor's personal development. One component of the selection plan should be another vitally important plan: a plan for training, developing, and evaluating the incoming CEO. Planning the successor's personal development is an integral part of the succession planning process, and the board must ensure that the CEO develops a comprehensive development plan for his or her potential successors. These development plans should be tightly linked to clear criteria established by the board for the next CEO at the time the development plan is made.

Choosing an unobtrusive selection or a competitive race. Most succession planning processes are quiet, orderly affairs in which the board goes about developing an appropriate cadre of candidates and then focuses on the few individuals most likely to reach the stage of being groomed for the CEO's position. However, some firms stage a competition to identify the best candidate in the field. This usually requires informing the competitors that they have been selected as candidates for the position.

Occasionally the rest of the world gets to witness one of these competitions (at least from a distance) as it is being played out inside a major corporation. This glimpse into corporate life at higher echelons happens because influences on major corporations excite extensive media coverage. The succession planning of General Electric, Coca Cola, Ford, Kellogg, Sony, American Express, and Lucent Technologies all have been highly publicized and widely discussed.

In the case of General Electric, an ongoing competition for GE's most coveted position became public after Jack Welch, GE's renowned leader, announced his planned retirement. Mr. Welch, the reports said, had led the GE board in the selection of three highly qualified candidates to replace him. These spirited executives were extremely qualified, obviously very talented, and very much desirous of the position.

Each of the candidates knew that, according to GE tradition, he would leave the company if he were not selected. As the candidates headed into the final stretch of the race in 2001, the board tried to assess which of these excellent executives would make the best CEO. While the board considered, the company risked losing one or more of the superstars to another company; any candidate who did not expect to win the competition would be considering all his options.

The board eventually selected Jeffrey R. Immelt to replace Jack Welch, an action that launched executive recruiting firms into a wild frenzy of effort to find great opportunities for two of the most available and qualified future CEOs in Corporate America. Home Depot managed to recruit Robert L. Nardelli to their top leadership spot, and 3M was thrilled to hire W. James McNerney, Jr. as chairman and CEO. (In 2005, McNerney resigned to assume the position of chairman and CEO of Boeing.)

While succession planning is purported to be understood, it continues to be a major challenge for many corporations. The announcement by Ford Motor Co. on September 5th, 2006, that it had hired Alan Mulally as the CEO, demonstrated the continuing succession planning challenges in corporate America. As noted earlier, 3M hired outsider CEO, James McNerney, who had been passed over for the top position at General Electric in 2001. Subsequently, McNerney was hired as the new CEO of Boeing. Interestingly, Mulaly, who was passed over for the top job at Boeing, was then hired as the CEO of Ford.

Plan for calamity. A comprehensive succession plan must include a plan to respond to an immediate need to replace the CEO. Lessons have been learned from the unfortunate and unexpected deaths of Jerry R. Junkins of Texas Instruments in 1996, Jim Cantalupo of McDonald's in 2004, and Charlie Bell of McDonald's in 2005.

In both corporations, the next CEO had already been selected and was in the process of being groomed for CEO position. In both corporations, several candidates were available so that the boards had selection options. These companies had boards who knew how to plan for calamity.

A solid succession plan by McDonald's board was able to put a knowledgeable leader in place just hours after a heart attack felled the company's chairman and CEO, Jim Cantalupo. The board swiftly appointed as replacement McDonald's president and chief operating officer, Charlie Bell, immediately reassuring employees, franchisees, and investors of the company's continuity.[xi] McDonalds again faced a succession challenge when Mr. Bell succumbed to cancer less than 18 months later. Most companies have only an interim succession plan for dealing with the sudden death of top executives. Enlightened companies plan for the unexpected.

Decide when to tell the selected successor. Some boards believe it is best to inform the selected successor as soon as the decision is made. Other boards believe it is best to wait until the opportunity to award the job arrives. Each board must determine the approach most appropriate for their company, and then methodically implement it.

Design a system to dispel rumors. When the CEO retires, voluntarily resigns, or is summarily dismissed by the board, a flurry of speculation radiates throughout the corporation and its shareholder community. Everyone wants to know why the CEO is leaving a great job, who will replace the CEO (an insider or an outsider), and how the CEO's departure will affect the company's short-term and long-term share prices.

For a variety of reasons—personal, competitive, and contractual—some corporations are not permitted to immediately disclose detailed information about the change of leadership. Unfortunately, when companies fail to provide timely information, stakeholders often extract answers through the deduction process. Because people will not go without information for long, they often will simply make up an answer that suits their logic. This answer usually is far from the truth!

Corporations cannot afford to hoard information about CEO succession. In the best interests of all stakeholders, including shareholders, employees, customers, suppliers, and communities, the better the quality of the information provided and the quicker it is supplied, the sooner the speculation ends. The wise board prepares to disseminate as much pertinent, reassuring information as possible as soon after the impending CEO transition is made public.

Review. Monitor. Review. Monitor. Prudence requires that the board frequently review the status of the succession-planning process and monitor its progress.

The Rules of Succession Planning

Some kinds of informal or formal rules no doubt influence the board's decisions about succession planning.[xii,xiii] Rules will "enable and constrain" the board's decisions."[xiv] Directors also are guided by tradition and history. Whatever rules and traditions influence a board, that influence boils down to: If it hasn't been done before, it probably won't be done now. If, for example, a company has never selected an outsider, the board will certainly feel constrained from doing so.

The old maxim that rules were made to be broken definitely applies to some of the traditional rules that have governed CEO selection. Rules need to be examined periodically to see if they still apply. They should be regularly challenged for validity, and they should be changed when appropriate.

IBM demonstrated the ability to take a fresh look at the old rules of succession. For the 118 years of its existence, IBM had never recruited an outside CEO, and then, after its unprecedented ousting of the company's chairman and CEO, John Akers, the board specifically pursued a candidate from outside the corporation because they thought that was what the company needed at the time. In retrospect, it was a brilliant move. During his tenure, Lou Gerstner did an outstanding job of rebuilding the corporation and building significant shareholder value. He also focused considerable energy on succession planning to ensure that an internal candidate for his successor would be available for the board to consider. When Lou decided to retire, he recommended as his successor an internal candidate, the company's president and CEO, Sam Palmisano. This experience of IBM demonstrates that no single answer is right or wrong in all cases of succession planning. Every board must evaluate the company's needs at the time and take the action they deem most appropriate for their company.

The Role of the CEO

In many ways, the level of quality and thoroughness of the succession planning process will be a product of the CEO's self-confidence. The more self-assured the CEO, the more robust the succession planning process will be. An actively engaged CEO definitely will enhance the succession planning process, and the board should inform the incumbent CEO that they expect his active engagement in developing the plan.

However, direction must emanate from the independent members of the board, and the board must set the tone for the CEO.

Many CEO's relish the process of cultivating a replacement. The board should expect such a CEO to favor insider candidates. (In most cases, the board also should prefer inside candidates.) However, some CEO's will regard succession planning as a threatening reminder of their own mortality or, perhaps worse, dispensability. In such a case, the CEO might develop a knack for driving off any promising heir, or casting potential successors in an unfavorable light. The actions taken by some CEO's who feel threatened by the succession process provide ample reasons why boards shouldn't allow CEO's to take the choose-your-own-successor approach. Starting a minimum of six years in advance, the board should demand that the CEO provide a list of candidates, plus regular briefings on how those candidates' skills are being tested.[xv]

Although the board may task the CEO to lead the effort, they never can abdicate their collective responsibility to own the selection process and deliver the results. As the top contenders emerge, the outside directors have a duty to meet with them alone for open-ended discussions.[xvi] This is demonstrating responsible board leadership.

Roger M. Kenny, the managing partner of Boardroom Consultants, a recruiting firm that places executives and directors, recently observed that:

> [B]oards have been social in nature. To be very outspoken against a C.E.O.'s wishes for succession, that's been a difficult thing. But it is happening. And some principles of succession planning are emerging. It has to be continuous. It has to be board-driven and collaborative. It has to be driven by corporate strategy.[xvii]

The Leadership Team's Succession and Responsibilities

Although planning the CEO's succession certainly is more important to the company than planning succession for any other company position, the board of directors should nonetheless concentrate succession planning efforts on the broader senior leadership team. To effectively develop a comprehensive CEO succession plan, the board must consider successors to the group of senior executives from which the next CEO is likely to be selected. The board also must ensure that the incoming CEO will have a supporting team capable of successfully supporting his or her direction.

Moreover, the board must make certain that the senior management team develops a comprehensive success plan for the company. Identifying, selecting, and training people to reach the high levels of performance expected by the company is the responsibility of line management and should not be delegated to the human resources arm of the company. However, the human resources experts should become an integral part in the development process.

Succession Planning for Directors

In the traditional corporate board environment, the director succession process is a straightforward and collegial one. The board seeking a director is likely to source their candidates from "friends of the family." In other words, through their professional relationships with other executives, directors leverage their access to personal information to help them identify people they believe would qualify as their colleagues on the board. Such network connections are part of the value proposition that experienced directors often are expected to bring to the corporation.

In the 1980s and 1990s, this type of process worked quite effectively because the supply of experienced directors willing and able to serve as directors usually exceeded the demand for qualified candidates. Unfortunately, given the substantial risks and formidable challenges associated with being a corporate director in the 21st century, the prevailing environment has changed. Today, more and more boards complement their informal "friends of the family" approach with professional executive searches in which an executive search or recruiting firm is retained to identify successor candidates through a formal search process. Although each of these approaches used to be reasonably effective, today they are insufficient even collectively because attracting highly qualified directors has become so difficult. Boards are searching longer and harder to find qualified directors that meet their needs. According to the latest data provided by the global executive search firm, Spencer Stuart, 8 of 10 potential candidates decline the opportunity to be considered for directorships, obligating boards to consider other creative approaches.

For qualified people with a passion and willingness to serve shareholders, opportunities have never been more available. Boards who establish director succession plans equal in rigor to those used for senior management team succession will enjoy vastly better access to talent than their competitors who rely exclusively on personal networking and executive search companies.

The Organizational Dynamics of Succession Planning

While undergoing the selection process, boards should not be unduly influenced or blindly guided by statistical analyses or study results. Directors should consider appropriate input from all reasonable sources to help them analyze their current situation and, relying on their best judgment, select the best candidate they can to lead the company at the given time.

That being said, a quick review of the numerous efforts made to understand the organizational dynamics of succession planning are in order. These efforts have led to four theoretical perspectives,[xviii] each of which attempts to explain CEO succession. According to these views, changing the CEO can be a rational attempt to create needed change, an unavoidable event that puts the company's performance at risk, an unavoidable event of almost no consequence to company performance, or an event that directors avoid at all costs.

From the *rational-adaptive perspective,* a board initiates CEO succession as an adaptive measure to ensure change needed for the company's survival.[xix,xx] The most likely cause for removal is poor company performance caused by the CEO's failure to effectively deploy the company's resources. Directors look for a replacement from outside the company in the belief that an outsider will be more successful at bringing about required change.[xxi]

From the *disruptive event perspective,* a change of CEO is a negative event caused by the environment; the change might alter the delicate balance between the company and the environment, resulting in the decline of company performance.[xxii]

From *the inconsequential event perspective,* company performance is caused solely by environmental factors, and changing the CEO has relatively little

influence on it. Thus the characteristics of the new CEO are of little consequence to the firm.[xxiii]

From the *inertial perspective*, the CEO has the ability to enact strategic
change in the company, but rarely does so. When the company's performance
declines, the CEO adheres to familiar practices. Whether or not resorting to
time-worn patterns initially leads to success, over time, resistance to change
might lead to the company's decline. The company's directors, who also
resist taking big risks even when poor company performance suggests that
significant change is required, are unlikely to select a replacement CEO from
outside the company.[xxiv]

These four contradictory academic perspectives aren't too much help in
the real world, but even in the most enlightened corporate boardroom, relatively little is known about the real effects of the many complex influences
that come to bear when a CEO is being selected.[xxv]

When scholars William H. Bommer and Alan E. Ellstrand studied 219
CEO succession events over a 2-year period, their complex data led them
to the conclusion that institutional shareholders "only flex their ownership
authority [on CEO selection] when firm performance is poor," and that they
do so by encouraging directors to select a new CEO from outside the company. Boards of poorly performing companies usually succumb to this pressure, but the data indicated that choosing an outsider is not likely to make a
difference to the company's future performance. What does positively affect
future performance is choosing a new CEO with existing ties to the board of
directors. Bommer and Ellstrand concluded that a board that resists pressures
to bring in an outside CEO and instead chooses a strong board member as
the CEO successor exhibits superior performance.[xxvi]

Summary

Despite a CEO's enthusiasm for—or avoidance of—the task of choosing his
or her future successor, corporate boards must resolutely and methodically
do the work of ensuring that the company will have an effective leader at all
times. This requires planning for the CEO's succession, and it even requires
making a plan that delineates the decisions that must be made to complete

that plan. The board also bears responsibility for making sure that the company will have a full complement of possible CEO replacements, senior executives, and directors. Active planning and oversight on the part of the board are needed to make sure that all responsible parties in the company are doing their part to develop senior executives and plan for their succession. In response to the current shortage of qualified directors, the board must make extra efforts to ensure that the board has an adequate pool of potential director candidates from which to draw.

The next chapter focuses on another critical board responsibility, CEO supervision.

Notes

[i] Lublin, J. S. (1997, July 3). Investors urge older directors to step down. *Wall Street Journal*, (E. E.) p. B1.

[ii] Lucier, C., Spiegel, E., & Schuyt, R. (2005, June 24). Why CEOs fall: The causes and consequences of turnover at the top. Booz Allen Hamilton Report Issue.

[iii] Krantz, M. (2005, February 11). Ousting CEOs often boosts stock price. *USA Today*. See also Lucier et al., 2005.

[iv] Lublin, June 24, 1997.

[v] Krantz, 2005; see also Lucier et al., 2005.

[vi] Reinganum, J. F. (1985). Innovation and Industry Evolution. *Quarterly Journal of Economics, 100*, 81-99.

[vii] Warner, J., Watts, R., & Wruck, K. (1988). Stock prices and top management. *Journal of Financial Economics, 20*, 431-460.

[viii] Borokhovich, K. A., Parrino, R., & Trapani, T. (1996). Outside directors and CEO selection. *Journal of Financial and Quantitative Analysis, 31*, 377-397.

[ix] Davidson III, W. N., Nemec, C., Worrell, D. L., & Lin, J. (2002). *Journal of Management & Governance, 6*(4), 295-321.

[x] Golden, B. R., & Zajac, E. J. (2001). When will boards influence strategy? *Strategic Management Journal, 22*, 1087-1111.

[xi] Hymowitz, C., & Lublin, J. (2004, April 20). McDonald's CEO tragedy holds lessons. *Wall Street Journal*, Dow Jones.

[xii] Ocasio, W. (1999). Institutionalized action and corporate governance: The reliance on rules of CEO succession. *Administrative Science Quarterly, 44*, 384-416.

[xiii] March, J. G., & Olsen, J. P. (1989). Rediscovering institutions: The organizational basis of politics. New York: Free Press.

[xiv] Ocasio, 1999.

[xv] Charan, R., & Useem, F. (2002). Why companies fail. *Fortune, 145*(11), 50-62.

[xvi] Charan & Useem, 2002.

[xvii] Holstein, W. J. (2004, April 25). Office space: Armchair M.B.A.; smoothing the way to a new C.E.O. *The New York Times.*

[xviii] Cannella, B., & Lubatkin, M. (1993). Succession as a sociopolitical process: Internal impediments to outsider selection. *Academy of Management Journal, 36*(4), 763-793.

[xix] Goodstein, J. & Boeker, W. (1991). Turbulence at the top: A new perspective on governance structure changes and strategic change. *Academy of Management Journal, 34*(2), 306-330.

[xx] Wiersema, M. & Bantel, K. Top management team turnover as an adaptation mechanism: The role of the environment. *Strategic Management Journal, 14,* 485–504.

[xxi] Walsh & Seward, l990.

[xxii] Friedman, S.D., & Singh, H. (1989). CEO succession and stockholder reaction: The influence of organizational context and event analysis. *Academy of Management Journal, 32,* 718-744.

[xxiii] Bommer, W. H., Ellstrand, A. E. (1996). CEO successor choice: Its antecedents and influence on subsequent firm performance. *Group & Organization Management, 21*(1), 105-123.

[xxiv] Cannella & Lubatkin, 1993.

[xxv] Bommer and Ellstrand, 1996).

[xxvi] Ibid.

Chapter 7

Supervising the CEO

Is an ace of hearts better than a king of diamonds?

A basic principle of general management is that people benefit from constructive feedback about job performance. Constructive feedback provides employees with opportunities to develop, improve, and broaden their skill sets. These are opportunities that should not be denied to any corporate employee, including the one who provides the corporation with overall supervision, the CEO. Obviously, those who provide feedback to the CEO should be extraordinarily qualified to give timely, meaningful reactions to the CEO's performance, whether that performance needs improvement or deserves congratulation. The people responsible for counseling, supervising, monitoring, evaluating, and compensating the CEO are the same people responsible for selecting and replacing that individual—the corporation's directors.

Directors need leadership too, and they elect their own leader in the person of the board chair. Whether that leader should be the CEO, another company insider, or an outsider with real independence of the company's management has become a hotly contested issue.

Holding Directors' Feet to the Fire

Corporate directors work at the discretion of the company's shareholders, and the CEO works at the discretion of the board. Old-style boardroom politics notwithstanding, there is no acceptable alternative to this approach, which began to become apparent in the United States during a period of economic turmoil starting in the mid-1970s, when a number of blue-chip American corporations began to decline. In the late 1980s, concerned pension and mutual funds, with huge sums of shareholder investments at stake, began actively working to increase board oversight of CEOs. By the early 1990s, when major layoffs by America's manufacturing giants had become commonplace, impatient institutional investors began to serve notice—in no uncertain terms—that they were holding boards responsible for ensuring that CEO's acted in the best interests of shareholders. In those early days of shareholder dissent, institutional investors generally placed blame on the systems by which corporations were run, but not on the people who ran them. M. C. Jensen summarized the concerns of the early investor activists quite well:

> Few boards in the past decades have done [their] job well in the absence of external crises. This is particularly unfortunate given the very purpose of the internal control mechanism they are entrusted to oversee, which is to provide an early warning system to put the organization back on track before difficulties reach a crisis stage. Bad systems or rules, not bad people, underlie the general failings of boards of directors.[i]

By holding boards accountable for CEO performance, institutional shareholders were able to force shake-ups once unthinkable in the cozy executive suites of giant companies. In 1991, General Motors' board responded to the highly visible impatience of activist shareholders by removing CEO Robert Stempel after a mere 27 months as GM's head.[ii] Then, in rapid succession, activist shareholders forced the ouster of the CEO's of Sears, IBM, and Kodak.

Three years later, investors began acting on the idea that sometimes people, not merely governance systems, were to blame for squandered investment dollars. In 1994, shareholders of Caremark International, a leader in the healthcare industry, brought a landmark lawsuit after the company was obliged to pay about $250 million in reimbursements and penalties when company executives were caught making illegal payments of Medicare and Medicaid patient-referral fees.[iii] Caremark's directors, the plaintiffs claimed, had breached their fiduciary duty of care by failing to monitor employee activities and by neglecting to institute corrective measures that might have prevented the unlawful conduct.[iv,v] Caremark's board was able to demonstrate to both the Court and the U.S. Securities and Exchange Commission that they indeed had made a good-faith attempt to assure that an adequate corporate information and reporting system existed at Caremark. However, had the board failed to equip themselves with a system to monitor management, the Court and the SEC might have held them responsible for failure to represent shareholders' interests.[vi]

Arthur Levitt, Chairman of the SEC observed:

> When a corporation finds itself in trouble, it often becomes clear that the board didn't fully discharge its responsibilities. What is obvious in hindsight, can be avoided through foresight. But directors can't stop there. If they have reason to know something doesn't seem right—or if the red flags are flying—they cannot avert their gaze.[vii]

The traditional power of CEO's over interlocking, closed-network boards whose members considered themselves employees of the CEO was under attack. Under pressure by activist investors, many boards attempted to align the interests of directors and investors and to enhance board oversight of CEO's. For CEO's, the results were unnerving. In the decade between 1995 and 2005, forced turnover of CEO's climbed 300%.[viii] During 2004 and 2005 alone, shareholder dissatisfaction and scandal resulted in the replacement of the CEO's of dozens of American corporations, including Coca-Cola, Fannie Mae, Disney, Hewlett-Packard, Boeing, and AIG.[ix] The primary reason for most CEO firings was poor shareholder returns; a 2004 survey conducted by Booz Allen Hamilton, a corporate strategy consulting firm, showed that CEO's who were fired generated 7.7% lower returns for their companies in the year before leaving office than those who left for other reasons.[x]

The CEO-replacement trend spread to Europe and Asia with a vengeance; in 2004, more than 14% of the CEO's of the world's 2,500 largest companies left office—4.4% because of disagreements with their boards, largely over issues concerning performance.[xi]

In the United States, following major crises at Enron, WorldCom, Quest Communications, Global Crossing, Tyco, and Adelphia Communications (among others), politicians and federal regulators joined the fray. In 2002, Congress passed the Sarbanes-Oxley Act, sometimes called SOX, which gave directors and their committees more power and required that boards include more *independent directors,* that is, directors who were not employees of the corporations they served.[1]

As of this writing, SOX hasn't yet affected CEO turnover in the United States, perhaps because, as suggested by strategists at Booz Allen Hamilton, boards of U.S. corporations already had increased their oversight of CEO's before passage of the Act.[xii] Meanwhile, institutional shareholders continue to work toward direct supervision of CEO's by their boards. The person most able to help provide shareholders with a point of leverage by which to influence the behavior of a CEO who has become too dominant, according to business scholar Youssef Cassis, is a board chair who is not the CEO and who comes from outside the company.[xiii]

---

[1] Under Section 302 of the Sarbanes-Oxley Act, the Securities and Exchange Commission was mandated to adopt rules requiring that CEOs and CFOs of publicly traded corporations certify financial and other information contained in their corporations' quarterly and annual reports. Although enthusiastically received by the broad base of shareholders, Section 302 was not nearly the watershed event it was purported to be because CEOs and CFOs had been responsible for signing these documents before passage of the Act. In essence, the Act merely required that these officers admit that they had signed these documents. Thus, Section 302 merely added yet another layer of bureaucracy and cost without creating substantial change. However, compliance with Section 302 does encourage CEOs and CFOs to reflect on related financial issues before signing certain documents, which offers some reassurance to the general investment community that most corporate leaders are paying somewhat greater attention to the businesses they run.

The Distinctly Different Roles of the CEO and the Board Chair

The roles of the CEO and board chair are distinctly different. The CEO is responsible for leading the company's management, whereas the board chair is responsible for leading the board in its supervision of the CEO. It is imperative that directors recognize and understand this difference.

Traditionally, in most U.S. corporations, one person serves in both capacities, with the CEO recognized as the preeminent leader of both board and management.[xiv,xv,xvi,xvii] An obvious weakness of the dual CEO/chairman role is that, when the CEO also chairs the board, the CEO becomes his or her own chief supervisor! This being the case, combining the two roles in a single individual is not a universally accepted governance method. In 2004, 74% of CEO's in North America chaired their boards, but only 40% did so in Europe (where the roles often are separated by law), and a mere 6% did so in Japan.[xviii]

In the pre-1980 days when directors of U.S. corporations routinely conducted themselves as rubber-stamp employees of the CEO, the risk posed by this weakness was considered to be more or less acceptable but, in the present climate of shareholder activism, this risk is taken very seriously, and the wisdom of combining the roles and functions of CEO and board chair in one person has evolved into a matter of contentious debate.

On one side of this debate are those who believe that most U.S. companies function best when CEO's also take on the board chair's role. Not surprisingly, the supporters of this position include the 150 CEO members of the U.S. trade group, The Business Roundtable, who hold that the dual CEO/chair role bridges companies and their boards, helping them to work together.[xix] These CEO's have a point. It is no secret that a great CEO clearly understands his or her accountability to the board and earns board support primarily through excellent performance. A CEO who chairs an energetic, highly enlightened board of directors can foster constructive dialogue and debate among board members and encourage them to engage in meeting challenges facing the company. A dual CEO/chair who wants to work with an effective, independent board certainly can eventually create one.

In decades past, most U.S. corporate boards agreed with their CEOs that companies work best when the CEO also chairs the board. In 1992, just a few years after the start of shareholder opposition to the dual CEO/chair role, a survey of boards by Korn/Ferry International disclosed that most of the boards surveyed did not believe that splitting the roles of chair and CEO was important.[xx] Statistics on board composition indicate that most boards probably still agree with this position. However, as discussed later in this chapter, this belief seems to be eroding, and many directors may be shifting toward the side of advocates of corporate governance reform in their discomfort with the risks of having one person lead both board and management. Playing into the apparent weakening of many boards' desire to maintain the dual CEO/chair role may be some new evidence that firms are more valuable and have better performance when the CEO and board chair are separate[xxi] and that "agency problems are higher when the same person holds both positions."[xxii]

When directors give traditional deference to the wishes of a CEO who also chairs the board, that CEO can dominate and suppress constructive dialogue, engagement, and debate among directors. The CEO who also chairs the board is, at once, chief architect of corporate policies, chief executive of these policies, and chief controller of the board's agenda and the information the board receives; he or she also makes recommendations on board composition, agendas, and priorities.[xxiii] Undeniably, if that CEO wants to fashion a passive board that will approve his or her decisions without argument, he or she eventually can do so.

As Sarah A. B. Teslik, executive director of the Council of Institutional Investors, pointed out, because the board exists to monitor the use of the great discretionary power held by the CEO, when the CEO chairs the board, management of the company is accountable to a body led by itself. Directors, she argued, rarely can know as much about the management of the company as the CEO, and even the most brilliant and motivated director can do little without accurate, timely information.[xxiv] Although I dispute her argument that motivated directors are relatively powerless in the boardroom, it is a fact that the board chair is responsible for the board's final decisions. The board is not permitted to debate the chair's rulings and decisions. To do so would seriously contravene *Robert's Rules of Order*. The only recourse to a wrong decision made by the board chair is to remove that person as leader of the board. Such considerations no doubt influenced Benjamin Rosen, at that time chairman of Compaq Computer, to argue that separating the two roles "is the single most important factor in creating the right balance of power needed for effective governance."

It is understandable, then, that such advocates of governance reform as Margaret M. Blair of the Brookings Institution and John Pound of Harvard University fear that the CEO who serves as board chair compromises the board's primary functions of assessing the CEO's performance and compensation and replacing the CEO when necessary. One indication of the weakness of many boards led by CEOs is evidence that CEO compensation is lower when the CEO and board chair positions are separate.[xxv] Combining the positions of CEO and board chair, Blair and Pound have argued, assigns too much power to a single individual, which may minimize constructive dissent and diversity of perspectives. When the CEO under review is the board's leader, Blair and Pound argued, the board cannot objectively carry out their duties.[xxvi,xxvii]

In the case of an ignorant, apathetic board whose members don't know much about their own duties and don't care to know more, such concerns are not misplaced. However, in the case of an enlightened board in which directors actively inform themselves and energetically fulfill their responsibilities, such fears amount to an unfortunate condemnation of the intelligence and integrity of directors quite capable of carrying out their responsibilities with or without the concurrence of the chair. Collectively, the members of a board are duty-bound to replace their board chair at any time they deem appropriate. Their authority to do so arises from their responsibility to evaluate the performance of the board chair and to assess compensation for fulfilling that role.

The willingness of an enlightened board to objectively carry out their duties when their leader happens to be both CEO and board chair has been demonstrated in a number of high-profile cases, including those involving AT&T, GM, IBM, and HP. In 2005, when Hewlett Packard's board differed with CEO Carleton Fiorina over methods of executing company strategy, for example, the board quickly moved the company's CFO, Robert Wayman, into the CEO job and elected a veteran HP director, Patricia C. Dunn, who will be further referenced later in this chapter, as non-executive board chair. xxviii The most effectively managed examples of performance management and succession planning by boards, however, never make the front pages of influential business publications because they are accomplished with minimal disruption to the corporations involved.

Creating a Healthy Relationship between the Board and the CEO

Most directors have been made painfully aware of what not to do in the boardroom by highly publicized examples of inappropriate behavior and ineffective practices that caused public outrage. However, in many boardrooms, what directors should be doing is not so clear! Gone are the days in which directors functioned mainly as deferential employees of the CEO, and the CEO who is largely unsupervised by the board is quickly becoming an anachronism. Recent changes in corporate governance have greatly increased the breadth, complexity, and responsibility of the director's job. In fact, it is fair to say that the role of corporate director has changed more in the few years since passage of the Sarbanes-Oxley Act of 2002 than in the entire preceding 3 decades. The chief rule of thumb for directors is that, to effectively govern, they must be highly visible in both their ability and their willingness to get engaged with problems and to lead their companies to solutions.

In contrast to a low-energy board that obviously tolerates director apathy and ignorance of the company's activities and directors' duties, a highly energized and effective board collectively expects each of its members to contribute intelligent, active leadership. Fortunately, energy can be transmitted, and transforming a lethargic board into an energetic one, although not easy, is quite possible if the ineffective board attracts into its ranks someone who really cares about the company and is determined to make a difference in it. Just one highly energized and effective director (who need not be the board chair) can raise the expectations of an entire board. By the same token, a self-serving director who is less interested in making a strong contribution than in rubbing shoulders with the winners on a board then can weaken the entire group.

M. C. Jensen defined the job of the corporate board quite well:

> The board is at the apex of the corporate internal control system and has the final responsibility for the functioning of the firm. Most importantly, it sets the rules of the game for the CEO. The job of the board is to hire, fire, and compensate the CEO and to provide high-level counsel.[xxix]

This vital job belongs not only to the person who chairs the board, but also to each and every individual director. In a healthy boardroom setting, of course, the directors, the board chair they elect, and the CEO they hire all support the belief that the board chair and the CEO serve at the discretion of the board and, ultimately, the shareholders. Enlightened directors are fully aware of their collective responsibility to select, supervise, monitor, and evaluate the individual performances of the board chair, the CEO, and each director, and to assess the compensation of every one of these individuals. It also is the board's duty to replace the board chair or CEO if necessary.

Once the board chooses a CEO, the board should define to that person clearly, and with great specificity, his or her duties in managing the activities of the corporation. Then the board's members should support that CEO in serving the best interests of the company and the shareholders, which includes providing the CEO with constructive feedback. This kind of support requires an atmosphere of trust between the CEO and the board. Although directors must exert strong leadership over the corporation's administration, they must carefully avoid involving themselves in the general management of the company's day-to-day operations.

Even in an ideal situation in which the CEO feels supported by the board and provides the directors with timely, accurate information, a wise board will expect tensions to arise between directors and the CEO because the board exists to satisfy the corporation's need for accountability and thus must monitor the use of the CEO's great discretionary power. It is vital that the board understand this tension because many abuses of management power and cases of board negligence stem from tensions inherent in the board-management relationship.[xxx,xxxi]

The board also should define clearly, and with great specificity, the responsibilities of the board chair they elect and should provide that individual with constructive feedback to help him or her serve the board well. When the duties of the CEO and the board chair reside in the same individual, the enlightened board makes certain that person receives constructive feedback about his or her performance in each of those separate roles. When the board chair is not the CEO—and even when the board chair is independent, that is, not a company employee, recent employee, or relative of an employee—the board should recognize that the board chair's role is not to act as "co-CEO" but to assist the CEO by managing the board's activities. (Even the activist pension fund CalPERS, which regards the role of independent board chair as vital, defines this role quite narrowly.) In any case, all of the board's responsibilities must be carried out even without concurrence of the board chair.

One of the biggest supervisory challenges a board can face is monitoring the activities of the rare CEO who boasts a larger-than-life performance record. Few shareholders are concerned about CEO supervision when they are consistently earning great returns on their investments; thus CEOs who consistently deliver exceptional shareholder value are quite able to reign with supreme control over their colleagues on the board. Even in such a case, however, directors must commit themselves to leading the corporate governance process, not merely participating in it. The board must not permit the CEO to avoid supervision. The fact that many boards do not adhere to this fundamental rule is no reason to suggest a substitute approach. Crooks and thieves will not be governed by rules and regulations that do not serve their purposes. It is up to the board to inspect and manage the governance process to ensure that the highest levels of integrity and honesty exist within the company they are responsible for governing.

Striking a Balance of Power between the Board and the CEO

In U.S. corporations, the dual CEO/chair position traditionally has been separated only temporarily to help a corporation through a crisis or a top management transition, but the 1980s and 1990s supplied examples aplenty of companies that suffered because these two roles were not delegated to separate individuals. The value of General Motors, for example, declined under the authority of Roger Smith,[xxxii,xxxiii,xxxiv,xxxv] and (as readers of *Barbarians at the Gate* will recall) RJR Nabisco pursued the doomed "smokeless cigarette" under Tylee Wilson without the board's knowledge.[xxxvi]

The board of the troubled construction materials giant, Lone Star Industries, invited trouble by failing to look into the expenses of chairman and CEO James Stewart until they read about his lavish lifestyle in *Business Week*; the board's belated inquiry uncovered that Stewart had billed the company for more than a million dollars of purely personal expenses. According to David Wallace, the company outsider who succeeded Stewart, the board had simply assumed that Stewart was honest and prudent.[xxxvii]

Admittedly, few boards allow themselves to be kept in the dark for long, but these cases illustrate what can go wrong when CEO's control boards. In a situation in which power is too greatly concentrated in the person of the CEO, the board's ability to guide and oversee that CEO undoubtedly is compromised. To achieve real independence and thus fulfill their roles as advisors and shapers of corporate strategy, boards must create a distinction between the board chair's role and the CEO's role. This is true whether one person or two fills the CEO and board chair positions. The strength of every corporation rests on its ability to strike a balance between the power of those who oversee the corporation and those who run it.[xxxviii,xxxix]

Activist shareholders and enlightened boards, with help from federal law and agencies, seem to be establishing a slight trend toward splitting the CEO/chair position and a quite pronounced trend toward providing independent leadership for independent directors in the form of a position called lead or presiding director, whose important responsibilities, discussed at greater length in the following section, provide a check on executive power. Just before the new millennium, in 1998, 18% of Fortune 1000 companies divided the board chair and CEO responsibilities between two people,[2] versus 69% that combined the CEO/chair duties in a single individual.[xl] Just after the turn of the new millennium, from 2001 to 2003, the percentage of companies (overall) having separate CEO/chair positions had increased by 5.4%.[xli] By 2003, 21% of Standard and Poor 500 boards had split the role; however, in most of these cases, the board chair was a former CEO or other former executive of the company.[xlii] In only 3% of S&P 500 boards was the board chair an independent outsider who never had been a company employee. By 2005, 27% of S&P 500 boards had separated the CEO/chair roles; but almost 70% of those with dual CEO/chairs had appointed a lead or presiding director.[xliii]

The slight trend toward division of the position is, in reality, not meaningful. Few corporate boards need separate persons in the two different roles of CEO and board chair. When a corporate board recognizes circumstances that warrant a separation of the two roles, they can implement the separation at any time. The following section outlines some circumstances in which the separation might be warranted.

Separating the Roles of CEO and Board Chair

To effectively oversee the management of a company, a board needs power, and splitting the roles of CEO and board chair is one way to strengthen the board's independence and prevent the CEO from acquiring too much power. However, no universal formula is available for determining whether or when the roles of CEO and chair of the board should be separated. Separation may work very well in some situations but not well in others. It is the board's responsibility to determine the appropriateness of combining or separating the roles of CEO and board chair.

In the United States, boards usually use separation as a means of helping corporations navigate through management transitions or crises, as was done by Dow Chemical, Humana, Home Depot, American Airlines, Hewlett Packard, MCI, American Airlines, McDonalds, and others. When one CEO is retiring and a new one is taking his or her place, the board may split the role so that the retiring CEO can stay on as board chair to assist the new "apprentice" CEO through the transition into the chief executive job.

---

[2] Of the Fortune 1000 companies, 13% divided the CEO/chair responsibilities using other arrangements.

McDonald's board earned praise for their foresight in splitting the CEO/chairman position to give their new, inexperienced CEO "a separate chair to mentor him and help him."[xliv] American Airlines' board waited until the company's newly appointed CEO made several missteps in bargaining with unions before splitting the role and electing one of their own members as board chair to work with the new CEO during the transition.[xlv] Perhaps providing experienced counsel for the CEO was what Dell Computers' board had in mind when they split the position and gave the chair to the company's founder, Michael Dell, who declared his desire to work on company strategy. On the other side of the coin, Oracle Corporation's directors obviously were unconcerned about CEO mentoring or oversight when the board split the position and gave the chair to one of the CEO's most trusted subordinates, Jeff Henley, the company's CFO.[xlvi]

Boards often are motivated to separate the positions as a watchdog measure. For example, when the CEO of Boeing stepped down from his position because of alleged violations of contracts with the federal government, Boeing's board elected a non-executive (non-management) board chair to provide a watchful eye over the activities of the company. In cases of public scandal, a government agency or court might require directors to split the two positions. When WorldCom emerged from bankruptcy, the Court demanded that a non-executive board chair work with the newly elected CEO, Michael Capellas; the board's choice was the highly respected outsider, former U.S. attorney general Nicholas Katzenbach.[xlvii] Fannie Mae, the biggest U.S. buyer of home mortgages, was forced by its governing agency to split the roles after the company's CEO, Franklin Raines, and CFO, J. Timothy Howard, involved themselves in an $11 billion earnings manipulations scandal.[3]

---

[3] After firing the company's CEO and CFO, Fannie Mae also agreed to correct its earnings, set up new policies to prevent the falsification of signatures in accounting ledgers, correct deficiencies in the company's mortgage-portfolio accounting systems, and create a new Office of Compliance and Ethics to hear and review complaints from company employees; Fannie Mae's general counsel was charged with reporting misconduct or suspected misconduct directly to the board (Fannie Mae agrees to put in new controls, March 9, 2004, Associated Press. Retrieved June 4, 206, from http://www.msnbc.msn.com/).

In a time of crisis, however, separating the CEO and board chair positions is not necessarily the most useful course of action.[xlviii] During bankruptcy reorganization, for example, dual leadership may be just as useful as split leadership; several studies have shown that the form of leadership presiding over bankruptcy reorganizations does not affect the outcome, perhaps because bankruptcy reorganization aligns the CEO's interests with those of the shareholders and because managerial self-interest is more easily monitored under the supervision of the bankruptcy court.[xlix] Another consideration during a corporate crisis is that, in the particular circumstances, the company might benefit from the CEO having more power, not less; for this reason, during times of crisis many boards tend to strengthen the CEO's leadership with greater autonomy.[l]

One technique for establishing the critical balance of power when the CEO also is the board chair is appointment of a lead or presiding director. This method has had many advocates for a long time and has been mentioned frequently in the governance literature.[li,lii,liii] A lead or presiding director generally is chosen from among the corporation's independent outside directors to create a balance in the boardroom and to work with the CEO. This director has some responsibilities that provide a check on executive power and put him or her in a better position to establish a system for evaluating the CEO, such as selecting board committee members and chairs, helping to set agendas for board meetings, ensuring that directors receive adequate information, and facilitating the board meeting process.[liv] Selecting a lead or presiding director is an effective way to improve oversight of board activities. This approach certainly is not nirvana, but it is a compromise acceptable to most stakeholders.

Despite CEOs' traditional aversion to splitting the CEO/chair role, there exist some excellent reasons why the wise CEO might prefer the split. Certainly, in the ever-increasing onslaught of pressures from investors, lenders, communities, employees, and customers—all of whom attempt to influence the corporation in different ways—the CEO frequently is called on to diplomatically negotiate with different parties on the corporation's behalf. The fact that the CEO is better able to fill this political role than anyone else in the corporation might motivate the dual CEO/chair to abdicate the role of monarch in favor of the more conciliatory role of mediator between the corporation and its various constituencies.[lv] In addition, although the CEO must be powerful enough to lead the corporation, wisdom dictates that he or she adjust to a more consensus-based governance structure, which in some cases might include relinquishing certain responsibilities of the board chair. In 1993, Ira Millstein, a long-time counsel to CEO's and boards, advised CEOs to determine how well their companies' board procedures encourage independence and thus credibility. If a CEO neglects for several years to make the necessary corrections, Millstein warned, shareholders, plaintiffs, or the government might do it for him.[lvi] (Eventually, passage of the Sarbanes Oxley Act in 2002 showed that Millstein's warning was right on target!) As the legendary investor and CEO, Warren Buffett, suggested, one of the best solutions for the problems of corporate governance is for corporations to select CEOs who can perform capably in situations of weak structural restraints.[lvii]

A Model for the CEO and Board Chair Positions: Some Basic Guidelines

Clearly, attempting to ascertain whether a company is best served by dividing or combining the CEO and board chair roles is difficult. This decision must be based on the realities of the given situation. However, regardless of how a board chooses to staff the two roles, the board as a whole must delineate the different responsibilities of each role. A few useful guidelines are available for directors to consider, as illustrated in Figures 7.1 and 7.2.

In general, when a corporation has a strong, seasoned, effective CEO and is governed by a more traditional, more passive board, the CEO and board chair positions should be combined. In such a case, the board is unlikely to have the strength or willingness to lead, and the CEO will find it necessary to provide leadership to the board. These circumstances indicate that it is time to begin developing an enlightened board of directors by attracting people to the board who are strongly interested in the corporation's success and have the energy and ability to learn and lead.

Board Leadership Decision Matrix
(The Roles of CEO & Chairman)

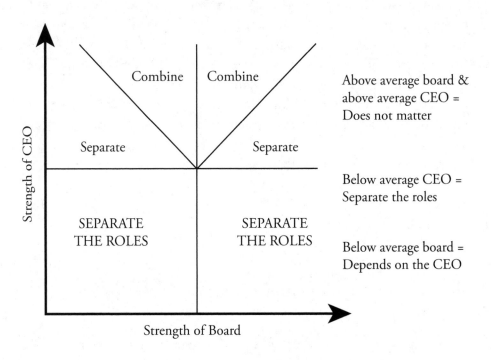

Figure 7.1

Examples of CEO Supervision

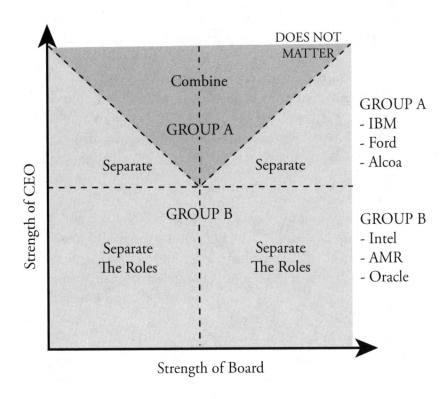

Figure 7.2

When the CEO is inexperienced or is performing marginally, the roles of the CEO and the board chair should be separated, whether the board is traditional or enlightened. The company is at risk, and this risk needs to be more appropriately balanced. An alternative action, of course, is to hire an experienced CEO. Of course, if the board is of the traditional variety, it is time to begin developing an enlightened board of directors.

It is interesting to note that the Ford board of directors deemed it appropriate in 2001 for William C. Ford to serve as CEO in addition to chairman of the board. However, they elected to separate the two roles when they hired Alan Mulaly in September of 2006. Is this a new strategy or merely an interim step toward recombining the roles? Only the Ford board knows, and only the Ford board should decide.

Conversely, following the recent debacle at Hewlett Packard involving inappropriate board behavior, Mark Hurd was named chairman and CEO. Was this a direct result of the board's dissatisfaction wtih the performance of chairman Patricia Dunn, or was it merely recognition that the chairman role and the CEO role should be recombined? Again, only the HP board knows, and only the HP board should decide.

If the corporation has hired or developed an experienced CEO whose performance is not as high as desired, and if the corporation has an enlightened board of directors, it does not matter whether the board chair and CEO positions are combined or separate. In this case, the board's paramount job is to improve the current CEO's performance! If the board's legitimate attempts to do so fail to yield the desired results, the CEO should be replaced.

A Closing Word

When all is said and done, and despite whatever transitions, crises, or power struggles are in play in the corporation, the board remains collectively responsible for the company's ultimate success. I write this from experience. I have had the privilege and pleasure of working with some of the most powerful and successful companies in Corporate America, including IBM, AT&T, Lucent, Dupont, and ITT. Over time, I have served as non-executive chairman of a public company listed on the NASDAQ; as chairman, president, and CEO of a public company listed on the NYSE; as director, CEO and president; and as director of a public company in which the combined role of CEO and board chair was shifted to separate roles of president/CEO and non-executive board chair. At this writing, I serve on four corporate boards. In three of these boardrooms, the CEO and board chair roles are combined. In one of these three situations, we elected a presiding director. In another, the chairman of the corporate governance committee serves as the lead director during executive sessions. In the other, the committee chairmen alternate that responsibility at each meeting. In the fourth boardroom, we elected a non-executive board chair and a separate CEO. In short, I have experienced every type of board leadership role, including presiding director and working with a lead director. In my experience, whether the CEO and board chair roles are combined is situation driven and company specific. If each director exercises his or her authority and responsibility, the chair will remain in check whether or not he or she has the additional role of CEO. Only irresponsible directors allow a board chair to rule the board without their collective involvement. Enlightened directors are neither weak nor apathetic. They are quite capable of dealing with any board chair. If they are not, they should not be serving on the board.

Another area in which board strength is needed is deciding executive compensation, which is the topic of the next chapter.

Notes

i Jensen, M. C. (1991). Corporate control and the politics of finance. *Journal of Applied Corporate Finance, 4*(2), 22-30.

ii Lohr, S. (1992, April 12). Pulling down the corporate clubhouse. *The New York Times,* p. B1.

iii Levitt, A. (1998, March 12). Corporate governance: Integrity in the information age. Remarks presented at Tulane University, New Orleans, Louisiana. Retrieved May 30, 2006, from http://www.sec.gov/news/speech/speecharchive/1998/spch206.txt.

iv Caremark International Inc. (1997, December). Securities class action alert. *Investors Research Bureau, 12*(12), 48.

v Levitt, 1998.

vi Ibid.

vii Ibid.

[viii] Lucier, C., Schuyt, R., & Tse, E. (2005, Summer). CEO succession 2005: The world's most prominent temp workers. *Strategy+Business, 39*. Reprint No. 05204.

[ix] Ibid.

[x] Ibid.

[xi] Ibid.

[xii] Ibid.

[xiii] Cassis, Y. (1997). *Big business: The European experience in the twentieth century.* Oxford, England: Oxford University Press.

[xiv] Lorsch, J. W., & MacIver, E. A. (1989). *Pawns and potentates: The reality of America's corporate boards.* Boston: Harvard Business School Press.

[xv] Ward, R. D. (1997). *21st century corporate board.* New York: John Wiley.

[xvi] Warner, M. (1996). Corporate governance. In *International encyclopedia of business and management,* (IEBM Series, 6 Vols.: Vol. 1, 777.) New York: Routledge.

[xvii] Ibid.

[xviii] Lucier, Schuyt, & Tse, 2005.

[xix] Iwata, E. (2004, March 16). To split or not to split? *USA Today.* Retrieved June 4, 2006, from http://www.usatoday.com/

[xx] Monks, R., & Minow, N. (1996). Watching the watchers: Corporate governance for the 21st century. Cambridge, MA: Blackwell.

[xxi] Brown, L. D., & Caylor, M. L. (2004). Corporate governance and firm performance. *Social Science Research Network,* p. 7. Retrieved June 3, 2006, from http://papers.ssrn.com/sol3/papers.cfm?abstract_id=586423.

[xxii] Rechner, P. L., & Dalton, D. R. (1991). CEO duality and organizational performance: A longitudinal analysis. *Strategic Management Journal, 12,* 120, 155-160.

[xxiii] Cadbury, A. (1997). Summing up the governance reports. *The Corporate Board, 18*(107), 6. Infotrac Article No. A20163324).

[xxiv] Teslik, S. (1993, August). The governance of Oozcskblnya. *CII Central Newsletter for the Council of Institutional Investors, 6,* 8.

[xxv] Core, Holthausen, & Larker, 1999, as cited by Brown & Caylor, 2004.

[xxvi] Blair, M. M. (1995). *Ownership and control: Rethinking corporate governance for the twenty-first century.* Washington, DC: The Brookings Institution.

[xxvii] Pound, J. (1995). The promise of the governed corporation. *Harvard Business Review, 73*(2), 89-98.

[xxviii] HP replaces CEO. (2005, February 9). *WebProNews.* Retrieved June 8, 2006, from http://www.webpronews.com/

[xxix] Jensen, 1991.

[xxx] Lorsch & MacIver, 1989.

[xxxi] Ward, 1997.

[xxxii] Ball, D. G. (1994). Revolution in the board room. *St. John's Law Review, 247,* 22.

[xxxiii] Clurman, R. M. (1993). *Who's in charge?* New York: Whittle.

[xxxiv] Coardiz, D. (1993). Corporate hangmen. Financial World 162, 24-28.

[xxxv] Lohr, S. (1992, April 12). Pulling down the corporate clubhouse. *The New York Times,* p. B1.

xxxvi Burrough, B., & Helyar, J. (1990). *Barbarians at the gate.* New York: Harper & Row, p. 75.

xxxvii Lublin, J. S. (1991, June 6). More chief executives are being forced out by tougher boards. *The Wall Street Journal,* p. A1.

xxxviii Carver, J. (1997b). *The chairperson's role as servant-leader to the board.* San Francisco: Jossey-Bass.

xxxix Swanson, A. (1992). *Building a better board: A guide to effective leadership.* Rockville, MD: Fund Raising Institute.

xl Directorship databank dividends. (1998, April). *Directorship, 24*(4), 13.

xli Dorf, P., & VanDeWalle, K. (2004, March 9). Splitting the roles of CEO and chairman of the board. Corporate Board Member Magazine. Retrieved June 2, 2006, from http://www.boardmember.com/network/index.pl?section=1086&article_id=11846&show=article.

xlii Ibid.

xliii Kopinksi, T. C. (2005). Independent board chair proposals get mixed reception. In 2005 postseason report: *Corporate governance at a crossroads,* p. 15. Rockville, Maryland: Institutional Shareholder Services.

xliv Holstein, W. J. (2004, April 25). Office space: Armchair M.B.A.; Smoothing the way to a new C.E.O. *The New York Times.*

xlv Ibid.

xlvi Whiting, R. (2004, January 19). Ellison now only CEO. *Information Week.* Retrieved June 4, 2006, from http://www.informationweek.com/

xlvii Iwata, E. (2004, March 16). To split or not to split? *USA Today.* Retrieved June 4, 2006, from http://www.usatoday.com/

xlviii Daily, C. (1995). The relationship between board composition and leadership structure and bankruptcy reorganization outcomes. *Journal of Management, 21*(6), 1041. (Infotrac Article No. A17792501).

xlix Ibid.

l Ibid.

li Cadbury, A. (1997). Summing up the governance reports. *The Corporate Board, 18*(107), 6. (Infotrac Article No. A20163324).

lii Conger, J., Finegold, D., & Lawler, E., III. (1998). Appraising boardroom performance. *Harvard Business Review, 98102,* 136-140.

liii Monks & Minow, 1996, p. 215.

liv Conger et al., 1998, p. 140.

lv Stewart, T. (1993). The king is dead. *Fortune, 34,* 40.

lvi Millstein, I. (1998). *Corporate governance: Improving competitiveness and access to capital in global markets.* New York: Organization for Economic Cooperation and Development (OECD), p. 87.

lvii Cunningham, L. A. (1998, July-August). Warren Buffet on the role of the board. *The Corporate Board, XIX*(111), 6-10.

Chapter 8

Executive Compensation

Should your opportunity to learn be limited by what others know?

Discussing executive compensation is like discussing politics and religion: everyone has a deeply entrenched opinion and no one expects the debate to end in agreement. Fascination with the wealth of high-profile corporate leaders no doubt leads many people to eagerly await the release of annual reports revealing the latest in CEOs' salaries, bonuses, and perquisites, served up by corporate proxy statements and nearly every major news journal or business publication in the world. However, for those interested in protecting their investments, this pastime has more serious consequences, and I confess to being among those who look forward with great anticipation to the annual ritual of reading about and discussing the new highs in CEO salaries and benefits!

This ritual began during the 1990s, when the business press responded virulently to rapidly growing CEO compensation packages that more and more often included lucrative stock options. Compensation had been an issue since the 1980's era of takeovers when disenfranchised shareholders watched highly paid directors rubber-stamp the questionable decisions of even more highly paid CEOs.[i] Americans were paying attention to CEO compensation for good reason: in the 14 years between 1980 and 1994, the total compensation for CEO's of the largest U.S. corporations increased by 209%![ii] Investors were demanding that CEO pay bear some relation to performance; by the 1990s, CEO compensation had become such a hot topic that *Business Week* began devoting an annual spring issue to it. This annual offering became an instant hit in the institutional investment community, especially among pension-fund managers.[iii] Lately, the spotlight's glare shines not only on the CEOs receiving huge compensation packages but also on the boards who awarded those packages.

On one side of the decades-old CEO compensation debate are those who wonder what a CEO actually is worth; on the other side are those who worry that a CEO might not be earning his or her compensation. At the very least, shareholders would like assurance that CEOs earn their huge paychecks. Especially considering the great power and influence that CEO's exert over their corporations, many corporate stakeholders are afraid that CEOs are not accountable to any higher authority.

A Look at What Research Reveals about CEO Compensation

When contemplating CEO compensation from a business perspective, it is important to recognize that corporations are not completely on their own when it comes to sorting out what works and what doesn't work when deciding compensation issues. Academic researchers have been studying top-executive pay for more than 70 years and have contributed more than 300 studies to increase understanding of what kinds of effects different types of packages have on corporate leadership and corporate success. The findings of these studies have given rise to a number of interesting theories that attempt to explain how executive compensation works.[iv]

Of these, a very popular and successful theory for explaining how companies decide what to pay their CEO's links pay and performance. This theory is called the agency theory because it deals with the relationships that an agent (such as a CEO or a board of directors) has with the people that agent represents (such as shareholders). With respect to CEO pay, the agency theory begins with the assumption that the CEO (as an agent) is self-serving and that those who design the CEO's reward structures intend to align the CEO's incentives with those of the shareholders; in other words, the board's compensation committee designs the CEO's compensation package so as to tie the financial gain of the CEO to the financial gain of shareholders.[v,vi]

The idea that the board will relate the size of a CEO's compensation package to how well the company does under that CEO's leadership is logical, but much depends on what kinds of company gains the package is designed to reward. Since the 1930s, research has revealed many instances in which the amount of the CEO's pay bore no relationship, or almost no relationship, to how well the firm performed over the long term. This finding is all the more noteworthy because it results from studies at different times by different researchers using different data sets, statistical techniques, variable measurements, and model specifications.[vii]

One of the more recent and often-cited investigations of the relationship between CEO pay and company performance was conducted by Michael C. Jensen of Harvard and Kevin J. Murphy of the University of Southern California, who found that CEO pay had low sensitivity to performance.[viii] Jensen and Murphy confessed surprise when they discovered that CEO's, despite their great influence on overall company operations, incurred about the same low risk of losing pay due to poor company performance as did common laborers.[ix] John E. Garen of the University of Kentucky, in a follow-up study of Jensen and Murphy's inquiry, also found that the concept of pay-for-performance had little effect on what boards chose to pay CEOs.[x] Later, in a 1998 study, a team of eminent researchers found that performance factors seemed to explain less than 5% of CEO pay.[xi]

Clearly, for compensation calculations to have a positive effect on a company's performance over time, the compensation committee must tie compensation to measures that meaningfully correlate with long-term growth. Convinced that CEOs are not necessarily paid in relation to company performance, Harry G. Barkema of Tilburg University and Gomez-Mejia of Arizona State University decided to look at other mechanisms and criteria that might be determining how boards set compensation for their company's top executives.[xii] Barkema and Gomez-Mejia reviewed and critiqued a collection of innovative studies that empirically tested other variables that might help to explain CEO pay, such as CEO influence, demand for the CEO's services, power relationships and social exchanges, upward and downward social comparisons, and human cognitive processes.[xiii]

Of the many pertinent findings of executive compensation research, one is particularly important for directors to contemplate: boards are more likely to link CEO pay to performance when the company's ownership includes large external block shareholders because these shareholders have both the incentives and the voting power to discipline CEOs.[xiv,xv]

How Much Is a CEO Really Worth?

Because everyone is affected by executive compensation in some way, it is understandable that people quickly form very strong personal opinions about it and bring these opinions to (often heated) discussions. People's opinions about CEO pay are likely to be tinged by their own unpleasant experiences with money shortages. When a person feels undervalued and underpaid, it is especially easy to see top executives as overvalued and overpaid; most people are quick to agree that CEOs make too much money in salaries, not to mention stocks, stock options, cash bonuses, and perquisites like use of corporate jets, rich severance packages, and exceedingly comfortable retirement plans. No matter how many years of extraordinary performance a CEO delivers, many people find it extremely difficult to understand why anyone might deserve to earn as much money as many CEOs do. While I was President and CEO of Lucent Technologies Microelectronics Group, one of my colleagues told me that if he were a CEO, he would awake every morning celebrating as though he had won the lottery!

It is not only a touch of envy that leads most people to question the size of many CEO compensation packages; some of these payouts are egregious by almost any measure. However, because each company must pay its talented CEO enough money to keep that person working for the company, examples of over-the-top CEO pay packages actually are fewer than most people think, especially when those packages are considered in light of the value CEOs generate for shareholders and all of the corporation's other stakeholders, particularly employees and communities.

Shareholders' Responsibility to Monitor CEO Pay

More than 2 decades ago, surfacing concerns about excessive executive compensation motivated the U.S. Securities and Exchange Commission to sharpen their focus on disclosure by corporate compensation committees. The heart of corporate governance and securities regulation in the United States has always been openness and disclosure, the purpose of which is to create informed buyers of a company's stock.[xvi] In 1934, when the SEC developed its first disclosure rules, the Commission realized that too much information could be as detrimental as none at all, particularly because the informed investors the SEC had in mind at the time were individual shareholders, not institutional investors,[xvii] whom the SEC deemed capable of taking care of themselves.

By the 1980s, however, executive compensation vehicles had become so complex that they were difficult even for institutional investors to understand. Institutional investors, although skilled in financial analysis, generally did not possess the specialized knowledge required to evaluate these vehicles. Institutional investors needed more disclosure if they were to monitor executive compensation and help shareholders review board performance.[xviii,xix]

In 1992, the SEC responded to these dramatically changed information needs with disclosure reforms specifically aimed at compensation issues. The SEC required that each corporate compensation committee state the basis for its decisions about executive compensation in its proxy statement. In a direct response to concerns of institutional investors, the SEC ordered significant deregulation of the proxy process. As a result, shareholders gained the freedom to raise issues, including those put to a vote of shareholders, without the SEC's prior approval.[xx] Although shareholders may still find it difficult to discern total executive compensation from proxy statements, the SEC did move away from its prior view of compensation as ordinary business in which the shareholders should not be involved to a view of salaries and benefits as raising important policy concerns for shareholder discussion. The SEC's new compensation rules also made it easier for shareholders to communicate with each other, thus increasing the possibility of effective oversight.

The SEC based its 1992 decisions on four guiding principles: protecting investors from information overload, making information understandable to unsophisticated individual investors, making information available to sophisticated institutional investors, and respecting the proprietary nature of executive compensation.[xxi,xxii,xxiii] The 1992 decisions fully addressed this last concern, but the remaining three principles may need ongoing examination.

The SEC recently required that a corporate compensation committee disclose the compensation of the company's five most highly paid executive officers, including the CEO and the CFO, and also describe the board's rationale for that compensation in easy-to-read language. These changes significantly improved the flow of information of executive compensation information to shareholders. Indeed, anyone with access to a computer can easily find compensation information on Yahoo! Finance or other financial Web sites.

For many reasons, broader corporate disclosures and greater availability of information regarding executive compensation have resulted in a feeding frenzy. Improving the flow of information about executive pay has not improved many people's understanding of the facts. Of course, sometimes the facts are not fully disclosed or are so poorly articulated that they are difficult to comprehend. However, with today's access to enormous amounts of information, individual investors are much more likely to suffer from information overload than from information shortages. Many times financial investors, corporate employees, and members of the general public ignore easily obtained, clearly expressed facts simply because they don't want to believe them!

Increased disclosure of CEO compensation packages will be of little use if shareholders do not use the available information to monitor the compensation decisions made by boards. As Supreme Court Justice Louis D. Brandeis wrote nearly a century ago, "there is no innocent shareholder." The person who takes a chance to profit by owning shares in an enterprise must take the fiscal and social responsibilities of his investment seriously.[xxiv] The investor who accepts the benefits of a system in which others take responsibility for managing his or her investment is obligated to ensure that those representatives act consistently with the public welfare. Shareholders are not innocent merely because they have had nothing personally to do with the business decisions of a company. Taken to its logical conclusion, this is simply absentee landlordism.[xxv]

Some governance experts believe that shareholders can most effectively ensure appropriate executive and director compensation by actively monitoring the board's performance and participating in elections. Robert A. G. Monks & Nell Minow, founders of The Corporate Library, an independent research firm dedicated to corporate governance, advised shareholders to review pay disclosures carefully, withhold votes for directors who approve poor plans, and submit resolutions to make sure that pay plans align the interests of directors with those of shareholders.[xxvi] By remaining vigilant, shareholders are likely to find that active oversight is more cost effective than its alternative, active trading.

In May of 2003, the stress and anxiety levels of compensation committees were elevated by a decision by the Delaware Court of Chancery that permitted some vigilant shareholders to sue Walt Disney's board of directors for breach of fiduciary duty. At issue was the board's decision to approve severance pay and other benefits equaling $140 million for former Disney president Michael Ovitz after he had served for only 14 months. With the Court's approval, Disney shareholders brought a suit accusing the Disney directors and officers of wasting the company's money.[xxvii]

In April of 2004, as the Disney shareholder lawsuit moved through the legal system, the travel and real estate giant, Cendant Corp., agreed to settle another shareholder lawsuit in Delaware that accused Cendant's board of breach of fiduciary duty. Shareholder ire had been aroused by changes to the pay package of chairman and CEO Henry R. Silverman, already the recipient of one of the richest executive compensation packages in the United

States.[xxviii] Cendant's compensation committee, the plaintiff complained, had agreed to amend Silverman's existing employment agreement without consulting compensation experts, an independent legal advisor, or even "any spreadsheets or other analyses showing the potential cost to Cendant of the new agreement." The plaintiff sought repayment of compensation that the suit termed "grossly excessive."[xxix] As part of Cendant's settlement, the compensation committee made "a significant majority" of Silverman's bonus "subject to the attainment of certain performance-based earnings per share goals," and cut his length of employment, severance pay, and post-termination consulting payments.[xxx]

Sixteen months later, in August of 2005, the lengthy trial of shareholders' claims that the Disney board had breached their fiduciary duty ended with the Court's rejection of that claim. The Court harshly criticized the Disney directors' actions in approving huge settlement benefits to the company's former President but acknowledged that the law "does not require corporate fiduciaries to meet current standards of ideal corporate governance or penalize them for failing to employ best practices."[xxxi] Disney's directors, the Court decided, were protected by "the business judgment rule," which "presumes that directors act in good faith in making business decisions in the best interests of the company." However, it seems clear that future shareholder plaintiffs could overcome this presumption by proving a breach of duty, fraud, bad faith, or self-dealing. In the Disney case, the business judgment rule protected directors, but it cannot be counted on to offer directors safe harbor from breach of the duty of due care through inaction.[xxxii]

The Disney case was not the only unsuccessful shareholder effort to curb excessive rewards for a poorly performing CEO. A number of boards have authorized millions in severance pay for CEOs fired for poor performance.[xxxiii] Nevertheless, boards are tending to take more seriously shareholders' desire that the compensation of CEOs, senior officers, and directors all be linked to shareholder value, and corporate governance reforms apparently have helped create this trend.[xxxiv]

Calculating CEO Pay

When excessively lavish executive compensation packages become the object of sensationalized news and cause public and shareholder alarm, it becomes clear that the boards involved should have aligned the total compensation of their senior officers with shareholder value. Such disturbing failures by inept or irresponsible boards should cause all directors to more carefully focus their executive compensation plans on performance. With few exceptions, when CEO compensation plans are linked to increasing shareholder value, everyone wins. Pay for performance should be every executive's mantra.

Federal tax law provides an opportunity for the creation of pay-for-performance executive compensation packages by permitting corporations to reduce their federal tax liabilities by using compensation packages linked to performance. Normally, executive compensation up to one million dollars is deductible as a corporate expense, but all executive compensation in excess of that amount must be paid from after-tax earnings. However, in an incentive provided by SEC rule 151 and Section 162(m) of the Internal Revenue Code, compensation programs that are at risk based on performance may be deducted as corporate expenses.[xxxv,xxxvi]

Clearly, however, corporate compensation committees must rethink the concept of performance.[xxxvii] Compensation has evolved as a key tool in business management, and translating corporate strategy into CEO rewards is becoming a top-priority goal of corporations. Although companies have traditionally judged performance in terms of what was happening at other companies in the competitive market, compensation committees should now be looking at pay packages from a broader perspective. As suggested by John A. Byrne, executive editor of *Business Week Magazine*, members of enlightened boards should place themselves in a good position to evaluate CEO performance by jointly establishing specific goals and strategies for their CEOs to follow.[xxxviii]

If it is true that the better an employee performs on the job, the more that employee should earn, it follows that the CEO's compensation should be directly related to the value that he or she brings to the corporation.[xxxix]

This brings up the question at the heart of the CEO pay issue: What level of performance-based compensation is reasonable? In other words, how much pay is too much pay?

Responsible Wealth, an organization of 400 wealthy individuals whose confidential membership includes sitting CEOs and corporate directors, promotes the notion that boards impose a ratio between CEO pay and that of the company's lowest-paid full-time employee. For many adherents to this notion, a CEO's pay should equal 6 to 10 times that of the lowest-paid worker. This formula, of course, is not very useful. If the lowest paid employee earns $20,000 per year, the CEO's earnings would be limited to 10 times $20,000. A salary of $200,000 will not attract a talented CEO competing among peers. Nonetheless, over the years, Responsible Wealth has filed resolutions at General Electric, Allied Signal, Citigroup, and AT&T asking directors to limit executive compensation packages.[xl]

Such proposals do not represent a carefully reasoned solution in an economic society founded on the principles of free markets and free enterprise, and the anonymity of this group is disturbing. It seems unlikely that members of Responsible Wealth would want their own wealth limited by a multiple of the minimum income of the average American or the minimum portfolio value of the average shareholder.

The real issue in corporate compensation is appropriate pay for performance and value, and many researchers and financial experts have attempted to find a uniform method of determining what a CEO should be paid. In our economic system, supply and demand determines the financial value of each job. Employees will be paid at least what other people who perform similar work are paid or they might be induced to leave the company, an obvious fact that happens to be substantiated by considerable research. When comparing social incentives that contribute over time to upward pressure on the pay packages of CEOs and their executive teams, the likely factors are market forces, social comparisons, and the advice of external consultants.[xli,xlii]

The Role of Stock Options in Executive Compensation

CEO pay specialist Pearl Meyer pointed out that CEOs have tremendous equity stakes in their businesses.[xliii] One outstanding example is Jerre Stead, former chairman and CEO of Ingram Micro, who accepted his job for a compensation package that included no salary but contained stock options with the potential of making him owner of 2.76% of the company after an initial public offering. [xliv] Many boards have implemented programs that require corporate directors and senior officers to own either a certain number of shares or a certain dollar amount in share value.

Stock options, which gave employees the right to purchase shares of the company's stock at a specified price within a set future period, became especially popular during the 1990s, when there seemed to be no end in sight for increases in share values. Stock options seemed to provide wonderful incentives for top managers to make outstanding improvements in shareholder value. If the company's share price rose above the CEO's share-grant price, that CEO's income increased, linking the interests of shareholder and CEO. Moreover, stock options redistributed the executive's total compensation by placing larger portions of his or her income at risk based on performance. The beauty of stock options seemed to be that no one was the loser. The stock market was hot and shareholders were thrilled with the wealth they were gaining. Senior managers and ordinary employees alike basked in the glow of stock option appreciation. The warning alarms of the Enron, Tyco, and Adelphia meltdowns had not yet sounded.

Stock options obviously can create positive inducements for better performance and oversight, but they are not a motivational panacea because they hold no real risk for the executives (or directors) who receive them. Compensation committees must guard against simply giving them away. Stock option awards should be used to create the same benefits and risks for executives and directors that are assumed by the company's shareholders. Stock option awards for corporate executives and directors are losing some popularity because they can tempt senior executives and directors to focus on short-term shareholder value, but, if properly used, stock option awards hold the possibility for changing the personality profile of the recipient.

Pay-for-Performance: A Two-Edged Sword

Pay-for-performance compensation packages are not without potential drawbacks. The primary focus of pay-for-performance efforts has been on the performance of the corporation and not on performance of the individual. It is possible for a CEO to do most of the right things in the short term and yet fail to produce the results expected by shareholders. When the board fails to link individual performance measures with appropriate measures of the corporation's success, individuals can be penalized for poor corporate results when in fact their efforts were largely in line with good practice. Such failures highlight the critical need for the board and CEO to be fully engaged in developing a strategic plan that is designed to yield positive long-term shareholder value and executive compensation together!

An important part of this effort is ensuring that executive management teams have the right incentives. They cannot be expected to undertake the difficult task of formulating and challenging corporate policies unless successful service is associated with real gains.[xlv,xlvi]

Few issues inflame those who follow the activities of corporations more than compensation that is seen as excessive.[xlvii,xlviii] Shareholders can easily relate to large compensations for CEOs and directors when the company involved is producing good share value; however, when CEOs and directors are compensated by large sums of money during a time that the company is producing poor returns or laying off workers, stakeholder anger and bad publicity ensue.

When making compensation decisions, the board's challenge is to select appropriate measures for success. The key indicator for measuring the corporation's success generally is share price, which should be measured as a reflection of long-term share price, not short-term price. Revenue growth, consistent earnings, and return on invested capital also are highly regarded indicators of long-term corporate performance. Compensation packages should reflect the board's clearly defined and articulated long-term objectives for building shareholder value.

Rewarding senior officers with share grants and options can be a very effective means of linking their long-term wealth directly to shareholder interests. It is the responsibility of the compensation committee, and ultimately of the entire board, to develop and implement the share plan, which will include the number of shares distributed to executives, the area in which excesses normally occur. If too many shares are awarded, any small increase in the level of performance can significantly reward executives and directors while non-affiliated shareholders experience very minor gains.

Pay for performance is a two-edged sword. Exceptional performance should be linked with exceptional pay, and when the corporation performs well, the board should reward its executives accordingly. However, the board should reward marginal performance with marginal compensation. If boards fail to structure compensation packages to reward long-term performance, small perturbations in the market can result in large compensation gains and losses. Boards must respond to the compensation challenge by designing appropriate, accurately calculated compensation programs inextricably linked with corporate performance targets.

Who Should Make Compensation Decisions?

Some corporate governance experts believe that the directors most likely to be complacent monitors of executive compensation are CEOs of other companies. In 1996, corporate governance researchers Robert A. G. Monks and Nell Minow reported that 86% of the boards of billion-dollar companies included at least one CEO of another company.[xlix] When CEOs and directors sit on each other's compensation committees, they create a strong perception that they are forming mutual protection societies.[l] Obviously, a CEO has a strong interest in providing high pay for another CEO or director who sits on his or her own compensation committee because it gives that CEO a place from which to negotiate with his or her own board. In some cases, activist investors have opposed such self-serving arrangements in lawsuits.[li] According to several researchers, a compensation committee's dependency on the CEO or appointment by the CEO predicts higher levels of CEO pay and lower levels of contingent pay.[lii]

Boards have learned to defend themselves from shareholders' dislike of high CEO pay (expressed through the annual shareholder proxy process) by thoroughly describing the roles and procedures of compensation committees in setting executive compensation. Enlightened directors aggressively attack shareholder dissatisfaction by dissolving interdependent relationships that create perceptions of mutual protection and lax monitoring.

Board independence in establishing compensation can be accomplished in a variety of ways that shareholders can monitor. Many governance experts, including Michael C. Jensen of the Harvard Business School, recommend diluting CEO power by separating the dual position of CEO/chair.[liii] (See Figures 7.1 and 7.2 in chapter 7.)

On November 4, 2003, the U. S. Securities and Exchange Commission culminated a rule-making process of nearly 2 years duration by approving new corporate governance listing standards proposed by the New York Stock Exchange. The new standards, which brought the NYSE into compliance with the Sarbanes-Oxley Act of 2002 and with other relevant standards, require a listed company to have an audit committee, a compensation committee, and a nominating or corporate governance committee, each composed entirely of independent directors and each having a charter describing its purposes and responsibilities.

Ironically, 7 months later, Eliot Spitzer, attorney general of New York State, unveiled a 55-page lawsuit against Richard Grasso, former chairman of the New York Stock Exchange, charging him with deception, conflict of interest, and receipt of excessive pay and demanding that Grasso return more than $100 million of $139.5 million paid to him by the exchange in the previous year.[liv,lv] Grasso immediately replied in a 1,400-word op-ed page in *The Wall Street Journal* in which he accused the attorney general of playing politics, called the deception charge baseless, and defended his compensation as just.

> I did not set my compensation. . . . Instead, the payments now under attack were decided by six different compensation committees and boards

of directors of the exchange, made up of more than three dozen of the most sophisticated, independent and knowledgeable executives in America. Every decision, every bonus, every contract, was decided by those directors in a series of unanimous votes.[lvi]

Incensed shareholders had expected the committees and the board of directors of the New York Stock Exchange to be role models for their customers, the companies listed on their exchange, but they were disappointed.

On the same day that the SEC approved the new NYSE corporate governance listing standards, the Commission also approved new listing standards of the NASDAQ Stock Market, which also had substantially altered its former listing standards.[lvii] The new NASDAQ requirements were designed to increase transparency and accountability for investors and harmonize NASDAQ rules with the requirements of the Sarbanes-Oxley Act and similar corporate governance proposals made by the New York Stock Exchange.

Under the new NASDAQ requirements, a compensation committee comprised solely of independent directors is required to recommend CEO compensation to the board for determination; lacking a compensation committee, a majority of a board's independent directors may determine the compensation. The CEO may not be present when his or her compensation is deliberated or decided. Independent directors must similarly determine compensation of other officers, but the CEO may be present at such deliberations and decisions. Under exceptional limited circumstances and time period, and with approval, a compensation committee comprised of at least three independent members may include one inside director who is not a current company officer, employee or family member of a current officer or employee.[lviii]

Compensating Directors

One of the most visible topics of corporate governance of late has been *corporate director compensation*, which generally refers to payments to outside directors. *Inside directors*, that is, company employees, normally do not receive additional compensation for board service.[lix] Unlike concerns about

147

CEO compensation, concerns about director compensation do not center on how much directors are paid but on whether their pay is linked to improved shareholder value.

In the traditional U.S. boardroom of not so long ago, a director's retainer fees and benefits bore no relationship to the director's performance or to the performance of the board or company. The director's compensation did not rise in good years or fall in bad years, and most directors did not hold significant shares of the company's stock to align their interests with those of shareholders.[lx] Today, most governance experts have concluded that directors should be paid for performance, and often directors are paid more for committee work.[lxi]

The important question in director pay is not necessarily how much directors are paid, but how seriously they take their duties and how well they perform these duties. While complacent directors might be overpaid for what they do, directors who take their duties seriously probably are not being paid nearly enough for their diligence and successful performance.

Director compensation should be modest, if only to reduce the inducement for professional *boardaholics* to serve on multiple boards as a way of making substantial incomes, and, relatively speaking, modest it is. Indeed, director pay originally was viewed as a sort of honorarium for people who made their living doing other things.[lxii] According to a 2005 survey by Pearl Meyer & Partners, of board-member compensation at the 200 largest U.S. corporations, over 8 years, total director remuneration averaged just 1.4% of the total collected by the CEOs.[lxiii] Not surprisingly, however, as directors' jobs become more complex and risky, demand for them rises and, according to the Pearl Meyer study, so does director pay. At present, only one board candidate in seven agrees to serve on a corporate board. Obviously, like CEO's and their teams, corporate directors must be offered good incentives to undertake the difficult task of formulating and challenging corporate policies.[lxiv] As Julie Connolly of *Corporate Board Member Magazine* reported:

> Total remuneration [for directors of the top 200 companies] grew 8.7% in 2004, to $191,971, on top of a 13% hike in 2003. The cash retainer rose by 14.2%, to $51,702, after a 17% increase the year before; the equity por-

tion was up 6.1% from an 8% expansion the previous year. Overall, cash accounted for 44% of the package, slightly more than in 2003, and equity was 56%. However, if you enlarge the sample size to 585 of the largest U.S. companies, . . . total compensation is up 20%. Some companies also offered stock options.[lxv]

More and more, boards pay their directors in shares versus cash, a technique that links director compensation more tightly with shareholders' economic value. In the average 2004 compensation package of a director of one of the 200 top U.S. companies, equity accounted for 56% and cash accounted for 44%.[lxvi] Stock options became popular inducements in director compensation packages in the 1990s at the time that they were widely used in executive compensation packages. If directors received real equity in the company, the idea went, they would watch CEO performance more closely. In the late 1990s, the most significant trend in director compensation was toward offering share grants and options in lieu of, or in addition to, cash compensation.[lxvii] More and more, however, boards are viewing share options as an inappropriate form of pay for performance.[lxviii] Between 2002 and 2005, the number of top 200 corporations granting options to their directors dropped from 75% to 50%, with 80% paying directors full-value shares.[lxix]

Although share grants as director pay are endorsed by the National Association of Corporate Directors (NACD), who see share ownership as a good way of getting directors to think like shareholders, this method of linking director interests to company performance also is somewhat problematic. One problem is that director compensation packages that do not emphasize long-term growth might induce directors to pursue short-term gain instead. Another is that assessing correlations between director performance and board performance is all but impossible during a bull market that raises all boats.

Business analyst Harry J. Bruce agreed that directors should hold shares, but disagreed with NACD's logic for doing so.[lxx,lxxi] Bruce reasoned that directors often are wealthy individuals with diversified portfolios whose financial wellbeing is unlikely to be affected by the performance of a company in which they own only few thousand shares. He proposed that directors need not feel any affinity to the common stockholder in order to perform their fiduciary duty, and that this duty compels directors to care for stakeholders' interests more diligently than they might care for their own property and interests. Whereas individuals reserve the right to neglect their own property, Bruce argued, they do not possess the right to neglect the property of others entrusted to their care. Bruce further proposed that governance policies should prohibit outside directors from directly or indirectly receiving any additional fees, such as consulting or legal fees, from the company whose board they join.[lxxii]

Tying the fortunes of directors to those of shareholders must be combined with appropriate disclosure and with careful monitoring of the board by shareholders. Lawrence Tucker, CEO of the international investment bank, Brown Brothers Harriman, related his experience on a board in which other outside directors had an average investment in the company of one million dollars. It was a board, Tucker said, that paid attention: "I've never seen the pocket calculators come out so quickly in my life!"[lxxiii]

Although share ownership may very well make better directors, stock programs must be carefully designed to deter possible board decisions that encourage short-term increases in stock value over long-term company viability. The board must decide to award directors with stocks or stock options only after careful consideration because profit-taking could be an issue. To reduce directors' temptations to create short-term profits, boards should measure director performance over the long term. Some observers have suggested that a director's pay baseline be set when the director joins the board, with adjustments made for retained earnings and inflation. Corporate governance pioneer Robert A. G. Monks recommended that resale of a director's stock should be restricted during his or her term in office[lxxiv] and, together with his associate Nell Minow, also suggested awarding a director with restricted stock that vests 12 to 36 months after he or she retires from the board.[lxxv] This technique, Monks and Minow suggested, puts enough of the director's financial future at stake to cause him or her to think like a shareholder.

Any comprehensive discussion of director compensation must follow the lead of activist shareholders in addressing the subject of benefits and perks, particularly when they take the form of retirement programs and free goods and services. Although director retainer fees are relatively modest, they often are supplemented by shares, life insurance, the use of corporate jets, retirement plans, and free or deeply discounted products or services such as free merchandise from a retail company or free use of a car by an auto manufacturer.[lxxvi] Occasionally boards have misused benefits and perks, but no evidence suggests that such abuse ever has been widespread. Providing a director with free transportation on a corporate jet for non-board-related trips is poor judgment and probably a violation of corporate policy. On the other hand, providing a director with a free pair of the tennis shoes manufactured by the company so that he or she can assess the product's quality or act as company spokesperson represents good judgment and hardly violates ethics. Most directors understand the difference between the two.

Summary

In the long run, the best interests of everyone affiliated with a public corporation are served when corporate directors, CEOs, and their executive teams, are compensated in ways that motivate them to seek long-term success for the company and its shareholders. Effective executive compensation depends on the board's ability to act independently. Director independence is discussed at length in the next chapter.

Notes

[i] Ellig, B. R., & Minehan, M. (1998). *Future focus on HR in the 21st century.* New York: Society of Human Resources.

[ii] Hall, B. J., & Liebman, J. B. (2000). The taxation of executive compensation (NBER Research Working Papers 7596). Cambridge, MA: National Bureau of Economic Research, Inc.

[iii] Crystal, G. (1995). Nowhere to go but down. *Financial Executive, 11,* 64.

[iv] See Gomez-Mejia, L. R. (1994). *Executive compensation: A reassessment and a future research agenda.* In K. M. Rowland & G. R. Ferris (Eds.), *Research in Personnel and Human Resources Management, 12,* 161-222; also Gomez-Mejia, L. R., & Wiseman, R. (1997). Reframing executive compensation: An assessment and outlook. *Journal of Management* 23(3): 291-374.

[v] Fama, E. F., & Jensen, M. (1983). Separation of ownership and control. *Journal of Law and Economics 26*(June), 301-325.

vi Jensen, M., & Meckling, W. (1976). Theory of the firm: Managerial behaviour, agency costs and ownership structure, *Journal of Financial Economics, 3,* 305-360.

vii For examples, see Jensen, M. C., & Murphy, K. J. (1990). CEO incentives: It's not how much you pay, but how. *Harvard Business Review, 90308,* 17; Kerr, J., & Bettis, R. A. (1987). Boards of directors, top management compensation, and shareholder returns. *Academy of Management Journal, 30,* 645-664.

viii Jensen, M. C., & Murphy, K. J. (1990). Performance pay and top-management incentives. *Journal of Political Economy, 98*(2), 225-64.

ix Ibid.

x Garen, J. E. (1994). Executive compensation and principal-agent theory. *Journal of Political Economy, 102*(6), 1198.

xi Tosi, H. L., Werner, S., Katz, J. P., & Gomez-Mejia, L. R. (2000). How much does performance matter? A meta-analysis of CEO pay studies. *Journal of Management, 26,* 301-339.

xii Barkema, H. G., Gomez-Mejia, L. (1998). Managerial compensation and firm performance: A general research framework. *Academy of Management Journal 41*(2), 135-145.

xiii Other tested theories include managerial discretion theory, social comparison theory, the marginal productivity theory, information-processing theory, and resource dependence theory.

xiv See the review by Gomez Mejia & Wiseman, 1997.

xv Shleifer, A., Vishny, R. (1986). Large shareholders and corporate control. *Journal of Political Economy, 94,* 461-488.

xvi Charkham, J. (1994). *Keeping good company: A study of corporate governance in five countries,* p. 175. New York: Oxford University Press.

xvii Vance, S. (1983). *Corporate leadership, boards, directors, and strategy,* pp. 152-156. New York: McGraw Hill.

sviii Jackson, T., & Lewis, W. (1995, June 19). Call to pay U.S. directors in stock. *The Financial Times,* p. 3.

xix Conger, J., Finegold, D., & Lawler, E., III. (1998). Appraising boardroom performance. *Harvard Business Review, 98102,* 136-140.

xx Maw, N. G. (1994). *Maw on corporate governance.* Aldershot, New York: Dartmouth.

xxi Blair, M. M. (1995). *Ownership and control: Rethinking corporate governance for the twenty-first century.* Washington, DC: The Brookings Institution.

xxii Brancato, C. K. (1997). *Institutional investors and corporate governance: Best practices for increasing corporate value.* Chicago: Irwin Professional.

xxiii deGruyter, W. (1994). *Institutional investors and corporate governance.* Berlin, Germany: WB-Druck Gmbh, Rieden.

xxiv Monks, R., & Minow, N. (1995). *Corporate governance,* p. 103. Cambridge, MA: Blackwell.

xxv Ibid.

xxvi Ibid.

xxvii Nussbaum, C. G., & Cummings, T. B. (2005, August 17). Decision in Walt Disney shareholder derivative suit criticizes but protects compensation decision of directors under business judgement rule. *Nixon Peabody LLD Corporate Responsibility Alert.* Retrieved July 12, 2005, from http://www.nixonpeabody.com/publications_detail3.asp?Type=P&PAID=&ID=1080.

xxviii Morgenson, G. (2004, April 20). Cendent chief takes pay cut. *The New York Times.* Retrieved July 12, 2006, from http://www.nytimes.com.

xxix Ibid.

xxx Crystal, G. (2004, April 28). Cendent's 'new' Henry Silverman cuts pay twice. *Bloomberg. com.* Retrieved July 12, 2006, from http://quote.bloomberg.com/

xxxi Nussbaum & Cummings, 2005.

xxxii Ibid.

xxxiii Bryant, A. (1998, January 5). How the mighty have fallen and sometimes profited anyway. *The New York Times,* p. D4.

xxxiv Detailed references can be found in Gugler, K. (Ed.). (2001). *Corporate governance and economic performance,* pp. 203-265. Oxford, England: Oxford University Press.

xxxv Brancato, 1997.

xxxvi Internal Revenue Service. (1993, December 20). *Disallowance of deductions for employee remuneration in excess of $1,000,000.* Federal Register (58 FR66310, EE-61-93). Washington, DC: Government Printing Office.

xxxvii Conger et al., 1998, 143.

xxxviii Byrne, 1997, 102.

xxxix Detailed references can be found in Gugler, 2001, 201-215 and 203-265. Oxford, England: Oxford University Press.

xl Wealthy crusaders combat CEO pay. (1999, February). *Directors Alert, 3*(2), 2.

xli O'Reilly, C. A., III, & Chatman, J. (1986). Organizational commitment and psychological attachment: The effects of compliance, identification, and internalization on prosocial behavior. *Journal of Applied Psychology, 71,* 492-499.

xlii Barkema & Gomez-Mejia, 1998.

xliii Meyer, P. (1997). *CEO pay: A comprehensive look.* Scottsdale, Arizona: American Compensation Association.

xliv Pereira, P., & O'Heir, J. (1996, September 2). Ingram taps Stead to lead global push: Beats 17 others for CEO. *Computer Reseller News,* p. 164.

xlv Pound, J. (1995). The promise of the governed corporation. *Harvard Business Review, 73*(2), 89-98.

xlvi See Jensen's agency theory, Jensen, M. C. (1993). The modern industrial revolution, exit, and the failure of internal control systems. *Journal of Finance, 48*(3), 831-880.

xlvii Brancato, 1997.

xlviii deGruyter, 1994.

xlix Monks, R., & Minow, N. (1996). *Watching the watchers: Corporate governance for the 21st century,* p. 188. Cambridge, MA: Blackwell.

l Ibid.

li Charkham, 1994, 179, 198-201.

lii Dalton, D., Daily, C., Ellstrand, A., & Johnson, J. (1998). Meta-analytic reviews of board composition, leadership structure, and financial performance. *Strategic Management Journal, 19,* 269-90.

liii Cadbury, A. (1997, November-December). Summing up the governance reports. *The Corporate Board, 18*(107), 6. (Infotrac Article No. A20163324).

liv Ackman, D. (2004, May 25). Spitzer vs. Grasso—For love or money. *Forbes.com.* Retrieved August 4, 2006, from www.forbes.com/

lv White, B. (2004, May 26). Grasso, Sptizer take it personal. *WashingtonPost.com.* Retrieved August 5, 2006, from http://www.washingtonpost.com.

lvi Ibid.

lvii Censoplano and Zuppone, 2003.

lviii Ibid.

lix Charkham, 1994, p. 189.

lx Ibid.

lxi Connolly, J. (2005, September-October). Why some board members are paid more than others. *Corporate Board Member Magazine.* Retrieved August 3, 2006, from http://www.boardmember.com/

lxii Ibid.

lxiii Ibid.

lxiv Pound, J. (1995). The promise of the governed corporation. *Harvard Business Review,* 73(2), 89-98.

lxv Connolly, 2005.

lxvi Ibid.

lxvii Significant data for directors 1999: Board policies and governance trends. (1999, January). *Directorship, 1*(1), 3.

lxviii Connolly, 2005.

lxix Ibid.

lxx Bruce, H. J. (1997). Duty, honor, company. *Directors & Boards,* 21(2), 12-16.

lxxi What the best boards do. (1996, November 26). *Business Week.* Retrieved from http://www.businessweek.com/

lxxii Bruce, 1997.

lxxiii Monks and Minow, 1996, p. 210.

lxxiv Monks, R. A. G. (1996). The American corporation at the end of the twentieth century: An outline of ownership based governance. A speech given at Cambridge University, July, 1996. Retrieved May 27, 2006, from http://www.lens-library.com/info/cambridge.html.

lxxv Monks and Minow, 1996.

lxxvi For current director retainer and per-meeting fees, see Investment Responsibility Research Center. (2002). Board practices, board pay, 2002, Author. Available from http://www.irrc.org/; and Connolly, 1995. for current per-meeting fees.

Chapter 9

Director Independence

Who you know does not always help.

On November 4, 2003, the U.S. Securities and Exchange Commission approved new corporate governance listing standards proposed by the New York Stock Exchange and the NASDAQ Stock Market requiring that the majority of directors of the corporate boards of listed companies be independent. This was a substantial change from prior listing standards that merely required independence of audit committees.

Before this change, the New York Stock Exchange had loosely defined *director independence* as having "no material relations" with the company; their new definition explicitly stated what was meant by "no material relations." A director could not qualify as independent if, during the previous 3 years, he or she:

1. had been employed by the listed company,

2. had received $100,000 per year in direct compensation from the listed company,

3. had been affiliated with or employed by a present or former external or internal auditor of the listed company, or

4. had been employed as an executive officer of another company where any of the listed company's present executives serve on that company's compensation committee.

The NYSE also disqualified a director from independent status if one of his or her immediate family members met one of these four criteria. In addition, a director was excluded if, during the previous 3 years, he or she:

5. had been employed by a company that made payments to, or received payments from, the listed company for property or services in an amount, which, in any single fiscal year, exceeded $1 million or, 2% of such other company's consolidated gross revenues (whichever was greater).

However, companies in which a single entity holds more than 50% of the company's voting rights (known as *controlled companies*) enjoy an exemption by which the board may opt out of some of the composition rules and some of the nominating and compensation committees requirements designed for companies with different ownership structures. The NYSE explained this exemption in a statement:

> Majority voting control generally entitles the holder to determine the makeup of the board of directors, and the exchange did not consider it appropriate to impose a listing standard that would in effect deprive the majority holder of that right.[i]

In some ways NASDAQ's new listing requirements were more stringent than those of the New York Stock Exchange. An independent director of a NASDAQ-listed company could not:

1. be currently employed or have been employed during the past 3 years by the listed company or any parent or subsidiary of the listed company, and in addition,
2. have accepted any payments from the listed company or any parent or subsidiary of the listed company in excess of $60,000 in the current or any of the past 3 fiscal years,
3. be a partner, controlling shareholder, or executive officer of any organization to which the company made, or from which the company received, payments for property or services in the current or any of the past 3 fiscal years that exceeded the greater of 5% of the recipient's consolidated gross revenues for that year or $200,00,
4. be an executive officer of another entity where any of the executive officers of the listed company served on the compensation committee of such other entity, if such relationship existed during the past 3 years, or
5. be a partner of the listed company's outside auditor, or a partner or employee of the company's outside auditor who worked on the listed company's audit at any time during the past 3 years.

A director also was ineligible for NASDAQ independent director status if a family member failed to meet the above restrictions.

Since 2003, both the NYSE and NASDAQ have refined their requirements for independent director status, partly because stakeholders have continuously redefined their definitions of independence.[ii] Court decisions often create subtle nuances that affect the current definition. In one example, at about the same time as the SEC was approving the new listing standards, a shareholder concerned about the actual independence of directors of Martha Stuart Living Omnimedia filed a lawsuit in the Delaware Court of Chancery against those directors as well as the founder, chair, and CEO of the company, Martha Stewart herself.[iii] The plaintiff alleged that the board's outside directors had business relationships before joining the board, moved in the same social circles, attended the same weddings, and described themselves as friends; in the plaintiff's view, these relationships, coupled with Stewart's 94% voting power, impeded the board's ability to make independent decisions.[iv] Delaware Chief Justice E. Norman Veasey ultimately ruled that friendship and social relationships—standing alone—did not rebut the presumption of director independence. Although such friendships may be relevant to determining director independence, the Court decided that the shareholder plaintiff needed more evidence to prove her claim.[v] Justice Veasey later explained:

> A variety of motivations, including friendship, may influence the demand futility inquiry [an inquiry of whether directors are incapable of making an impartial decision[vi]]. But, to render a director unable to consider demand, a relationship must be of a bias-producing nature. Allegations of mere personal friendship or a mere outside business relationship, standing alone, are insufficient to raise a reasonable doubt about a director's independence.[vii]

Since passage of new Security and Exchange Commission rules governing corporate boards in 2003, ownership of a significant amount of the company's stock also is a definitive bar to qualifying as an independent director.

The new emphasis on director independence also affects not-for-profit organizations and private corporations because the independence of a majority of directors on a board is important to all stakeholders of the corporation. When directors have no conflicting indebtedness to anyone associated with the company, they are more likely to be objective. Interestingly, a 2004 study of non-profit firms conducted by Judith Saidel, executive director of the Center for Women in Government, reinforced the conclusion that independence helps produce non-subjective decisions grounded in merit.[viii] Corporations that are not publicly traded are considering new rules for nominating directors, such as separate nominating committees, defined processes for identifying and evaluating candidates, and more transparency for stakeholders. More than 22% of private companies already have hired independent consultant firms. At present, boards of not-for-profits and private companies can hold their companies to the standards required for publicly held companies without submitting to burdensome required oversight.[ix,x]

Independence in the Boardroom

Director independence brings value to the board because better thoughts and ideas flow from a group of independent thinkers. In the boardroom, independence can feel like a double-edged sword. Although shareholders expect their representatives to exercise independent judgment when overseeing investments, they also expect them to work as a team toward a common set of objectives that maximize shareholder value. Obviously, exerting independence in the boardroom may include voting against issues that are not aligned with the director's carefully considered views even when this means voting differently from trusted colleagues. However, a necessary balance must be struck between director independence and the board's intimate relationship with corporate strategy.[xi]

Thus, director independence does not imply that the director must always be different in his or her thinking. The board as a whole and each individual director should stay attuned to signs of misalignment among the directors and consider what this misalignment indicates. If, for example, a director finds himself on the opposite side of the board on most issues, it might indicate that the director is not the right person to serve on that particular board. On the other hand, the misalignment may be a warning sign that the board is heading for trouble.

As indicated in Figure 9.1, the traditional path to enlightenment goes in two different directions. In general, there should always be a certain degree of alignment amongst all board members, and frequently they should be completely aligned. However, continuing to be fully aligned on all issues, at all times, can lead to an unhealthy board environment. Therefore, it is important for board members to demonstrate their independence by reevaluating their position dynamically around issues as those issues evolve.

If directors are continuously aligned around all issues at all times, they may miss strategic opportunities to generate substantial shareowner value because of their inability to see things from a different perspective. Therefore, as highlighted in Figure 9.2, the enlightened alignment phenomenon suggests that directors calibrate their levels of engagement and knowledge

Traditional Path to Alignment

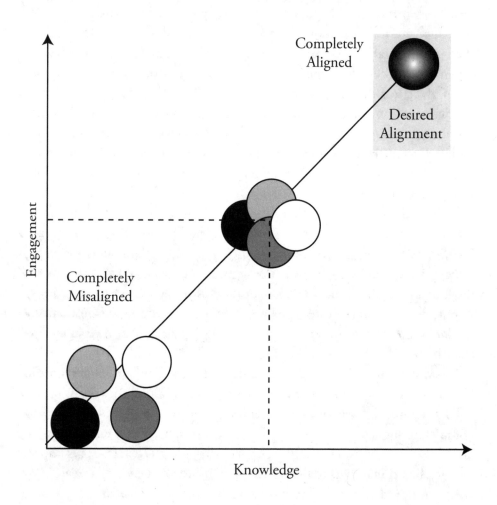

Figure 9.1

Enlightened Alignment Phenomena

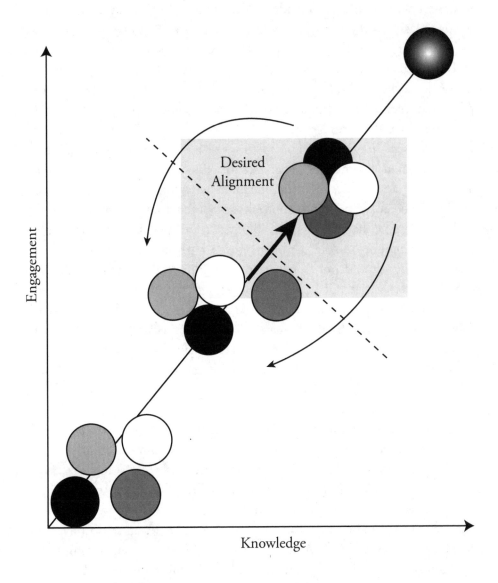

Figure 9.2

around unique events and challenges. As a consequence, directors will modulate between full alignment and partial alignment on a regular basis. While full alignment should be considered desirable and achieved most often, it is not necessarily the most productive position to always be in. Sometimes being less aligned will provide opportunities for growth and creativity that will help directors better serve their shareowners.

When a director accepts the responsibility of serving on the board of a publicly traded corporation, he or she must either accept the values of the organization as they are or work to change them. Every director should strive to set a leadership example for the senior executive team and its constituencies. Congruence should exist between the director's professional behavior as a board member and his or her personal behavior.

Inside the boardroom, it is appropriate for each director to wear his or her badge of independence. However, directors should be careful not to flaunt this independence outside the boardroom. With rare exceptions, internal disagreements should not be revealed in public. Unless the differences in opinion are the result of legal issues or significant differences in strategic direction, director independence should remain in the forum of the boardroom because bitter infighting on a public stage can reduce shareholder value. Shareholders expect teamwork, and directors who elect to continue in their directorship should respect the principle of cabinet solidarity and should allow this principle to bind the board's decisions. Again, the recent debacle at HP demonstrates the importance of teamwork inside of the boardroom. The board's responsibility is to strive for increased shareowner value . . . not destroy it! There was an obvious lack of leadership from the chair.

Governing and regulatory agencies, such as the New York Stock Exchange, the NASDAQ Stock Market, the U.S. Securities and Exchange Commission, Institutional Shareholder Services, and Moody's Investors Service have tended to assess director independence using traditional measures such as work history, number of shares owned, and relationships with the company. The new corporate governance listing standards substantially altered these standards and otherwise implemented SEC Rule 10A-3 under Section 10A(m) of the Securities Exchange Act of 1934 (which was added by Section 301 of the Sarbanes-Oxley Act of 2002). The new standards were intended to enhance the accountability, integrity, and transparency of NYSE listed companies.[xii,xiii]

These very important parameters are not the only measures that an enlightened board of directors should use. In any given situation, some directors might act independently whereas others might not. Director attitudes and behaviors are more important to board independence than other factors, but unfortunately these elusive characteristics are quite difficult to measure. Because most shareholders have no idea how much director attitudes and behaviors contribute to share value, it is up to the enlightened board to influence director attitude and modify director behaviors through intense levels of engagement designed to maximize focus on shareholder and stakeholder value.[xiv]

In fact, some evidence indicates that director independence does not necessarily correlate with increased shareholder value. In the first large-scale test of whether American corporations improve when large-stake, long-term investors actively monitor management performance and engage with management in setting corporate policy, three researchers investigated ownership and performance data for more than 1,500 large U.S. companies from 1983 to 1995, and got mixed results. Sanjai Bhagat of Leeds School of Business, Bernard S. Black of University of Texas at Austin School of Law, and Margaret M. Blair of Vanderbilt University School of Law found that, during the hostile takeover period of the late 1980s, the influence of a high-stake outside investor was associated with higher stock market returns, perhaps because such influence induced corporate restructuring, whose principal effect was to reduce growth rates while improving profitability. However, the researchers were unable to find this pattern in the early 1980s or in the early 1990s.[xv] Some other studies also have undermined security in the notion that director independence correlates with increased shareholder value.

All considered, it is more important that directors be enlightened than independent. A truly independent board is likely to include a number of similarly enlightened directors able to assess the board's strengths and determine what the board needs to maximize their service to shareholders. Although all directors are not equal and, certainly, all directors are not enlightened, real acceleration occurs in the boardroom when most of board members demonstrate extreme personal leadership, independent thinking, and enlightened perspectives.

One board criticized by shareholders for lack of independence due to board composition was that of Walt Disney. In 1988, the College Recruitment Equities Fund, the powerful owner of nearly 19 million Disney shares, issued a proposal urging Disney to reconfigure its board to achieve greater board independence.[xvi] Soon after, Disney added two independent directors to its board and the fund withdrew its proposal.[xvii]

Director independence has been called into question in other types of situations, for example when directors are professional service providers such as bankers, attorneys, and consultants whose own companies earn substantial fees from the company they direct. Consider for example, the board service of prominent attorney Larry W. Sonsini, who leads Wilson Sonsini Goodrich & Rosati, a Silicon Valley law firm that employs about 600 lawyers, serves numerous blue-chip corporations, and helped launch several technology startup companies including Apple Computer. Sonsini, who has served on corporate boards that paid his law firm millions of dollars each year for legal services, maintains that his director independence is unharmed by such relationships. "Often," he said, "my interests are aligned with the shareholders." "A lawyer serving on the board does not, in itself, compromise the concept of independence because the lawyer represents the organization and must act in the best interest of the shareholder," he added. Some clients agree. "My sense is that he's one of our more outspoken board members," says Ron Epstein, general counsel of Brocade Communications Systems Inc.[xviii]

Such challenges to the independence rule precipitate debates that cause people to reconsider their thinking on the gray areas of director independence. Being outspoken and engaged in confronting the corporation's problems does not necessarily mean independent behavior in the boardroom. Independence must be found elsewhere than behavior; it must be present in directors' perceptions and the influences they feel from outside the boardroom.

Institutional investors generally regard director independence as a cornerstone of fairness and justice in the corporation. This respect for director independence has raised the priority placed by directors on dealing with board independence, board composition, and board activities in general. The importance of enlightened independent directors to long-term shareholder value is matched by the importance of enlightened, independent shareholders and stakeholders. Effective corporate governance is enhanced by active engagement by the general community. In corporate governance, just as in politics, individual participation does make a difference. Just as it is very important that Americans understand the basic principles of the U.S. Constitution to protect their individual personal property rights, it is very important for Americans to understand the principles of corporate governance to protect their wealth and economic value.[xix]

Independent Directors and Day-to-Day Company Operations

Although the collective board and individual directors are expected to play much larger roles in the overall supervision of the corporations they serve, it still is unwise, inappropriate, and probably ineffective for directors to get too deeply involved in the general management of the day-to-day operations of the company. This is true even in situations where substantial fraudulent activities have occurred within the company.

Regardless of the list of credentials and worldly experiences they bring to the board, all non-employee directors must resist the temptation to leap in and attempt to manage the companies they serve. However, they certainly should exhibit their willingness to engage with the CEO and his senior team to help *lead* the company. This is an idea challenged by management consultant Paul Coombes when he was director of McKinsey & Company. Coombes suggested that boards move away from directing day-to-day operations *and* from directing strategy.[xx] Enlightened directors who agree with Coombes that staying out of day-to-day operations is important for directors will respectfully beg to differ with his recommendation that directors stay away from strategy development.

What Sets Effective Boards and Directors Apart?

Ineffective management and weak boardroom leadership are hardly unique to the 21st century. During the past 5 years alone, numerous examples of unprecedented negative impacts on stakeholders have demonstrated that some corporate boards were not engaged deeply enough with CEOs and their senior teams to discover their fraudulent activities. More stringent rules and regulations and heightened levels of scrutiny by stakeholders, have informed directors of what to avoid doing in the boardroom. However, the fundamental debate over what directors should do in this new environment of heightened interest in corporate governance continues in earnest.

What not to do constitutes the baseline for fundamental compliance with corporate governance practices, but passionately pursuing *what should be done* constitutes the baseline for extreme personal leadership in the boardroom. Maximizing long-term shareholder value in this way embodies the spirit of enlightened independent directors and fully implies compliance and conviction!

The independent thinking and personal responsibility exhibited by directors in the enlightened corporate boardroom are not driven by regulatory mandates. Although enlightened directors fully understand and respect the need for corporate governance regulations, they are motivated by a need to excel in producing long-term shareholder value.

Notes

i Solomon, D. (2004, April 4). Loophole Limits Independence. *Wall Street Journal*, p. C1.

ii Delaware court spurns claims in Stewart case. (2004, May 3). *Corporate Governance Report.*

iii Beam v. Stewart, Del., No. 501. [2003. 3/31/04].

iv Ibid.

v Veasey, E. N. (2004). Musings From the center of the corporate universe. Remarks made at Section of Business Law Luncheon, American Bar Association Annual Meeting, August 9, 2004, Atlanta, Georgia.

vi Roberts, H., & Owen, L. L. P. (2004, December 3). Not as independent as you thought? *HRO Alert.* Retrieved July 18, 2006, from http://www.hro.com/

vii Veasey, E. N. (2004, November). Juxtaposing best practices and Delaware corporate jurisprudence—part II. *The Metropolitan Corporate Counsel*, p. 46.

viii Saidel, J. R. (1991). Resource interdependence: The relationship between state agencies and nonprofit organizations. *Public Administration Review 51*, 543-53.

ix Interdependence, stock ownership key to corporate governance. (2003, January 6). *Corporate Governance Report.*

x Murry, M. (2003, July 22). Private companies also feel pressure to clean up acts. *Wall Street Journal,* (S.W. Ed.), p. B1.

xi Oliver, R. (n.d.). The push towards greater independence for boards of directors doesn't relieve the board's important role in formation of corporate strategy. *Corporate Governance.*

xii Zuppone, 2003.

xiii Kirwin, J. (2004, June 7). EC to set criteria for independent directors. Published by BNA, Inc.

xiv SEC proposes disclosure rules on directors' nominations. (2003, September 1). *Corporate Governance Report.*

xv Bhagat, S., Black, B. S., & Blair, M. (2004). *Journal of Financial Research, 27*, 1-30.

xvi Lublin, J. S. (1998, December 4). Major Disney investor scraps calling for greater board independence. *The Wall Street Journal,* p. B6.

xvii Ibid.

xviii Lublin, J. S. (2003, July 22). Boardrooms under renovation. *Wall Street Journal.*

xix Solomon, D. (2003, October 3). SEC faces criticism of board-of-director proposal. *Wall Street Journal,* p. C5.

xx McKinsey & Company. Governance beyond the board—Interview with Paul Coombes. *Managing in Turbulent Times.* Retrieved July 18, 2006, from http://www.mckinsey.com/ideas/MITT/govbeyondboard/

Chapter 10

Board Composition

Successful teams can only afford to accommodate one Michael Jordan.

In an increasingly globalized and socially conscious world, today's corporate boards must keep pace with changing environments, markets, and technologies while simultaneously streamlining, downsizing, and refocusing corporate operations. In this sea of change, boards interested in corporate reform have little choice than to study their own behaviors amid these changes and then restructure themselves. Through this process, boards increase their likelihood of producing the accountability, liability protection, and strategic audits stakeholders expect, and they also help CEOs restructure their executive teams.

With the right people on the board and a sharp focus on corporate governance, teamwork among board members becomes not only possible but also likely. Directors who work as a team spend most of their board meetings identifying the company's critical issues, demanding and reviewing information about those issues, and producing solutions to the challenges raised by those issues. An important feature of the teamwork-oriented board is that its members protect the company from drawn-out decision-making (which harms the company's strategic market position) by controlling the kinds and numbers of its committees.

Most directors, I am convinced, dedicate themselves to their jobs on the board and strive to do everything stakeholders expect of them. There are hidden risks in doing so, however, one of which is that different stakeholders have different expectations of directors and doing what is expected might not always be the wisest course of action. It is important that directors remember that attempting to do what is expected is *never* sufficient when the company is competing against world-class global enterprises and highly motivated start-ups! When the stakes are this high, merely fulfilling the requirements of the director's job is not enough! Directors' passion for building stakeholder value must propel them to do much more than is expected of them.

Tactics of Board Restructuring and Reform

Some basic board-restructuring tactics include recruiting independent directors, limiting the number of boards on which directors may sit, and instituting term limits for directors. A major tactic of board reform is to require directors to own shares in the companies they serve (equaling, for example, a minimum of 2 to 3 years of their retainer fees). As important as these tactics are, many corporate boards have yet to fully implement them. Enlightened boards, however, have been instituting these reforms for some time as part of their ongoing efforts to maximize shareholder value. Respondents to a 1996 *Business Week* survey revealed that the best boards already had adopted all of these reforms and several others a decade ago.[i]

Other board-restructuring tactics are essential for bringing corporate boards into tip-top condition. These include optimizing board size, balancing board composition, and diversifying board talents and experiences, all of which are discussed in this chapter.

Optimizing the Board's Size

Corporate boards typically range in size from 5 to 15 or more directors. Size is an important factor in board performance because the effectiveness of each director is strongly influenced by the number of other directors with whom each individual must interact. A director on a board with too few members will experience isolation, limited input, interaction with a narrow field of vision, and pressure to reduce his or her independence. A director on a board with too many members will find it very difficult to participate in the full board's proceedings, confront the company's challenges, and build solutions. If the board is composed of an even number of directors, directors will have more trouble reaching consensus,[ii] which is one reason that some small corporations limit the size of their boards to a small odd number, often 5, 7, or 9.

The changing nature of markets and the uncertainty of the global economy have forced companies to look at ways to enable their directors to give them the best possible advice, and experience suggests that one way to do so is to maintain a smaller number of directors who get to know each other, discuss issues fully, work productively as a team, and are able to reach consensus.[iii] According to findings by Spencer Stuart Executive Search Consultants, smaller board size might be correlated with company ability to move quickly to gain or hold a position of market leadership.[iv]

One positive effect of smaller board size is that it deters the formation of hierarchies in the board.[v] It is to be expected that some directors will be more opinionated and determined to exert their will, even at the expense of losing opportunities to hear and benefit from the opinions of others. By its mere size, a large board encourages formation of an inner cabal of directors with an "insider" mentality that stifles the exchange of ideas.[vi,vii] When this inner board (often called the *executive committee*) takes over as the functioning center of board control, other members of the board are deprived of equal representation.[viii] To avoid this scenario, most boards have abandoned executive committees or restructured them to fill roles very clearly defined and approved by the full board. As part of this type of restructuring, full representation of all the directors on the board often is somewhat protected by a requirement that the minutes of the executive committee be circulated among all directors well before meetings of the full board.

When corporate governance experts focused their attention on board size in the mid-1990s,[ix] they concluded that most boards were too big.[x] Martin Lipton of the law firm, Wachtell, Lipton, Rosen & Katz, and Jay W. Lorsch of the Harvard Business School recommended that, in the interests of building an effective team, board size should be restricted to no more than 10 directors or, even better, 9 directors.

Why have larger boards at all if smaller boards are more effective and also less expensive in terms of costs and benefits? The answer is that, although boards must be small enough to promote timely discussion and efficient decision-making, they also must be large enough to gain sufficient input and encourage debate.[xi] One risk of small board size is that the board may be too tightly knit to have diverse perspectives.[xii] Financier Warren Buffet has opinions on board size, according to his biographer, Lawrence A. Cunningham, author of *The Essays of Warren Buffett, the "Sage of Omaha":*

> [A] corporation without a controlling shareholder . . . is where management problems are most acute, Buffett says. It would be helpful if directors could supply necessary discipline, but board congeniality usually prevents that. To improve board effectiveness in this situation, Buffett believes the board should be small in size and composed mostly of outside directors. The strongest weapon a director can wield in these situations remains his or her threat to resign.[xiii]

In other words, the board's membership should balance congeniality with independence.

In general, boards should have a minimum of 7 directors and no more than 15 directors. At least 7 directors are needed to effectively staff the three required standing committees, which are the audit committee, the compensation committee, and the nominating/governance committee. Some boards (typically those of high-tech start-ups and majority-controlled firms) believe that 5 to 7 directors are best because board members become very deeply engaged and scheduling meetings is relatively easy. Boards with more than 15 directors (typically those of financial institutions, utilities, and philanthropies) aim to gather together as many qualified participants as the board can reasonably accommodate to involve as many smart and caring people in helping to oversee the company. The large size of these boards, however, can deter directors from adding value to the board's governance process and outcome.

Today's corporate boardroom is the setting for serious work, not friendly chitchat. Despite differing opinions to the contrary, to operate effectively most boards need at least 7 directors, and no board should have more than 15 members.

Enlightened boards typically limit their sizes to about 10 to 12 members. This size is large enough to staff several board committees, but also is small enough to offer each board member the opportunity to participate fully in the board's leadership process, which includes intense listening, thought-provoking questioning, and adding insightful comments and perspectives. To offer knowledge and perspectives of value to the corporate management team, enlightened directors must join board discussions.

Over the past 2 decades, a trend toward smaller boards has affected corporate boards overall. In 1998, the average board had 12 members; in 2005 it had 10.7 members. By 2006, two-thirds of all corporate boards had 12 or fewer directors."[xiv] Technology companies led this trend. In 1998, technology companies surveyed by Spencer Stuart had 1 to 6 fewer directors than companies overall.[xv] Their directors also were younger and more likely to be paid in shares than in cash.

The reasons for these differences are unclear. Perhaps technology leaders, believing that larger traditional boards are too unwieldy to be effective in their volatile sector, are purposefully developing a smaller, younger, less entrenched kind of board. Technology boards may believe that compensating directors with shares instead of cash more directly connects directors with the company's future. Possibly, however, technology boards are small for a more pragmatic reason: fewer executives may be qualified to direct them.[xvi] Certainly, the pool from which corporate directors in general usually are selected includes many males over the age of 50 who acquired much of their leadership experience before the introduction of newer high technologies; today's technophiles are mostly to be found among a younger group of executives who have been conversant with many of today's high technologies from their youth.[xvii]

Technology firms are not the only firms experiencing difficulty recruiting active CEOs as directors. One factor influencing the trend toward smaller boards across all sectors is the result of restrictions imposed by the Sarbanes-Oxley Act. Before its passage, CEOs traditionally sat on two or more boards of publicly traded outside companies, but the post-SOX revised listing rules of the New York Stock Exchange and NASDAQ Stock Market now suggest limiting each CEO's board participation to one publicly traded outside company. Moreover, the competition for adding independent directors to boards makes recruiting such directors more difficult.

Balancing Board Composition

One of the most pivotal tactics for making boards more independent, effective, and influential is balancing board composition.[xviii] Corporate directors are chosen from a pool of highly qualified people, and being selected as a shareholder representative is a very significant achievement that demonstrates that the director has cleared a high hurdle of competence. However, although directors are all high achievers with equal legal responsibilities to serve, exercise duty care, and act in good faith, they differ substantially in the kinds of value they can contribute to the board. Each director embodies differences in experience, background, interests, and tenure, which is a good thing considering that multiple talents are necessary for the board to properly do its job.

No mandate requires directors, however talented, to qualify as effective servants of shareholders. Directors do not share the same level of interest in high performance, have the same amount of time available for attending to board matters, or feel equal devotion to the company's success. Some directors prefer to contribute to the company's overall performance; others would rather focus on contributing value to the board. Directors also vary in their willingness to prepare for board activities and in their ability to effectively govern others. Some directors bask in the well-earned confidence of their fellow board members in contrast to some who prefer to avoid board assignments.

The lead/presiding director, or the chair of the corporate governance committee, is responsible for working with the CEO to schedule and restructure board meetings, for maximizing the overall effectiveness of the group by making the best use of the contributions of each director. Although this person is duty-bound to assess the strengths of each of the board's individual members, it is unnecessary for that person to publicly quantify or qualify the value of each board member—directors generally know where they stand relative to their colleagues.

Although directors understand that it is extremely naïve to assume that all directors are equally capable in every respect, many boards find it useful to maintain the polite fiction that all of their fellow board members are just that. Maintaining this position is an excellent way to enforce a status quo that limits the board's performance by deterring directors from rocking the boat. Enlightened directors reject this proposition because they constantly want to lead their companies to the next higher level of performance!

Diversifying the Board's Contributions

Diversified boards have an array of executive members, and may include specialists in finance, technology, marketing, employee relations, ecology, management, and corporate governance. Microsoft's board provides an excellent example of the power of diversification to help drive extraordinary growth. Microsoft's domination of the PC software market and inroads into the telecommunications industry resulted in part from the diversity of the network of advisors cultivated by the company's CEO, Bill Gates.[xix] Microsoft enlisted the advice of John Malone, long-time chair of Telecommunications Incorporated, and of Warren Buffet, the powerful financier who recently made headlines by announcing his plan to give shares worth at least $30 billion to the Bill & Melinda Gates Foundation.[xx,xxi] Microsoft's board members included a venture capitalist, a general partner of a management group, the chair of a timber company board, and former executives of the information technology giant Hewlett-Packard and the industrial chemical distributor

Univar Corp., as well as company insiders.[xxii] Other boards of major corporations that consistently welcome directors with diverse skills are DuPont, ITT, American Express, Alcoa, and PepsiCo.

The enlightened board includes both male and female executives from the racial, ethnic, and cultural backgrounds most relevant to the company's operations and present and anticipated customer base. Board composition that reflects more of the global ecology raises the professional tension of constructive debate among board members and introduces directors to more taxing challenges, making board meetings more interesting and rewarding. Boards with access to diverse expertise are better qualified to advise management on the most pressing issues of corporations in today's highly competitive global markets.

Although many societal needs provide the basis for persuasive arguments for board gender, racial, and ethnic diversification, my arguments for these kinds of board diversification are based on labor force and domestic and global market demographics. Of the more than 6 billion people in the world, fewer than 5% are residents of the United States, and many of these are aging Baby Boomers. The U.S. labor force, unlike the populations of most boardrooms, includes very high percentages of people of diverse minority groups. In fact, nearly half (46.4%) of American workers are women and almost a third (30%) are non-white.[xxiii] Moreover, in an era of global markets, it makes good business sense to appreciate the thinking and cultures of people in other regions of the world, including those who populate the most rapidly advancing underdeveloped countries.

Gaining Competitive Advantage through Minority Directors

The enlightened board seeks diversity as a competitive advantage. An excellent strategy for adding diverse strengths to the company is to recruit directors who are women and/or members of minority groups with backgrounds that complement the board's composition. To direct the corporation more effectively, its board should reflect the customers and communities that the company serves. To this end, boards should seek out more members of groups currently underrepresented in their ranks.

Obviously, during the last 2 decades, many boards have been changing their gender and ethnic diversity. The *2005 Census of Women Board Directors of the Fortune 500* by the research and women's advocacy organization, Catalyst, showed a 10-year trend of progress toward fuller representation of women on corporate boards.[xxiv] In 2005, women held 14.7% of all Fortune 500 board seats, up from 13.6% in 2003 and 9.6% in 1995. However, progress has been slow. In 2005, women of color held only 3.4% of the board seats, and women as a group were underrepresented significantly on audit, compensation, and governance committees. At the average rate of increase in women's representation on Fortune 500 boards, one-half of 1% per year, Catalyst predicted that it could take another 70 years for women to hold 50% of Fortune 500 board seats and thus achieve parity with men in the boardroom.

According to Susan Willett Bird, president of the American Mediation Council, boards tend to look for women board candidates in the same places from which male directors have come,[xxv] producing numerical diversity that does little to give corporations access to the kinds of diversity they really need. Bird advised boards to start their searches for new directors by analyzing the dramatically changed business environment in which their companies operate. Even if such searches were conducted on a gender-blind basis, Bird argued, the number of women directors of corporate boards would increase. In a similar vein, Lawrence A. Cunningham pointed to Warren Buffett's belief that corporations create problems when they select directors merely to add diversity or prominence to the board. Corporate governance works best when directors are selected for business savvy, shareholder orientation, and high interest in both the corporation and their responsibilities.[xxvi] In my view, however, seeking diversity for diversity's sake is good business, and a board seeking diversity in its membership is engaging in reasonable and expected behavior. In other words, whether in gender, ethnicity, or other dimensions, diversity always should be pursued as an opportunity to broaden the perspectives at the boardroom table. Diversity is too important an ingredient of success to be pursued casually!

Catalyst also analyzed the composition of Fortune 500 boards in terms of gender and race or ethnicity, using data from 2003. In that year, white men held 73.1% of seats, white women held 13.1%, African-American men held 6.8%, Latinos held 2.4%, African-American women held 2.3%, and members of all other racial or ethnic groups held less than 1% of the seats. Latinas held .3% of the Fortune 500 board seats.[xxvii]

Spencer Stuart performed a similar study measuring gender, racial, and ethnic diversity in 2005 among the boards of the top 200 companies in the Standard and Poors 500. Women held 16% of those seats; African-American, Hispanic, Asian, and members of other minority groups combined held 15%.[xxviii]

Interestingly, the three fastest-growing populations in the U.S., namely Hispanic Americans, Asian Americans, and Native Americans, are the groups most significantly underrepresented on corporate boards. The challenge of developing a board that reflects the customers and communities targeted by the company is amplified by the preference of most corporate boards for mining the wealth of knowledge and experience offered by current and retired CEOs; among minority groups in the United States, more white women and African American males have this kind of experience.

Boards undoubtedly need directors with leadership experience, but enlightened boards recognize that all great directors do not necessarily run publicly held corporations. Moreover, as we have learned from recent corporate disasters at Enron, Tyco, Global Crossing, Computer Associates, and WorldCom, not all CEOs are great leaders! In fact, even CEOs who are genuinely great leaders do not necessarily make the best directors. Great directors are to be found not only in corporate settings, but also in government and in not-for-profit cultural and academic settings. Given the substantial shortage of CEOs available to serve as directors, it is high time for boards to develop strategies for tapping into the eclectic pool of highly qualified candidates working in non-traditional settings. No board should accept the assertion that qualified candidates for directorships cannot be found.

Enlightened boards ensure that their focus on diversity reaches deep into the DNA of the corporation by leading the management team to application of *workplace-flexibility programs*, such as flextime, job sharing, and telecommuting programs, as well as programs that permit employees to move from full to part-time employment and back again without jeopardizing advancement. These programs, of course, should be driven by business cases, and contribute directly to the bottom-line performance of the corporation. The difficulty of achieving diversity at the corporate level through workplace flexibility demonstrates yet another reason why the board should develop a more diverse slate of exceptionally qualified and highly enlightened directors. The advantages that flow from the board's diversity can help inspire the company to claim market share through diversity.

Gaining Competitive Advantage through International Executives

One way of broadening the potential director pool is to consider qualified foreign executives as potential candidates. For a company with global reach, there is no substitute for a director with current, real-life, day-to-day experiences outside the United States. Although directors wanting greater insight into an established or emerging foreign market initially might feel more comfortable recruiting an American executive who has lived and managed operations in that market or a foreign national of that market currently residing in the United States, recruiting a foreign national living in that foreign market instantly expands the board's point of view. Such a director possesses cultural insights that can prevent operational misunderstandings and marketing blunders in the market he or she represents. He or she also can provide access to key foreign decision-makers and industry leaders that can help the company forge new business alliances.

During the 1980s and 1990s, America's corporate boards made very little real progress in recruiting foreign directors. In the 5 years between 1992 and 1997, for example, the number of foreign directors serving on the boards of Fortune 1000 companies increased by only one, from 199 to 200.[xxix] By 2004, however, acceptance of foreign directors in the United States had risen over 50%, with 30% of corporate boards having at least one foreign director.[xxx]

Progress in this direction has been impeded by several difficulties in recruitment and implementation. Identifying foreign candidates who are both interested in and able to serve on boards of U.S. corporations is difficult, largely because corporate governance structures in many regions of the world make it difficult or impossible for foreign executives to serve on corporate boards. For example, although directors of European supervisory boards and corporate management boards can be excellent candidates for U.S. corporate directorships, many European companies prohibit their senior executives from serving on other company's boards. The pervasive Japanese corporate tradition in which a company's senior executive officers function as its corporate board of directors prevents Japanese executives from serving as directors of other publicly held corporations. (In Japan, the move toward independent directorships has gained little interest except at Sony and perhaps one or two other Japanese corporations.)

Time-zone differences present another barrier to the recruitment of foreign executives by U.S. corporate boards because scheduling meetings for a set of directors residing in different time zones around the globe is extremely difficult, even if the meeting contemplated is only a conference call.

Language differences once impeded recruitment of foreign executives to American boards because many otherwise desirable foreign candidates were not fluent enough in the English language to communicate easily and openly in an American boardroom. However, with English now quite well established as a global business language, language barriers have faded as a reasonable rationale for failing to achieve global representation on the board. Most European, South American, and Asian senior executives are capable of full engagement in the boardroom, along with many of their counterparts from other corners of the map.

Differences in national corporate governance models and time zones can seem to be formidable barriers to the inclusion of foreign executives on the board, but these are challenges that can be successfully addressed. Companies such as DuPont and Eli Lilly have consistently been able to attract foreign directors on their boards. If the board recruits the right foreign director, he or she very likely will need to visit the U.S. a few times each year in the usual course of business. A European director generally will be able to participate in six or seven board meetings per year without undue burden on his or her travel schedule if the board schedules one meeting per year in Europe, one on the East Coast of the U.S., and one as a conference call. Similar accommodations can be made for Asian or South American senior executives. Canadian executives should be only slightly disadvantaged by meeting locations in the U.S.

Although U.S. corporate boards do recognize global diversity as a competitive advantage, they obviously need to accelerate their efforts to identify and attract a more diverse population of executives to their ranks. The benefits of the value-added knowledge and experiences of senior executives in other parts of the world can be well worth the extra effort it takes to incorporate foreign executives into the board process. To start the ball rolling, the chair of the corporate governance committee should establish a process to identify interested and qualified foreign candidates. This process should include scheduling meetings in parts of the world that account for significant portions of the corporate operations. Much work needs to be done. For the highly enlightened corporate board of the 21st century, developing global diversity will be imperative.

Adding Prominent Directors to the Board

Boards seek prominent directors for a number of reasons, including attempting to gain better insights, seeking improved access to customers, developing an image, or merely making the board and company seem more notable than they really are. Adding prominent people to the board of directors can be important, but, in general, boards should require much more of their directors than fame or celebrity. The core selection criteria of competence and experience in areas of importance to the company never should be compromised for show. The chairman of the corporate governance committee is responsible for working with the CEO to attract and recruit directors with a comprehensive set of skills and experiences. In this regard, the needs of the board should be clearly defined and measured against the profiles of its current directors. When recruiting new members of the board, companies should use a matrix, such as the one featured in Figure 10.1, as a roadmap to identify where expertise gaps exist. This tool will help them focus more crisply on the types of individuals they need to effectively carryout their duties.

Director Experience Matrix

Skill/Experience/Other Consideration	Director												Potential Candidates
	1	2	3	4	5	6	7	8	9	10	11	12	
Lead Large Organizations													
Global Perspective and/or Non-U.S. Region													
Sales & Marketing Experience													
Science/Technology Orientation													
Manufacturing/Operations													
Finance/Accounting													
Gender/Racial Diversity													
Academia													
Consultancy													
Public Policy/Government Service													
Nonprofit Sector													
Environment/Sustainability													
Industry Knowledge													
Customer Knowledge													
Independence													
CEO													
Other													

Figure 10.1

Deploying Committees

Board committees are separate entities that work on behalf of the entire board to increase the time and attention the board pays to specific board responsibilities. When properly focused by a charter and staffed with the right people, board committees improve the board's overall effectiveness and efficiency. Board committees have become a major force in contemporary corporate governance because, when properly deployed, they facilitate improved board oversight.

One reason that boards need a minimum of 7 directors is that at least that many are needed to effectively staff the three standing committees required for listing in the New York Stock Exchange, namely, the corporate governance/nominating committee, the compensation committee, and the audit committee, each of which must be composed entirely of independent directors and follow a charter describing its purposes and responsibilities.[xxxi]

Although it is the duty of the nominating/governance committee to define a board committee's role, each committee should develop its own mission and charter to guide its work. This is an important job because any committee's success depends on the clarity of its mission and charter. Each committee also should implement a set of activities by which to carry out its defined responsibilities.

It is important to note that committee members and their chairs serve at the pleasure of the full board. It should be perfectly clear that no committee should be considered more important than the board. Although some board committees (such as the compensation and audit committees) operate independently, the broader board elects the committee members in and the board can elect them out.

Committee structure is an integral part of board structure and its management must be an on-going process. An important part of this process is that each committee chair provides the full board with an update of the committee's activities at each meeting of the full board. In some environments, it might be appropriate for the board to delegate a broad set of authorities to a committee so that the committee need only update the board with brief periodical reports. In other environments, it may be more appropriate for a committee to report to the board for approval of its actions. Committees also may invite the full board to participate in some committee meetings.

The chairs of the full board and of the nominating/corporate governance committee are responsible for working together to coordinate the balance between cooperation and independence among the various board committees. It is extremely important that these two chairs understand each board member's talents, experiences, and potential contributions so they can appropriately position each director to contribute maximum value to the company.

One area of significant challenge for all boards is the staffing of required and optional standing committees. The size of the board is always a factor in this task. As mentioned above, the board's size should be large enough to staff a minimum of the three required standing committees. However, larger and or more complex corporations will most likely need the services of a least one or two additional committees, requiring a larger size board. Boards responding to stakeholder concerns might enlist the aid of corporate responsibility or environmental policy committees. Boards examining very complex products and service issues or substantial new opportunities might want additional information from science and technology committees.

Protecting Board Composition through Regular Evaluations

A major key to board renewal and reformation is a regularly occurring board evaluation.[xxxii] A thorough review and evaluation of the board's role and performance will reveal when the board requires new talents and skills, when the talents of one or more directors no longer fit the company's needs, and when one or more ineffectual board members are weakening the effectiveness of the entire board. Self-evaluations and periodically commissioned external evaluations help directors identify the board's role and have become regulatory requirements.

Boards encounter the need to replace incompetent or indecisive directors with surprising frequency. In a 1996 survey of corporate boards conducted by Korn/Ferry International, a majority of respondents reported firing a director for poor attendance, inattentiveness, or poor decision-making.[xxxiii] The presence of an ineffectual director on the board is a good reminder of why every board should possess a process by which the full board, individual directors, or the CEO can seek the resignation or termination of an ineffectual board member.

Broadening the Board's View through a Board of Advisors

The board can broaden its view of the company's industry and stakeholder community by enlisting the aide of a board of advisors comprised by volunteer "directors." Because corporate advisors have no official responsibilities to the company, they are not subject to the same set of risks and restrictions as elected directors; thus, professionals who elect not to serve as directors often can be persuaded to act as advisors. Advisors can provide enormous value to a CEO in a variety of situations and can provide independent input to the board without compromising the board's independence. DuPont's chairman and CEO, Charles O. Holliday, Jr., described DuPont's excellent biotechnology advisory panel as follows:

> The unique, diverse and global perspectives of our panel members have proven to be valuable assets to our decision-making process as we bring new products to market. They provide a thoughtful, global perspective to the opportunities and concerns associated with biotechnology and its careful and deliberate application.[xxxiv]

Summary

Boards can improve their functioning in a radically changing environment by maintaining an effective number and mix of directors that encourage communication among members. A wisely selected group of directors representing a diversity of experiences, opinions, and cultures should act as resources for the CEO and representatives of long-term shareholder interests.

Seriously intent corporate boards should be able to identify the quality of governance they are providing to the companies they direct. In the next chapter, the earmarks of three levels of corporate governance are explained: traditional, standard, and enlightened.

Notes

[i] New expectations for directors. (1996, November 26). *Business Week*. Retrieved from: http://www.businessweek.com.

[ii] Houle, C. O. (1989). *Governing boards: Their nature and nurture*. San Francisco: Jossey-Bass.

[iii] Lipton, M., & Lorsch, J. W. (1992). A modest proposal for improved corporate governance. *The Business Lawyer, 48*(11), 59.

[iv] Spencer Stuart Executive Search Consultants. (1996). *Board trends and practices at major American corporations. 1996 Board Index*. San Francisco: Author.

[v] Bruce, H. J. (1997). Duty, honor, company. *Directors & Boards, 21*(2), 12-16.

[vi] Ibid.

[vii] Cordrey, T. (1994, June). Who rules the boardroom? *International Management, 49*(5), 32-33.

[viii] Houle, 1989.

[ix] Cadbury, A. (1997). Summing up the governance reports. *The Corporate Board, 18*(107), 6. (Infotrac Article No. A20163324).

[x] Monks, R., & Minow, N. (1995). *Corporate governance*. Cambridge, MA: Blackwell.

[xi] Dolan, T. C. (1996). Observations on governance. *Health-care Executive, 11*(5), 5.

[xii] Spencer Stuart, 1998.

[xiii] Ibid.

[xiv] Citizen Works. (2006, January 3). Report finds plenty of room for improvement in corporate governance. *The Corporate Reform Weekly, (5)*1, p. 2.

[xv] Spencer Stuart, 1998.

[xvi] Ibid.

[xvii] Kotz, R. F. (1998, Spring). Technology company boards: In search of a new model. *Directors & Boards, 22*(3), 26-28.

[xviii] Daily, C. M., & Dalton, D. R. (1998). Does board composition affect corporate performance? No! *Directorship, 24*(7), 7-9.

[xix] Darrow, B. (1995, April 24). A view from the biggest software maker. *Computer Reseller News*, p. 110.

[xx] Ibid.

[xxi] Loomis, C. J. (2006, June 25). Warren Buffet gives away his fortune. *Fortune*. Retrieved July 18, 2006, from http://money.cnn.com/

[xxii] Darrow, 1995.

[xxiii] Bureau of Labor Statistics. (2006). U.S. Department of Labor. http://www.bls.gov.

xxiv Catalyst. (2006, March 29). Catalyst census of women board directors of the Fortune 500. [Press release]. Author. Retrieved July 21, 2006, from http://www.catalystwomen. org/pressroom/

xxv Bird, S. W. (1999, January). Marketplace revolution calls for entrepreneurs on boards. *Directorship, 25*(1), 1.

xxvi Cunningham, L. A. (1998, July-August). Warren Buffet on the role of the board. *The Corporate Board, XIX*(111), 6-10.

xxvii Catalyst. (2006). 2005 Catalyst census of women board directors of the Fortune 500: Ten years later. *Catalyst.* Publication Code D43. Retrieved July 21, 2006, from http:// www.catalystwomen.org/

xxviii Daum, J. H., Neff, T, & Norris, J. C. (2006). *Spencer Stuart 2006 board diversity report.* Retrieved July 21, 2006, from http://www.spencerstuart.com/research/articles/955/

xxix Significant Data for Directors. (1999). *Directorship.*

xxx Spencer Stuart. (2004). Spencer Stuart board index, 2004. Retrieved August 3, 2006, from http://content.spencerstuart.com/sswebsite/pdf/lib/SSBI-2004.pdf.

xxxi Fein, D. B., & Roer, P. L. (2004). New NYSE and Nasdaq listing standards designed to enhance corporate governance at public companies. *GC New England Magazine*, First Quarter. [Reprint]. Retrieved August 5, 2006, from http://www.wiggin.com/db30/cgi-bin/pubs/New%20NYSE%20david%20patti.pdf.

xxxii National Association of Corporate Directors. (1996). *Report of the NACD blue ribbon commission on executive compensation guidelines for corporate directors.* Washington, DC: Author.

xxxiii Listen up. (1996, November 26). *Business Week.* Retrieved from http://www. businessweek.com/

xxxiv DuPont names new biotechnology advisory panel members. (2004, July 19). Retrieved August 4, 2006, from http://www2.DuPont.com/Media_Center/en_US/news_releases/2004/nr07_19_04a.html.

Chapter 11

Evolving from Tradition to Enlightenment

The opportunity to choose FedEx, UPS, or the U.S. Postal Service.

The ultimate objective of publicly owned companies is to maximize returns to shareholders in the form of share price appreciation and dividends. In the late 1980s and 1990s, many U.S. corporations worked to raise their share prices by squeezing costs out of their businesses, using their assets more efficiently, and divesting.[i] However, as management consultant Jude Rich of Sibson Consulting pointed out, companies that don't grow their top lines eventually run out of opportunities to improve their profitability and drive up their share prices. Ultimately, the boards of most of these companies will bring in new CEOs or watch other companies acquire their businesses. In the long run, Rich concluded, it's grow or die.[ii]

In contrast to companies that concentrated on cutting costs, some companies worked to grow their top lines *while* producing better shareholder returns.[iii] Coca Cola, General Electric, DuPont, ITT Industries, and IBM all are recognized as some of the world's

189

best-managed companies because their boards and management focused for decades on global strategic plans, outstanding performances, and shareholder value appreciation. Their boards also led the way in corporate governance by paying their directors with mostly equity shares, reforming their compensation committees to make them independent, and diversifying their board rosters to include some of the world's most talented women and minority executives, as well as executives from Asia, Europe, and Latin America, thus capturing a very large share of investment funds. They recognized the risk of losing much of their board talent if they failed to attract a world-class executive team. Their boards also conscientiously planned executive succession and regularly evaluated board efficacy. As a result, institutional investors did not have to prod them into major shifts in behavior, although pressure from investors did increase these boards' attention to board independence, board composition, and the speed at which they addressed these issues. The boards of these very well managed corporations kept their lead in corporate governance by aligning their board structures with guidelines proffered by institutional investors. In the past, some of these companies' boards included two or more inside directors, but today most of them have only one employee director, the current CEO. (None have separated the dual CEO/chair position.)

The directors of these outstanding corporations clearly understood their responsibilities to shareholders and recognized their duty to involve themselves in the process of determining corporate strategic direction to create long-term value as well as short-term gains. Their adoption of this enlightened approach seems to have been driven much less by investor activism or the threat of legal ramifications than by the realities of global competition and the changing dynamics of the marketplace. When an enlightened board directs a company, it will outperform its industry competitors while providing a fair rate of return to shareholders.

Reaching far beyond Compliance . . . toward Enlightenment

In the area of corporate governance, process does matter! In fact, in many respects, the very important series of actions called *process* might be more important than the results of the action taken. Driving long-term value requires change, which in turn demands major shifts in behavior. This is why a board must be vigilant in its pursuit of excellent corporate governance. An important question then becomes: Does process drive behavior?

The drafters of the Sarbanes-Oxley Act of 2002 aimed to restore investor confidence in Corporate America by reforming corporate process and structure. SOX established new standards of compliance with some governance practices and significantly increased penalties for security violations. This value-add comforted some shareholders but caused others a great deal of concern and discomfort. On the comforting side, Sarbanes-Oxley provides marginally performing directors with a sense of empowerment; they can regard SOX as shield protecting them from a burden of guilt if they ask the management team tough questions! Perhaps by raising directors' levels of personal responsibility, accountability, and liability (thus making the director's job somewhat riskier) SOX inoculated directors with a new sense of responsibility for monitoring and truth-telling. On the disquieting side, SOX did not (and cannot) address the issue of personal integrity and thus does not assure investors that the right things are getting done.

Of course, it is not only SOX and other laws and regulations ushered in by a flurry of corporate frauds and questionable schemes that make the director's job seem vaguely perilous of late. Contributing to directors' unease is the intensification of public scrutiny of nearly everyone highly placed in Corporate America. All major institutional investors, including CalPERS and TIAA-CREF, are heavily engaged in this scrutiny, and even credit-rating agencies such as Moody's and Standard and Poor's include corporate governance measurements in their evaluation and rating criteria. In this environment of continual criticism of corporate leadership and corporate practices, an important concern is how shareholders will attract the right talent to provide them with the necessary oversight of their investments. This concern is addressed in more detail later in this chapter.

The Three Types of Corporate Boards

Corporate boards have many distinguishing characteristics, and researchers over the decades have amassed a substantial body of research studies examining many of these attributes to discover how they affect board performance.

191

In their efforts to find out what makes the best boards tick, researchers have analyzed many details of board composition, size, and location (East Coast versus West Coast, for example). Much of this research has been helpful. However, I believe that the most revealing features of corporate boards are attitudes and behaviors. Why is it that some boards are conservative in their approach to company management whereas others are forward-looking and have far-reaching influence? What benefits and disadvantages flow from different attitudes and behaviors?

In my view, board attitudes and behaviors lend themselves to classification into three distinct categories: traditional, standard, and enlightened. *Traditional boards* are guided by the ways of the past, *standard boards* toe the line through compliance with laws and regulations, and *enlightened boards* propel themselves and their companies beyond expected performance.

Because boards are reflections of the directors who comprise them, the behaviors of individual directors can be classified into the same set of categories. *Traditional directors* think and act conservatively, *standard directors* conform their board activities to laws and regulations, and *enlightened directors* seek to excel.

In defining these three categories, of course, I am not suggesting that the distinctions between traditional, standard, and enlightened boards and directors are functions of any lack of healthy sensitivity to shareholder interests. In many important ways, the three categories of corporate boards are very alike, most importantly in that boards of all three categories are, each in their different way, working to carry out their responsibilities to shareholders.

The *traditional board* does so primarily by providing support for the CEO and acting as a very important resource for the senior management team as these executives carry out their responsibilities. This type of board is highly concerned about the care and feeding of the CEO, largely because the CEO, who generally handpicks the members of the board, expects it. Members of the traditional board provide valuable linkages to customers and community leaders as well as access to product and service partners, personal mentors, and potential funding sources. The traditional board of directors is equally concerned about fiduciary oversight and duty of care. Meetings are held regularly, are well organized, and are executed according to plan. For many decades, most boards operated in the traditional mode, and traditional directors often regard the Sarbanes-Oxley Act of 2002 as a constraining or inhibiting influence on their attempts to increase shareholder value. Traditional boards, tend to be large, serve larger corporations, and have more directors with more tenure in their respective industries, whether or not their experience is relevant to current company needs.

The *standard board* is more centered on insuring that they are doing what the company, shareholders and stakeholders, and regulators expect of them. This type of board has a heightened awareness of director's legal obligations and the board's obligation to comply with laws and regulations. Because the standard board stays sharply focused on regulatory compliance, senior management is likely to view the board as a monitoring agency that oversees the senior management team's general performance in ways that comply with the board's legal and regulatory responsibilities. Standard directors often feel mandated to support the company, which causes them to engage more deeply than traditional directors in oversight of the corporation's general well-being. Standard directors may regard the Sarbanes-Oxley Act as a liberating influence that frees them to engage in company oversight.

The *enlightened board* intently focuses energy on the company's shareholders and doing what is necessary and appropriate to maximize shareholder value. Like traditional and standard directors, enlightened directors feel duty-bound to support and help the CEO. Like standard directors, they maintain a firm commitment to all board obligations, including ensuring full compliance with laws and regulations, and engaging with the CEO's problems, aspirations, and plans. However, the enlightened board differs from the other two types in possessing a strong sense of company ownership that is appropriately aligned with the shareholder's ownership of the company and other stakeholders' connectedness with the company. Enlightened boards live neither on tradition nor standards, but on strategy!

The enlightened board sees their mission as helping management lead the company toward maximum share performance by engaging the challenges facing the company. They tend to be quite supportive of the senior management team. Because enlightened directors strongly believe that it is their duty to involve themselves in an intellectual analysis of how the company should move forward into the future, most of the time the enlightened board is aligned on the critically important issues facing the company.

Unlike traditional boards, enlightened boards do not feel hampered by the rules and regulations of the Sarbanes-Oxley Act! Unlike standard boards that aim to comply with regulations, enlightened boards regard compliance with regulations as merely a baseline for board performance, and enlightened directors go far beyond merely meeting the requirements on a checklist. Nor do they need Sarbanes-Oxley to mandate that they protect values and ethics or monitor CEO performance. They recognize that these are services valuable to the CEO and his or her executive team. At the same time, they recognize that it is not their role to be involved in the day-to-day operations of the corporation. They lead by example, knowing that the company's future success (or lack thereof) will be strongly influenced by what they do. Overall, what most distinguishes enlightened directors from traditional and standard directors is the passionate obligation they feel to engage in the day-to-day challenges and strategizing of the company. Enlightened boards can be found in very large, complex companies, however, they are most likely to be found in smaller companies. The boards of smaller companies tend to be collegial groups with younger members.

As I discussed in the previous chapter, although directors from all three types of boards are almost always talented people, directors are never equal in any capacity, including their willingness to view intricate corporate governance issues from a wide perspective. That being the case, I am very emphatically suggesting that directors and boards, by changing their attitudes and behaviors, can propel their companies toward substantially enhanced long-term shareholder value.

Board Attitudes and Behaviors in Action

In some ways traditional, standard, and enlightened boards think much alike; however, on many issues their attitudes diverge. In this section, I compare the attitudes and resulting behaviors of these three different board types as they approach nine very important board activities, namely, planning management succession, developing strategy, configuring the board, choosing the board chair, coaching and mentoring the CEO, managing stakeholders, supporting customers and managing suppliers, prioritizing activities, coping with risk, and rewarding directors. (Determining CEO compensation is discussed at length in Chapter 8.)

Succession planning. When it comes to succession planning, all three types of boards—traditional, standard, and enlightened—expect the CEO to develop his or her successor. However, the traditional board is likely to relegate the responsibility of developing the succession planning process and of identifying future CEO candidates to the current CEO and will approve his selection provided that it can be credibly justified and that the CEO has not lost the board's confidence.

In contrast, the standard board dealing with succession planning recognizes that directors are responsible for engaging in the process of selecting his or her successor. Thus, standard directors will feel obligated to question the CEO more deeply about the candidates he or she proposes and are likely to suggest alternate candidates for the board to consider. Standard boards are comfortable abdicating the responsibility of succession planning to the CEO.

The enlightened board readily accepts full responsibility for CEO succession planning and takes ownership of the responsibility for selecting the next CEO. The board seeks the CEO's advice and counsel in their selection of candidates and expects the incumbent CEO to submit the names of nominee candidates and to make other significant contributions to the selection process as both a board member and a management participant in the selection process. However, the enlightened board does not permit the CEO to choose his or her successor or to take the lead in making that selection.

Clearly, when dealing with a very strong CEO, the selection-process approaches of the three different categories of boards are quite different. The traditional board follows the strong CEO's lead. The standard board does the same, but its members first engage with the CEO as he contemplates the selection. The enlightened board does not relinquish their responsibility to make the selection, but does seek the strong CEO's input and recommendations.

Best governance practices suggest that, when choosing directors to fill the nominating/corporate governance committee, the board select directors who will lead the rest of the board through the selection process. Every director shares in the CEO selection responsibility and thus should be given an opportunity to participate in the decision-making process. It is important that the board not delegate to the nominating/corporate governance committee the responsibility for (or authority to) make a CEO selection decision. Instead, the board should empower the committee to make recommendations that must be approved or rejected by the full board of directors.

By the way, long before the nomination and selection process begins, the enlightened board enthusiastically accepts accountability for ensuring that an effective CEO succession plan is developed and implemented. The enlightened board does not wait for a crisis to ensue before planning the CEO's succession.

As concerned as the enlightened board is about CEO succession, its members are equally concerned about developing and executing a comprehensive senior executive succession-planning process. Certainly, the enlightened board understands that it is not their job to select the CEO's team; however, they recognize that they are responsible for providing input that adds value to the CEO's efforts to identify and select highly qualified senior managers for the company. In the course of this process, the enlightened board learns the CEO's logic for selecting his or her team.

Strategy development. The three types of boards and directors also have different attitudes and behaviors when it comes to strategy development. The traditional CEO is unlikely to want directors to delve too deeply into the company's strategic thinking, and thus the traditional board is unlikely to engage in developing the company's strategic direction. Traditional directors are not interested in becoming deeply involved in the overall strategic direction of the company, which, in their view, is the domain of the CEO and the management team.

The traditional board's disengagement from strategy development seemed to work in the days when boards primarily were comprised by providers of services to the company, such as bankers, lawyers, and community leaders.

With little knowledge about the company's industry, these directors could be influenced easily by the recommendations of the CEO and the senior management team. Even today, traditional directors expect the CEO and his or her team to perform a thorough market analysis and to understand the direction that the company should be headed.

After the CEO and his senior team develop the company strategy, the traditional board reviews and then approves it. Although traditional directors participate in periodic reviews of the company's strategic direction, they believe themselves responsible for supporting the CEO's strategy provided that it seems logical and in the best interests of shareholders. Traditional directors do not accept ownership of the company's strategy creation process or believe that they should direct the CEO in developing company strategy.

The standard board exhibits similar attitudes and behaviors when it comes to corporate strategy development. However, although the standard board does not acknowledge significant ownership of the corporation's strategy, standard directors will insist that the CEO develops a strategic plan and executes it to produce the desired results.

In contrast, the enlightened board fully acknowledges part ownership of the corporation's strategic intent and will partner with the CEO in developing that intent! The board and CEO believe themselves to be collectively responsible for defining and articulating a corporate strategic intent that maximizes shareholder value. The CEO and senior management team feel responsible for leading strategy development, implementation, and execution.

Clearly, enlightened directors go much beyond reviewing the company's quantitative financial performance and annually reviewing the company's strategic plan; they support the CEO's aspirations for the shareholders and help the senior management team conceptually design strategies to achieve those goals.

Board configuration. The major distinction between the three types of boards is who comprises it. The traditional board most likely includes the CEO, one or two additional senior executives of the company, and lawyers, bankers, other providers of services to the company, and local community leaders. The standard board is most likely similar in structure to a traditional board.

The enlightened board includes the CEO (but probably not other company employees), other corporate CEOs and industry leaders with experience in critical issues relevant to the company's success, and executives with broad global perspectives. In general, the enlightened boardroom contains a broader array of talent and leadership than is expected (or necessary) in a traditional or standard boardroom. The enlightened board commits to establishing a group of appropriately experienced independent directors with complementary areas of expertise.

Enlightened directors structure the board so as to leverage the strength of each board member. For example, in addition to staffing the three required standing committees, enlightened boards establish other standing committees necessary to complete their oversight responsibilities, such as technology, environmental, intellectual property, or public policy committees.

Enlightened directors know that the board's ability to maximize shareholder value rests on effective recruitment of the diverse talent needed by the company as well as ongoing director education to make the best use of that talent. Under the leadership of the nominating/corporate governance committee, the enlightened board takes complete responsibility for board configuration and committee assignments, and then works in very close concert with the CEO to make sure that the board's composition will match the senior management team's needs as they execute the company's strategic plan. Together, the board and CEO specify procedures for identifying and recruiting candidates that complement the existing board members' abilities to monitor and help the CEO.

Board chair selection. Traditional boards award the CEO and board chair position to the same person. Standard boards usually do the same, but directors feel mild pressure from some regulatory agencies, such as the New York Stock Exchange and the U.S. Securities and Exchange Commission, to staff these two positions with two different individuals. Enlightened boards base their decision to separate or combine the roles of CEO and board chair on the current situation because enlightened directors tend to concentrate their energy on what they deem to be most important and most effective for that company at the time. As a general rule, it probably is fair to say that most enlightened directors believe that a dual board chair/CEO arrangement usually best serves shareholder interests.

CEO coaching and mentoring. Members of the traditional board often lack the experience, interest, or perhaps even capacity to mentor and coach the CEO. Very often, they have little experience in the company's industry. This is not surprising because most traditional boards are led by a very successful, very powerful CEO who has selected the directors partly based on their deference to his or her success and power.

Enlightened boards, on the other hand, are comprised of independent directors selected for their leadership abilities and expertise. They are quite willing to give the CEO honest, constructive feedback about his or her performance and professional development relative to the CEO's own personal aspirations and expectations. In other words, the directors help the CEO to understand how the company's internal and external stakeholders view him (or her). This generous mentoring and coaching (which is not to be confused with obligatory supervision) greatly helps the CEO improve his or her job performance.

Stakeholder management. Traditional boards, standard boards, and enlightened boards all place high value on management of the company's relationships with stakeholders. Most traditional boards place strong emphasis on stakeholder management because the directors themselves are members of the stakeholder community and have a vested interest in ensuring that the company pays attention to the stakeholders that they represent. Enlightened boards value excellent relationships with company stakeholders as a function of their strong focus on achieving long-term shareholder value; often the most efficient path to this goal is a well-maintained relationship with a vital company stakeholder, such as a community. Inextricable linkages often exist between company issues and the issues of communities or other stakeholders. When the genuinely responsible company is viewed as a good corporate citizen, stakeholder support for the company flourishes, providing many opportunities to maximize shareholder value.

Customer support and supplier management. Traditional boards often are filled with company customers focused on customer service, company suppliers focused on supplier support, and industry associates focused on industry relations. Naturally enough, the traditional board spends considerable time on all three of these endeavors. Standard boards are less sensitive to this role. Enlightened boards do not consider customer support or supplier management as top priorities in their value-add effort. At times, of course, standard and enlightened directors share their access to customers and suppliers as well as information of potential value to the CEO or management team. When appropriate, they also offer supplier or customer perspectives or engage with management in supplier activities. Generally speaking, however, enlightened directors are much more intent on planning activities and supporting the CEO.

Prioritization. When comparing the three categories of corporate boards, it is fair to say that traditional boards allocate more time to supporting the management team through customer support and industry support, standard boards allocate more time to assessing rules and regulations and bringing the board into compliance with them; and enlightened boards allocate more time to succession planning and developing strategic directions for the corporations.

Enlightened boards' first priority—on which they spend the majority of their time—is fulfilling their duty of care, during which activities they make quantitative assessments. They give next-highest priority to activities that they believe will maximize the long-term returns to shareholders; these activities often rely on qualitative assessments made as part of strategy development. Equally important to enlightened boards is overall supervision of the CEO. Enlightened boards dedicate significant amounts of time to coaching their CEOs and to providing them with consistent, candid feedback about current performance and ways to improve it. The enlightened board's support of the CEO is highly visible both within and outside the corporation;

enlightened directors believe that everyone should know what they expect of the CEO and exactly how much they support the CEO.

Board perquisites and benefits. The three types of boards differ in their views of perquisites and benefits for senior managers and directors. During the 1970s and 1980s, many traditionally oriented, very large market-cap companies, as well as some much smaller ones, rewarded their directors for board service with retirement plans. By serving a specified number of years on the board (usually a minimum of 5), a director earned a vested retirement benefit, typically paid after the director became retirement eligible and completed his or her board service to the company. These usually were warranted, unfunded plans in contrast to defined benefit plans.

Today's standard board generally does not offer directors a retirement plan. Instead, as partial compensation for board service, the standard board rewards directors with opportunities to invest in the company through stock options or restricted shares of the company's common stock. These stock options or shares vest over a long period of time, thereby providing a much tighter alignment with the interests of long-term shareholders, while, at the same time, providing directors with future compensation that may be used for retirement income. Often the standard board helps the director facilitate his or her retirement investing if he or she elects to do so.

The enlightened board replaces retirement plans and stock options with restricted shares, but, in addition to compensating directors with equity in the company, the enlightened board requires directors to maintain a minimum level of ownership of company shares of common stock, usually the equivalent of 3 to 5 times the director's annual retainer fee. Thus, enlightened boards take director compensation to a higher plain by requiring directors to invest in the company above a certain level until they retire from the board.

Coping with risk. Whereas the traditional board supports the CEO and the standard board seeks regulatory compliance, the enlightened board seeks maximum shareholder value *while* in regulatory compliance. Thus, the enlightened board is not averse to risk. As Thomas Jefferson was quoted as saying, "In order to enjoy the fruits of freedom, we must endure its occasional abuse." This is abundantly true in corporate governance. As directors fully engage to add value to the company, mistakes will be made because nobody is perfect. In their pursuit of maximum shareholder value, enlightened directors are not afraid to do what is right, to do what is ethical, and to act in a manner surrounded by a high level of integrity.

Knowing Where Your Board Stands

Even boards that share a common set of objectives, similar attitudes, and comparable behaviors and practices execute their responsibilities in unique ways. At some point in time, the expectations of shareholders, the opinions of investment bankers, the attitudes of employees, and the mind-set of customers will significantly influence every board's actions, as will the state of the general economy and events in the legal arena. Just as no two directors can be the same, no two boards can be the same. Moreover, just as people's attitudes and behaviors vary from circumstance to circumstance, so do the attitudes and behaviors of boards. For the board to be self-aware, it is imperative that the board's members understand which category the board is functioning in at any given time. Equally important, they must understand which classification the board aspires to achieve and why!

Because all members of the board definitely are not equal, each board member should assess his or her positioning on the board. Listed below are some earmarks by which to recognize whether a board's activities in an area are traditional, standard, or enlightened.

Energy level. The board's levels of energy and engagement offer important clues to board mode. When the board is in traditional mode, directors ask questions as needed; when in standard mode, directors ask questions as required; when in enlightened mode, directors ask questions to gain understanding and to add perspective. Staid discussions signal traditional mode, whereas high levels of energy, interaction, and engagement signal that the board likely is in enlightened mode.

Information flow. The quality of information distributed to the board before and during board meetings, the relevancy of that information, and the constancy of the information flow are all good indicators of board mode. When directors receive a lot of documentation that they are not encouraged to understand or research, the board is in traditional mode. When directors receive a great deal of information for the purpose of ensuring that they are in full compliance with regulations, the board is in standard mode, particularly if the directors are not encouraged to delve into the information. If, however, directors insist on receiving timely and substantial information that helps them strategize ways to support the CEO's efforts, the board is in enlightened mode.

One aspect of information flow is the frequency and length of scheduled board meetings. If directors meet for 4 hours at a time less often than once per quarter, that board obviously takes a passive approach to corporate governance and must be considered traditional. Highly enlightened boards meet long and often to exchange ideas and address challenges. Meeting locations and agendas also affect information flow. So does who is included in board meetings. In an enlightened boardroom, the company's senior leaders attend appropriate sections of meetings to give directors opportunities to engage with a broader set of management.

Intensity. When the board is in traditional mode, directors are relatively passive in their approach, which means, of course, that they are not likely to be adding significant value to the company's success. When the board is in enlightened mode, directors seem to have a compelling need to contribute to the overall effectiveness of the meeting in maximizing shareholder value. In this mode, directors constructively challenge management to gain better understandings of the issues at hand so they can add value to the process.

As mentioned above, just as there are significant differences in board attitudes and behaviors, there are significant differences in the performances of individual directors. These differences also can be classified into the three categories of traditional, standard, and enlightened. Like board entities, individual directors execute their responsibilities in unique ways, which is the topic of the next section.

Focusing on Director Attitudes and Behaviors

Although following process is an important path to good corporate governance, statistical measures used to assess board effectiveness are far less useful to directors than a solid focus on director attitudes and behaviors. Although every director must understand post-Enron corporate governance and regulatory reforms and how they affect his or her boardroom responsibilities and activities, no director should allow himself or herself to be deterred from effective service by overreactions to new governance requirements and procedures or by concentrating on process to the exclusion of the board's fundamental functions.

Certainly, all 21st-century directors are expected to meet a common set of expectations. For example, every director is expected to attend a minimum number of board meetings, do what is in the best interest of company shareholders, and keep in mind the implications of their actions for all company stakeholders. Every director is expected to use the experiences that justified their selection as a candidate for the board (and ultimately solidified their election as a board member) to contribute some value to the company's ongoing enterprise. Because all 21st-century corporate boards cope with a common set of issues and challenges, each director is expected to maximize the value of the board by engaging those issues and challenges at a certain level of inquiry and constructive inspection.

Directors being people, their responses to these expectations differ considerably! As corporate directors do their best to fulfill their obligations to shareholders, they rely, as they must, on the personal attitudes, behaviors, and practices that they developed during lifetimes of unique individual experiences. Although all members of a board share equally in the board's obligations and risks, they never can be equal in their contribution to the board or their value to the company.

To raise the company to unexpected heights, directors should practice thinking and behaving like extreme personal leaders. X-Leaders are powered by creativity. This might make their thinking unconventional, but by channeling their creativity through discipline, they are able to apply it appropriately and effectively. X-Leaders also are bold. They identify problems that others don't dare to perceive, and they connect ideas that others regard as unrelated. The X-leader understands that the quality of a question might be more valuable than its answer. After an X-Leader solves a problem, their competitors ask: *Why didn't we think of that?* To move into enlightened leadership, directors must keep their eye on the ball, which is the essence of shareholder value creation.

The value of a director's service rises or falls dramatically as that director moves across the continuum of engagement. The value of the director's service rises as the director creates effective relationships with other members of the board. That value rises again as the director earns the opportunity to have constructive dialog with management. Increasing one's level of engagement requires much more than becoming cognizant of issues of concern to audit and compensation committees. It requires actively increasing one's knowledge and understanding of the activities taking place in the committee rooms deemed important by the board.

Tools for Enlightenment

Obviously, I advocate superior corporate governance leadership—as opposed to merely acceptable performance—in the boardroom. In my view, directors should seek opportunities far beyond those that are conveniently available to fulfill their basic responsibilities. They should expect to exceed the standard. By seeking the best possible corporate governance and operating with the conviction that principled, constructive leadership requires action, they secure a foundation on which the company can build more shareholder value.

To assist boards in achieving these goals, my associates and I at XCEO, Inc. developed a set of measurement tools for assessing their current and desired states of performance. These tools, which are discussed in the following chapter, are useful in appraising a board's potential attitudes and behaviors and also for assessing director's general attitudes toward engagement in board meetings. Directors also can use these tools to assess their individual performances in the boardroom. One of our instruments can help the collective board evaluate current behaviors as precursors to desired future behaviors.

Notes

[i] Rich, J. (1998). Find a way to grow. *Perspectives.* Sibson and Company, *8*(2), 6.
[ii] Ibid.
[iii] Ibid.

Chapter 12

Evaluating Board and Director Performance

Does anyone ever really win if no one is keeping score?

Corporate governance leadership has become a leading corporate performance indicator. Effective governance structures focus the board's attention on trend monitoring, strategic planning, and succession planning. This increased attention to keeping the company healthy and flexible through changing markets and economic conditions helps ensure that investors receive appropriate returns on their investments and protects directors from legal actions claiming dereliction of duty. An overwhelming majority of investors surveyed in 2002 reported being willing to pay premiums of 12-14% for American companies with high governance standards.[i]

Not surprisingly, then, enlightened boards are looking for new opportunities to generate significant competitive advantage and maximize long-term stakeholder value through their corporate governance. In a 2004 survey of more than 1,000 corporate directors, McKinsey & Company found that, after years of being put on the defensive by accounting scandals and charges of inadequate governance, directors were looking for ways to accelerate and deepen their engagement with core areas of corporate performance and value creation.[ii] Many of the surveyed directors, McKinsey reported, having focused for a time on accounting-compliance issues, were determined to play active roles in setting the strategy, assessing the risks, developing the leaders, and monitoring the long-term health of their companies. Directors who want to do much more than meet the minimum requirements of their jobs are likely to become the enlightened X-Leaders of their boards.[iii]

Enlightened directors and enlightened boards, as I have pointed out repeatedly in this book, believe in compliance, but they strive to exceed it. For them, Sarbanes-Oxley, with all its strengths and frailties, is a convenient stepping-stone to higher levels of engagement. They also believe in intense commitment, and theirs is to working with the CEO in the passionate pursuit of increased long-term shareholder value. In their zeal to engage in complex issues, they are careful not to give management the incorrect impression that they would like to take on day-to-day operational roles. They keep their thinking fresh so they can make strong contributions to the board's culture and agenda.[iv]

Boards are in charge of supervising the CEO, but who supervises the supervisors? In some ways, the board chair oversees the board by organizing and leading board activities in conjunction with the chair of the nominating/corporate governance committee and the lead or presiding director, if the board has one. Some federal and state regulatory agencies, such as the U.S. Securities and Exchange Commission, the New York Stock Exchange, and NASDAQ are chartered to oversee corporate boards through rules and policies meant to encourage appropriate behaviors. Other watchdog organizations also keep track of corporate board behaviors, including corporate credit rating agencies such as Moody's and Standard and Poor's and shareholder special interest groups such as CalPERS and International Shareholder Services. Despite considerable internal and external oversight of boards, however, in reality, boards supervise themselves.

Boards function as self-directed workgroups. Most boards today are stepping-up their activities to maintain full regulatory compliance, exercise their newfound powers and authority, and more openly show their conviction to shareholders. They have taken on new challenges, such as risk assessment, whistle blowers, and heightened stakeholder initiatives. As a result, directors meet more frequently, burrow more deeply into their corporations, and review increasingly complex subjects.

All this activity means that many standing board committees no longer meet 5 or 6 times each year but at least 8 to 12 times per year. According to a 2004 survey by the executive search company, Korn/Ferry International, the average commitment of a director of a U.S.-listed company increased from 13 hours per month in 2001 to 19 hours in 2003 (before falling to 18 hours in 2004). Clearly, boards must improve their efficiency, and one of the best ways to do this is through self-evaluation.

Monitoring Board Performance

Acknowledgment of the need for regular board evaluations was a major milestone in the evolution of enlightened corporate governance. In 1998, only 25% of corporate boards conducted board performance evaluations.[v] Many of these were boards that, having had to replace ineffective CEOs and cooperate with institutional investors on monitoring corporate performance, finally took seriously their need to appraise their own performances.[vi] Of course, since the 2004 New York Stock Exchange mandate that companies listed on the Exchange conduct at least annual board performance evaluations, board evaluations have become much more common. This relatively recent NYSE requirement constitutes recognition that regularly scheduled board evaluations are major tools for accomplishing the board renewal and reformation critical to improving corporate governance.[vii]

For the last decade at least, however, the National Association of Corporate Directors has recommended that boards conduct their own annual evaluations and that they periodically commission external evaluations. Between formal evaluations, the Association advises, the board should meet in executive session on a regular basis to monitor board performance. In this monitoring process, every director is responsible for being open and honest about the board's collective performance.[viii]

Board evaluations help identify the board's current role and determine its future role.[ix] Done properly, they help the board run more smoothly and ensure a healthier balance of power between board and CEO. Board evaluations also improve the board-CEO relationship by providing a set of defined, agreed-upon objectives and performance expectations.[x] Once in place, board evaluation processes become institutionalized and difficult to dismantle, making it difficult for new CEOs to dominate boards.[xi] Board evaluations clarify directors' individual roles and responsibilities, giving each director a much better understanding of what is expected of him or her. One of the most consistent benefits observed in companies where board evaluations are performed is a commitment by both directors and the CEO to devote more attention to long-term strategy—reason enough to implement regular board appraisals![xii]

A thorough evaluation of the board's role and performance can indicate when the board requires new talents and skills and when director's talents no longer fit the company's needs.

Although board performance evaluations are gaining acceptance as important tools for corporate governance, another, extremely powerful, tool is so underutilized that its use is still considered "quite rare."[xiii] This tool is the individual director evaluation.

Monitoring Individual Performance

The essence of enlightened leadership is the ability to motivate people to continually learn how to be more effective in their work. As corporate boards evolve from traditional passivity to enlightened pro-activity, they learn how to create boardroom environments that encourage each director to perform at the highest level of his or her capability, resulting in maximum individual effectiveness. The first step in any organizational learning, of course, is evaluation of current performance. The results of performance evaluations point the way to better methods for achieving goals. Interestingly, according to data gathered by Korn/Ferry International, directors gave significantly higher effectiveness ratings to boards in which individual directors were evaluated.[xiv]

To help directors reach higher levels of effectiveness, the board should develop a set of expectations and guidelines against which each director can evaluate his or her performance. Directors will be greatly aided in their self-policing efforts if, once each year, the chair of the corporate governance committee meets with each director to discuss individual performance and contribution issues.

Board service is a privilege that should be available only to those qualified to serve. Obviously, a prerequisite for continued board service must be continuing contributions to the board. *If* the board has done a good job of recruiting talented directors who are well matched to the needs of the company and the board, the issue of a poorly performing director is unlikely to be raised. This, however, is a big *if.* Even a decade ago, a majority of corporate boards surveyed by Korn/Ferry reported having fired a director for poor attendance, inattentiveness, or poor decision-making.[xv] As fewer directors take on more board work, directors will demonstrate a much broader range of attitudes and behaviors. Most of these will be positive and constructive, but some of the emerging thinking and conduct will be negative and destructive.

When negative feedback concerning a director's performance or contribution occurs, or if the board no longer has need of a director's area of expertise, the chair of the corporate governance committee should bring this to the individual's attention as soon as possible. One reason that directors think that boards become more efficient when individual directors are evaluated may be that, when director evaluation is not part of the regular board process, the board's members rarely are given an early warning about inappropriate conduct and a chance to improve.[xvi] In most cases, boards reactively wait for under-performing directors to retire and replace them only for extreme offenses such as criminal misconduct, conflict of interest, active disruption, or a very poor attendance and participation record.[xvii]

When a director's performance problem comes to light and the director shows unwillingness or inability to remedy the problem, he or she should be encouraged to resign from the board in the best interests of the corporation. In the unlikely event that the director refuses to resign, the chair of the corporate governance committee must exercise the full responsibility of that office and recommend that the board not propose the under-performing director for re-election. All boards should possess a process whereby the CEO, individual directors, or the complete board can seek a director's resignation or termination.[xviii]

Clearly, full board evaluations and individual evaluations provide directors with information they can use to serve the long-term interests of shareholders. However, to periodically assess how well their efforts on behalf of shareholders are progressing, both boards and the individuals who comprise them need efficient evaluation tools.

Tools for Evaluating Boards and Directors

A number of tools are available to assist corporate boards in performing board and director self-evaluations, including those recommended by feedback specialists, 3D Group, or by CEO consultant, David Nadler. Among the available tools are a set of two profiles constructed by XCEO, Inc., namely, the *Enlightened Corporate Governance Profile®* (for full board self-evaluation) and the *Enlightened Individual Director Performance Profile®* (for individual director self-evaluation). Directors complete these profiles anonymously and in private. These tools reflect a straightforward model easily implemented by any board desiring to establish a director-attitude baseline.

The *Enlightened Individual Director Performance Profile®* includes an option for a voluntary *360-degree evaluation* in which the director solicits perceptions about his or her performance from the board chair, two or more director colleagues, and appropriate committee chairs. Using this option, the director also may solicit input from the CEO or other members of the management team with whom the director has substantial interaction as part of his or her board activities.

Both the *Enlightened Corporate Governance Profile®* and the *Enlightened Individual Director Performance Profile®* are designed to help boards evaluate their current attitudes with respect to current board practices. Using these tools helps boards improve boardroom interrelationships, which moves directors toward deeper engagement and better contributions.

To evaluate the full board using the *Enlightened Corporate Governance Profile*®, (See Figure 12.1), each board member is asked to weight and prioritize the importance of the items in a set of prescribed board activities and responsibilities. The collective tally of all board member input is compared against an XCEO, Inc. benchmark. (See Figure 12.2)

To perform an individual self-evaluation using the *Enlightened Individual Director Performance Profile*®, (See Figure 12.3), the director weights and prioritizes the importance of his or her boardroom behaviors or performances in relation to a set of prescribed boardroom activities and responsibilities. The director's score then is compared against an XCEO, Inc. benchmark. (See Figure 12.4.)

All qualitative comparisons used in the profiles are based on XCEO's empirical research combined with nearly 2 decades of experience in various boardrooms. The baseline for comparison was developed using characteristics of the standard board and standard director described in the previous chapter. Thus, the score of a traditional board (or a director closely aligned with traditional board attitudes) will be lower than the standard measure; the score of a highly enlightened board (or a director practicing extreme personal leadership) will be higher than the standard measure.

Summary

The collective behavior of a corporate board substantially influences the attitudes of the board's individual directors. The reverse also is true. The levels of engagement of the directors who take leadership positions in board activities have great influence on the collective board. The wise board makes every effort to compose itself in such a way that the CEO's needs for talented counsel and direction are met by a reservoir of strengths and talents of individual directors. To keep this system running smoothly, boards need a systematized process of regularly occurring board and director evaluations.

The next chapter gives the reader a glimpse into the minds of people who deal with corporate governance issues on a daily basis.

Enlightened Corporate Governance (ECG) Profile

Item	Score	Activity
1.	–	Duty of Care (Shareholder representation)
2.	–	Supervising the CEO (Coach/Council/Support)
3.	–	Senior Executive Succession Planning
4.	–	Board Configuration
5.	–	Mentoring/Coaching CEO
6.	–	Corporate Strategic Direction
7.	–	Stakeholder Management
8.	–	Industry Support
9.	–	Senior Management Selection/Coaching
10.	–	Supplier Support
11.	–	Customer Support

Figure 12.1

Enlightened Corporate Governance (ECG) Graph

Types of Boards

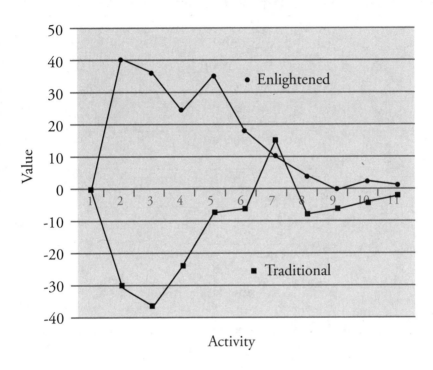

Activity

Figure 12.2

Enlightened Individual Director Performance (IDP) Profile

Item	Score	Activity
1.	–	Regular attendance at board and committee meetings
2.	–	Attentive: Consistently asks constructive questions
3.	–	Perspective: Regularly offers real value-added insights
4.	–	Arrives at all meetings on time and stays until the end
5.	–	Actively participates in committee assignments
6.	–	Fully engaged throughout the meetings
7.	–	Provides personal mentoring and coaching to the CEO
8.	–	Willingly accepts special assignments for the board
9.	–	Provides personal mentoring and coaching to senior managers
10.	–	Occasionally participates in company site visits
11.	–	Represents the company at industry or customer events

Figure 12.3

Enlightened Individual Director Performance (IDP) Graph

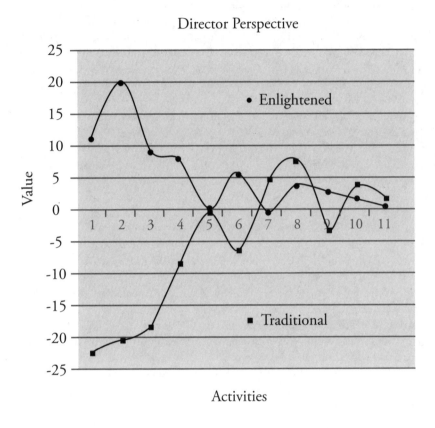

Director Perspective

Figure 12.4

Notes

[i] McKinsey & Company. (2002, July). Global investor opinion survey: Key findings. Retrieved August 5, 2006, from http://www.mckinsey.com/governance.

[ii] Corporate governance: The view from the boardroom. (2004). *The McKinsey Quarterly, 2004*. Available from McKinsey & Company, http://www.mckinsey.com/governance.

[iii] Crawford, C. J. (2005). Corporate rise: *The x principles of extreme personal leadership*. Santa Clara, CA: XCEO, Inc.

[iv] Corporate governance, 2004.

[v] Conger, J., Finegold, D., & Lawler, E., III. (1998). Appraising boardroom performance. *Harvard Business Review, 98102*, 136-140.

[vi] Conger et al., 1998, p. 136.

[vii] National Association of Corporate Directors. (1996). Putting board evaluation to work. Washington, DC: Author.

[viii] Ibid.

[ix] Ibid.

[x] Conger et al., 1998, p. 148.

[xi] Ibid., p. 136.

[xii] Bassett, L. C. (1998). Putting board evaluation to work. *The Corporate Board, 19*(109), 20.

[xiii] Nadler, D. A., Behan, B. A., & Nadler, M. B. (Eds.). (2005). *Building better boards: A blueprint for effective governance*. San Francisco: Jossey-Bass.

[xiv] Korn/Ferry International. (1998). Board meeting in session: Evaluating the board of directors. Retrieved August 5, 2006, from http://www.kornferry.com.br/site/pdf/mediapublications_b292.pdf.

[xv] Listen up. (1996, November 26). *Business Week*. Retrieved November 20, 2000, from www.businessweek.com/

[xvi] Korn/Ferry International, 1998.

[xvii] Ibid.

[xviii] National Association of Corporate Directors, 1996.

Chapter 13

Close-Up Views of Corporate Governance: The Real Impact of Investor Activism

Your critique of the performance will be influenced by your view in the theater.

Corporate governance is a topic rich in controversy. After decades of debate, scrutiny, suggestions, and demands, what impacts have institutional investors actually had on the attitudes and behaviors of American corporations?

On the surface at least, institutional investors seem to have very successfully influenced the thinking and actions of America's corporations, the CEOs who manage them, and the boards who direct them. Corporate governance has improved immensely since the mid-1970s. [i] Institutional investors and other stakeholders are able to monitor CEO performance, see that boards are properly composed of active directors, and bring social and performance issues to the attention of CEOs and boards. In the end, the test of activist success will be whether boards stand up to CEOs whenever it is necessary.[ii]

Our research at XCEO, Inc. revealed that the corporate governance issues of most interest to boards are company linkages with their demographically and culturally diverse stakeholders, correlations between pay and corporate performance in the compensation packages of CEOs, separation of the dual role of CEO and board chair, optimal board size, and using directors' knowledge and talents as competitive advantages. To crosscheck our research findings, we interviewed a group of corporate directors and governance experts in a series of interviews on the effects of institutional investor efforts on corporate behaviors. We looked for professional views about CEO supervision, boardroom composition, corporate strategy, and succession planning. This chapter presents some of the experiences and expert opinions we gathered during these interviews, together with some analysis of them.

Interviews with Corporate Governance Practitioners and Experts

We interviewed current or recently retired CEOs of major U.S. corporations or executives actively engaged in practicing or monitoring corporate governance. Some were CEOs of multi-billion dollar global enterprises, some were non-executive chairs of small high-tech companies, and the remainder included a board executive recruiter, an attorney, and a journalist, all highly regarded experts in corporate governance. The views of these practitioners and experts provided us with further insight into the ongoing evolution of highly enlightened corporate governance.

An executive recruiter. The vice-chair of a leading global CEO recruiting and training firm reported that corporate governance has changed at "glacial speed" since the mid-1970s. For this executive recruiter, watching corporate governance change was "like watching ice melt." Nevertheless, this executive recruiter thought that several high-profile disasters resulting from CEO succession-planning debacles had finally accelerated profound governance change being driven by institutional investors, the media, enlightened CEOs, and board compensation.

This CEO recruiter thought that institutional investors were most responsible for profound governance changes because they had forced directors to listen to their demands by means of proxy battles. The press, especially the business press, helped by attacking the secrecy of corporate operations taking place in what this respondent called the "club-oriented atmospheres" of boardrooms. By crying "foul" when attacking interlocking directorates, special benefits for directors, lagging corporate performance, CEO succession, and CEO compensation, the press managed to focus attention on boardroom activities.

Another chief cause of major change in corporate governance, this recruiter thought, was the emergence of a new generation of enlightened CEOs who believe that the board should be instrumental to the company's success and who value directors' contributions of added intelligence, peripheral vision, and networks for on-going counsel and advice. A new generation of CEOs at companies like American Express and IBM, this recruiter said, created a "sea-change" inside their boardrooms by significantly reducing the number of insider directors from the standard four or five of the mid-1970s to the one or two of today. They also recruited more CEO directors and fewer lawyers, accountants, and investment bankers, who now are seen as having potential conflicts with board activities and therefore should be treated as service providers to the board.

This recruiter foresaw profound corporate governance changes in Europe and Asia.

A business journalist. The senior journalist of a major business publication also believed that corporate governance is changing for the better. However, this journalist believed that the effect of institutional investors on board behavior has been minimal, less real than perceived. Nevertheless, CEOs are working much harder to develop better relationships with institutional investors. The changes, this journalist said, are being driven by CEOs who are responding to their boards because they recognize the penalty of not responding. In addition, many new, enlightened CEOs also value director input and are aligned with the notion of increasing value.

This journalist supported the concept of pay for real performance. In this journalist's opinion, CEO compensation plans are still unbalanced because CEOs are not penalized for corporate failures and poor performances. When CEOs do not meet the performance requirements of their jobs, they should have their salaries reduced, their bonuses reduced or eliminated, and their share options withdrawn. Losing a job generally is not in the cards for a CEO, and boards give CEOs "a lot of rope before they hang themselves." When CEOs deliver outstanding performance, however, they should be paid accordingly.

Board diversity, thought this journalist, is a desirable state because it should bring more "out-of-the-box thinking." When recruiting directors, most companies wait to find the right person who brings a total package of experience, value, and diversity.

The retired CEO of a pharmaceutical company. The former CEO, president, and board chair of a major pharmaceutical company thought that institutional investor involvement had a positive impact on the corporate governance process, making corporations more sensitive to linking pay and performance. As a result, boards are making compensation plans more specific, with both goals and timetables. During the past 5 to 10 years, this CEO reported, total compensation for CEOs and senior officers has become highly leveraged and tightly linked to shareholder interests via simpler share options that no longer include restricted stock with advantageous terms and conditions. Except for a few examples of excessively large grants of share options, most share-option grants to employees represent a very small percentage of the total outstanding shares.

This CEO also expressed the belief that boards are—and should be—more involved in ensuring that corporations have executable corporate strategies. Because boards have limited time and knowledge, they are not capable of developing corporate strategy, but boards should monitor strategy and challenge its substance. Effective use of board committees, this CEO observed, has increased board influence on development of strategic direction.

The CEO of a large computer manufacturer. The leader of a computer company with more than $10 billion in annual revenues thought institutional investors have had no impact on boardroom operations. The influence of influential investors on major decisions by competent corporate directors, this CEO said, is non-existent for companies with both good and bad performances. Although institutional investors sometimes express concerns about share-option grants, for this respondent's industry, share-option grants were a moot issue because base compensation often is less than 25% of total compensation.

This CEO believed that boards should not be responsible for establishing company strategy but should be deeply involved in reviewing it. The board's responsibility is to hire and develop the right people to form an appropriate strategy for the company. This CEO believed that the board should develop a broad global perspective, but this CEO saw no critical need for a director from outside the United States. Instead, the board could seek a local person for advice as needed and gain a global perspective from the management team, who meets with customers around the world.

The CEO of an airline. The CEO and board chair of a major U.S.-based airline serving domestic and foreign travelers believed that the opinions of institutional investors have increased board focus on CEO compensation, However, these opinions do not drive boards to do anything inconsistent with their strategic plans to increase shareholder value. Corporations view institutional investors just like other large shareholder groups: "When they talk, we listen because we should be aligned to achieve the same results." This CEO believed quite strongly that CEO compensation should be tied directly to share price and that all shareholders and employees (including the CEO) should participate in company share programs.

This CEO was very partial to keeping the CEO and board chair positions combined, although this decision does depend on the individuals involved. This CEO thought that the airline board needed representation from U.S. communities with large populations of airline employees. Global board composition should be driven by the nature of the business and, although the airline board would not gain value from a foreign director, other companies might.

The CEO of a computer manufacturer and distributor. The CEO of a very large computer manufacturer and distributor who had chaired 5 of the 24 boards he served on during his career (including 4 boards of international corporations) expressed the belief that most boardroom activity today focuses on establishing appropriate objectives and reward plans, establishing leadership and succession plans, and developing strategic directions. In the 1980s, this CEO recalled, 80% of board time was dedicated to reviewing the numbers after the fact, with the other 20% allocated to reviewing audit plans and legal-exposure issues.

This CEO agreed that boards should not develop company strategy but instead should be deeply involved in assuring that a thoughtful strategic plan is in place and in monitoring the company's performance against the fulfillment of that strategic plan.

This CEO strongly believed that only one insider should be on the board, and that the audit, compensation, and corporate governance committees should be made up entirely of outside directors. Combining the roles of CEO and board chair, this respondent held, is the most effective solution, particularly when the board sets the right objectives for the CEO. When the two positions are separated, this respondent believed, the CEO must spend too much time trying to prepare for the board meeting instead of concentrating on running the business. However, this respondent would strongly recommended an outsider chair for a board with a high percentage of inside directors.

The CEO of a metals company. The CEO and board chair of a large metals company believed that institutional investors did have a major impact on the behaviors or performances of corporate boards, particularly early on. Unfortunately, some boards perceived institutional investors' actions as non-constructive and resulting in negative value. Nonetheless, this CEO thought, institutional investor activism caused some boards to be more introspective.

Keeping the CEO and board chair roles combined, according to this respondent, is the right approach. The chair needs to be well-informed about the operations of the company, which is a far larger role than convening the board, and the CEO should not be spending time trying to educate the chair on the details of the business. The CEO's job is to manage, and the board's job is to direct. Therefore, the board should focus on strategy and not management of day-to-day operations.

Although this CEO did not favor splitting the dual role of CEO/board chair, this CEO had accepted the challenge of making such a split work for "a while" based on a board recommendation. In some situations, this CEO believed, separating the two roles is appropriate. Another, less attractive, option is designating a lead director, which also can be quite effective in certain situations at certain times.

This CEO believed that board size is important, Keeping a board small, with 12 to 14 directors, can help make the board more effective. The board, this CEO said, should be like a group of "your most trusted critical friends." Directors "should care enough about what you are doing to ask you tough questions and to tell you things that help you improve even when you do not want to hear them."

This CEO recommended board evaluation programs, which, if managed effectively, should obviate the need for director term and age limits because an evaluation program allows a board to adjust its membership based on contribution rather than on age or tenure. Directors, this CEO thought, should stay on the board as long as they add real value.

The retired CEO of a pharmaceutical company. A retired CEO and board chair of a second major pharmaceutical company thought institutional investors had little impact on board activities. From a distance, this CEO thought, institutional investor activism seemed more ceremonial than substantive and might have done more harm than good.

After giving considerable thought to the issue of separating the dual CEO/board chair position, this retired CEO had concluded that separating the two roles has no real value except possibly for a company in a transitional period. In that situation, the two roles should be specifically defined, with clear distinctions, to prevent the company from spending too much time and energy communicating what is going on. The CEO should concentrate on managing the business, not on managing the board. If the two roles need to be split, the board should ask: Do we have the right CEO?

This retired CEO was strongly committed to boardroom diversity in all its manifestations, including racial, gender, professional, global, technical, and consumer diversity. Having a non-American director who is not based in the U.S. would be advantageous to the board, this retired CEO thought, because the greater the diversity, the greater the opportunity for creative solutions to business problems. However, any non-American director must be fully qualified to offer the value expected by shareholders.

This respondent did not favor either age or term limits for directors because "you could lose great people for the wrong reasons." However, boards do need some benchmarks for assessing directors' on-going contributions, including benchmarks that address alertness, involvement, and currency of knowledge. If forced to decide between age and term limits, this retired CEO would choose age limits because assessing director's contributions and managing those assessments might be difficult. Retiring CEOs should retire from their own boards, this respondent thought, but they should not be required to resign from other boards if they can continue to contribute. Because retirement frees up much of a person's time and energy, a director's value might actually increase upon his or her retirement.

The CEO of a medium size *manufacturing company.* The CEO and board chair of a medium size manufacturing company believed institutional investor activism did change the behavioral patterns of boards. Although boards had been behaving responsibly and therefore did not need guidance from institutional investors, this CEO thought, pressure from institutional investors caused boards to somewhat modify their practices and to be more engaged in discussions of boardroom reform and corporate strategy.

Like several other CEOs interviewed in this study, this CEO reported having held both the dual CEO/chair position as well as the separated CEO role. Separating the two roles, this CEO thought, usually creates more disruption than added value because the CEO ends up concentrating too much time on board issues and deciding to whom he or she is accountable. Because few companies see value in separating the two roles, the shift away from the dual CEO/chair position has reversed.

Also like several other interviewees in this study, this CEO saw a significant link between executive compensation and shareholder interests. Pay for performance, this CEO reported, is a commonly accepted practice in industry, and boards are linking executive compensation more tightly to share price than to management objectives. With regard to strategic plans, this respondent held, the board's job is to ensure that the corporation has strategic plans that work and the CEO's job is to develop and execute those plans.

The CEO of a large manufacturing company. The CEO and chair of a very large manufacturing company thought that institutional investment activism mostly impacted the behaviors and practices of corporate boards of poorly performing companies, but that even this impact was not large. This CEO was disappointed that institutional investors recommended board practices for good-performing companies that essentially had been designed for under-performing companies. A positive outcome of institutional activism was increased interest in shareholder value. Another benefit is the current recognition of pay-for-performance as the appropriate driver of executive compensation. However, in the view of this CEO, executive compensation certainly is not perfect. During times of great market performance, executives are well paid, but when the market suffers a down-turn, their bonuses and share payoffs are negatively affected.

This CEO strongly characterized separation of the dual CEO/chair role as absolutely wrong for most enterprises because it creates communication problems between the CEO and board chair. An effective board evaluation process in which director performance is reviewed makes role separation an unnecessary issue. Moreover, if all of the board's members take on special assignments when required, a lead director also is unnecessary. The key to getting something done in the boardroom is to find the right director for a desired project and to ask that director to take the lead and report his or her actions back to the board. Independent directors, this CEO recommended, should schedule appropriate meeting times, as they deem necessary, to discuss pertinent issues outside the presence of the CEO/chair.

Each board, this CEO said, should develop a plan to compose board membership to reflect the realities of the company's marketplace, representative communities, and employee population mix. Although boards generally have become more diverse, they must aggressively improve their diversity without compromising their director qualification goals, which however, should not be so strict that diversity becomes unachievable. For example, a board requiring that all directors be current CEOs will probably not find a large enough pool of African American, Hispanic, or women candidates.

A corporate governance attorney. An internationally prominent corporate governance activist and partner of a major New York law firm was absolutely convinced that institutional investors significantly impacted the behaviors and practices of corporate boards, resulting in increased shareholder value.

In today's compensation plans, this activist stated, a theoretical connection exists between pay and performance, but during bull runs in the stock market, it is difficult to distinguish real performers from those who are merely riding on the market's good fortune. Many things happening in the market have no connection with the individual performances of CEOs. Share prices have nothing to do with performance and, when the market turns south, price/performance theory fails to match actual performance. This activist recommended that boards tie executive compensation directly to "increased" economic value added (EVA), even though this value is complex and therefore difficult to measure and track, based on the concept that good performance maximizes the return on the total invested capital. Generally, positive EVA is generated when the corporation makes enough income to cover the cost of the capital needed to operate the business.

Another effective method for linking pay to performance, according to this activist, is peer ranking, in which a corporation benchmarks its performance to the rest of its industry in such areas as revenue growth, operating margins, expense management, etc.

A former CEO of a Fortune 15 company. The former CEO/chair of a U.S. Fortune 15 company and board chair of a small manufacturing company believed that institutional investors have had some effect on the changes taking place in the boardroom, but that their impact has not been nearly as significant as institutional investors have suggested. Institutional investors, this director believed, lack the element of credibility because the investment money at risk generally is not their own. This former CEO, having witnessed profound corporate governance changes since the mid-1970s, believed that these changes were driven by business leaders and have been for the good. Organizations such as the Business Roundtable and the U.S. Securities and Exchange Commission, this director thought, led the way for corporations to substantially improve the way they operate.

According to this director, since the mid-1970s, executive pay is more tightly linked to shareholder value but not necessarily linked to individual performance. A director's most difficult assignment is the corporate compensation committee. Historically, compensation committees have not done their jobs well, although they are rapidly improving. Although most boards do a fine job of managing the executive compensation process, too many boards don't manage this process appropriately. This former CEO saw a conflict of interest between CEOs and the consultants they hire to provide comparative market data for establishing senior executive compensation. "It is amazing," this director exclaimed, "that the system works as well as it does."

Concerning board diversity, this director suggested that boards that don't reflect the communities that their companies represent and operate in might be out of touch with their own businesses. However, boards should require all directors to meet the minimum desired director qualifications.

Analysis of Interview Results

Michael Novak of the American Enterprise Institute warned that those who clamor for a "stakeholder" society, in which citizens make claims of entitlement against the corporation, threaten to dampen ambition, imagination, and personal independence.[iii] Business leaders, Novak observed, "underestimate the size, intensity, intelligence, and commitment of the forces determined to undermine corporate independence." The CEOs interviewed in our study generally agreed that institutional investors have not significantly impacted the behaviors or performances of boards. Of the three non-CEOs we interviewed, one believed that the impact of institutional investors has been minimal; one believed that the impact was profound, but extremely slow to take effect, and one believed that institutional investors drove major change in the practices of corporate boards.

Most of the group believed that supervising the CEO by separating the dual role of CEO/chair is unnecessary, and most very strongly opposed separating the dual role because they thought it would make corporations less effective. A minority of the group voiced moderate support for separating the two positions.

According to our interviewees, diversity in the corporate boardroom is growing, albeit at a slow rate, and greater representation of women and minorities on boards is important. The primary focus of board diversity, in the view of our study's respondents, should be to link the board with the constituencies served by the company. With two exceptions, they showed very little passion for pursuing diversity to achieve a desired state as opposed to improving the makeup of a board. Only one respondent passionately expressed the need for more diversity in corporate boards for both social and business reasons.

All of our study's respondents recognized the importance of corporation participation in the global market, but none of them strongly supported a major effort to add foreign directors to corporate boards. Most believed that corporations could gain the needed global perspectives through some other means, and most seemed quite comfortable gaining international insight and perspective from directors who operate on a global scale in their own companies and who have lived and worked in foreign countries.

Perceived Impact of Institutional Investors

Not surprisingly, the CEOs we interviewed did not believe that institutional investors substantially impacted board activities. Nor did a prominent journalist. A global executive recruiter credited institutional investors with precipitating profound change in corporate governance, but also credited the business press and, especially, a new breed of CEOs with great respect for the potential contributions of director talent and intelligence. Of all our interviewees, only an internationally acclaimed corporate governance attorney placed responsibility for improved corporate governance directly on institutional investor activism.

These findings lead to the observation that practicing directors generally believed that, pre-Sarbanes-Oxley, they drove corporate governance trends and changes in board behaviors. Their discussions of board practices with respect to board size, director age, and term limits for directors indicated that directors did not consider these board practices to have been influenced by institutional investors, the media, or shareholders. CEOs regarded corporate governance changes as opportunities for boards to improve their efficiency and effectiveness.

These beliefs notwithstanding, the significant increase in shareholder activism since the mid-1970s obviously heightened corporate boards' awareness of corporate governance. The changes in corporate governance since the mid-1970s are too significant to have been driven only by internal forces. However, institutional investors were not necessarily the only external drivers of change. The globalization of business enterprises (resulting from expanding new technologies) and governmental policy changes playing out on the world stage also might have been driving corporate governance reform, along with other powerful forces. In general, people are not likely to change unless the pain of not changing becomes greater than the pain of changing. That makes survival a great motivation for change. The passage of the Sarbanes-Oxley Act of 2002 supported the notion that human beings are more driven by fear than opportunity, and whatever successes SOX has achieved suggest that corporate directors changed board behaviors because they feared the results of not changing them.

In the final chapter of this book, I summarize the experiences of U.S. corporate boards over the last 3 decades, discuss the corporate-governance scenarios likely to occur in the wake of Sarbanes-Oxley, and discuss how directors can best come to terms with them.

Notes

[i] Brancato, C. K. (1997). *Institutional investors and corporate governance: Best practices for increasing corporate value.* Chicago: Irwin Professional.

[ii] Ibid.

[iii] Novak, M. (1996). *The future of the corporation. Washington, DC: AEI Press.*

Chapter 14

Corporate Governance:
A Work in Progress

Principled leadership requires continued action beyond obligation.

The last quarter of the 20th century witnessed the emergence of a global economy and an international movement toward free trade. From the mid-1970s through the year 2000, robust change in the high-technology industries fueled enormous global economic growth, and sharply increased competition from Japanese, German, and U.K. corporations ended the United States' post-war dominance of the global economy. By the dawn of the new millennium, the Industrial Age had evolved into the new Information Age. Today, the major force of competition comes from China and India.

For most corporations and their long-term shareholders, the 20th century ended on a high note. The final years of the millennium had witnessed phenomenal growth in corporate market capitalization of both large and small companies, as well as extreme increases in personal wealth for many corporate leaders. In general, at least on the

233

charts, everything seemed to be moving in a great direction—up and to the right.

However, this colossal corporate success and exuberance might have been at the root of many of the substantial corporate failures in the first decade of the 21st century. Most corporate stakeholders were totally oblivious to subtle cracks in the foundations of major corporations driving much of the excitement. To some extent, continued pursuit of exaggerated growth trends contributed to the demise of these major corporations, precipitating, perhaps inevitably, a renewal and transformation of corporate governance around the globe.

During these exhilarating and frightening years, the role of the U.S. corporate board substantially changed. Intense global competition forced U.S. corporations to act more nimbly and to take more calculated risks. As corporate boards evolved, they assumed accountability beyond their traditional duties of overseeing company management and performance and ensuring corporate social responsibility. To take accountability for overall corporate performance, enlightened boards began selecting and supervising CEOs, linking executive compensation plans to company performance, and monitoring corporate strategy development and implementation. Corporate boards became smaller, started including fewer inside directors and more independent outside directors, and recruited a slightly higher percentage of women, minorities, and foreigners. They faced increasing pressure to evaluate new financial opportunities that developed more and more quickly. Regulatory requirements for board committees increased, thereby expanding the importance of those committees. In general, boards became more accountable for creating processes by which to exercise the power granted to them by company shareholders and other stakeholders.

Several of the nation's largest and most successful corporations exemplified the changes occurring in corporate governance. In the 1990s, the boards of IBM, GM, and Campbell Soup became models for many other boards by redefining their roles. By 2000, most boards were dealing with corporate board size and diversity, talent availability, compensation, corporate mission, and market globalization. In the 21st century, the public got an inside look at accounting scandals at Enron, WorldCom, Global Crossing, Tyco and other major corporations that showed the kind of devastation that could ensue when corporate governance fails.

Today, some of the most pressing questions demanding the board's attention concern directors' broader accountability. The Sarbanes-Oxley Act of 2002 helped conservative boards break through well-entrenched traditions by requiring all corporate boards to conform to certain changes in corporate governance. Equally important, many directors expressed willingness to drive significant corporate governance reform using board self-evaluations.

The current generation of more enlightened directors face greater challenges than their predecessors. Their jobs are more difficult, their risks are more substantial, and their critics are more knowledgeable and determined. The broadened focus of the corporate board, however, rewards directors with a much more satisfying set of experiences. For the boards that most effectively execute their responsibilities, opportunities to contribute substantial value to their corporations are increasing. The rewards and recognition for these boards likewise will be plentiful.

The Sarbanes-Oxley Act has a long reach. Increased focus on corporate governance in the United States has significantly impacted corporations around the globe, and foreign companies listed on U.S. stock markets are being required to demonstrate the same internal controls required of American companies. This increased financial transparency will increase costs for these foreign companies but also should provide their American investors with greater confidence.

Corporate governance plays a very serious role in today's competitive environment. Arthur Levitt, 25th Chairman of the United States Securities and Exchange Commission, pointed out that, when our entire corporate system lives up to the highest standard of integrity, it inspires deeper public faith that our marketplace is sound. The task of upholding the integrity of our corporate system begins with the work of directors, Levitt observed, because the task of corporate governance is the director's legal mandate and must become a fundamental part of every director's mission. The responsibilities, characteristics, and behaviors of today's corporate directors should be substantially different than in the past.[i]

The Main Patterns of Potential Reform

In theory, corporate governance exists to protect shareholders by providing for an elected board of directors who are accountable to the shareholders to monitor management activities and decisions. Also in theory, information flows from shareholders to the board to the management team and back again, and should result in plans and decisions that favor the long-term interests of shareholders. However, some corporate governance experts, such as Jonathan Charkham, former member of the Cadbury Committee and former adviser in industry to the governor of the Bank of England, believe that corporate governance, in practice, may fall so dismally short of theory that effective oversight fails to occur and shareholders are disenfranchised.[ii]

No doubt. However, partly as the result of highly publicized failures of corporate governance that caused experts like Charkham to doubt the reliability of corporate governance, things have changed in the boardrooms of enlightened corporate directors. CEOs no longer simply fill boardrooms with other CEOs who reciprocally sit on each other's boards and compensation committees. Enlightened directors enthusiastically support their CEOs, but they do not feel beholden to them. They want the CEO to be successful, but they are willing to make changes that they believe are in the best interests of their long-term shareholders.

Today's classic investor is much more than the historical single small shareholder. In the mid-1970s, institutional investors owned about one-fourth of equities; by 2004, they owned 50% of outstanding equities. By 2005, institutional investments accounted for more than 59.2% ($7.974 trillion) of outstanding equities in the U.S., up from 51.8% ($6.4 trillion) in 2004.[iii,iv] Unlike traditional single shareholders, these large institutional investors are exceptionally well positioned and thus able to monitor the performance of companies in their portfolios, as they are obligated to do.

Public pension funds, such as CalPERS, TIAA-CREF, and other very large private, municipal, state, and federal operators are some of the largest investment entities. Just 1% of U.S. pension funds currently is invested in hedge funds.[v] Because pension fund operators are heavily invested with money held for an average of 30 years, they generally hold investments for decades. As a result, they face substantial difficulty in identifying new investment opportunities that represent secure investments, and they carry enormous fiduciary obligations. Rather than sell stocks in poorly performing companies, pension fund operators chose to become activist investors. Their size, knowledge, and power make it possible for them to influence the direction of corporate governance issues. Of late, they have focused their efforts on the corporate board's obligations to monitor management on behalf of shareholders.

In most industries, both the number and the quality of competitors have increased dramatically in the last 2 decades. The end of the Cold War, major technological advances, increasing free trade, greater capital mobility, and a more equally distributed source of qualified talent lessened the effects of geography and national identity as impediments to global commerce. According to U.S. Department of Labor statistics cited by the Heritage Foundation, the U.S. has been losing an average of 7.71 million jobs every quarter for the last decade at least.[vi]

The competitors challenging U.S. corporations are a new breed. To win market share, U.S. corporations must have a mindset for growth, be results-oriented, and maintain an obsession for customer service. They also must develop and implement plans to address the decreasing availability of talented workers by exploiting the advantages of diversity in the workforce. By 2014, white non-Hispanics are expected to account for less of the U.S. workforce, about 65.6% down from 70% in 2004. Blacks share of the workforce is expected to grow a bit from 11.3% to 12%; but Hispanics, whose share of the workforce is growing at a rate of 33.7%, will hold at least a 15% share. Although the total size of the workforce will grow, men's share of it is expected to drop a bit from 53.6% to 53.2% as women's share increases.[vii] By 2034, Asians share of the workforce is expected to expand to 5% of the workforce, up from 4.3% in 2004.

Today's corporations cannot afford to be complacent. They must act with a sense of urgency. The astonishingly rapid pace of change of today's economic world is demonstrated by the fact that the life cycles of many high-technology products are as short as 6 months. In today's environment, speed is a defining characteristic of winners.

The Future of Corporate Governance Research

Corporate governance has the potential to become one of the most interesting research topics of the 21st century. Tremendous opportunity exists for corporate directors, CEOs, and scholars to add value to the domain of corporate governance by sharing their perspectives more openly. Because the number of investors in the stock market is growing through increasing use of mutual and pension funds, more and more people of average income will find themselves engaging in discussions about share values, executive pay, and succession planning. As commerce continues to globalize, average consumers will become more sophisticated in their investment selections. To maximize their investments, these consumers can be expected to look to corporate boards and CEOs to create outstanding corporate performance.

Firsthand Observation of Corporate Governance

Scholar L. G. Thurman argued that the ideal way to study directors and their processes is not by studying publicly available data but by getting behind boardroom doors to observe corporate governance firsthand. Corporate governance researchers, Thurman argued, should step beyond the academic purview and observe corporate governance as it is conducted by hands-on business professionals, the very people who have real-world insight and are most able to develop methodologies and instruments to investigate corporate governance. Directors, Thurman concluded, are "unquestionably one of our nation's most valuable resources." "Corporate America, and therefore all of America," Thurman stated, "needs them to be performing at their best."[viii]

When my team at XCEO, Inc. followed through on some of Thurman's research recommendations, we found, as we expected, that most published corporate governance studies were performed at a considerable distance from real-world corporate governance. Only very limited inside experiences were used to validate the accuracy of most researchers' views of the workings of board operations. As a result, much of the available literature was heavily slanted toward the perspectives of either academics or institutional shareholders. The perceived ideals of corporate board operations contrasted sharply with reality.

Our findings do not constitute a criticism of the authors of the literature but merely reflect fact. Historically, the authors sufficiently concerned about corporate governance to investigate and report on it were not practicing experts on their issues of concern. However, the intense outside focus placed on corporate governance issues has motivated corporate governance practitioners from inside the boardrooms of Corporate America to add to the literature being developed by scholars.

Likely Future Scenarios in Corporate Governance

On the surface, much progress seems to have been made in improving the quality and effectiveness of corporate governance. Yet, much work needs to be done. Consider the following questions. Has the Sarbanes-Oxley Act constructed a sufficiently strong foundation to keep Corporate America steady in its pursuit of shareholder value? What additional leverage is needed to keep corporations from settling in at a new level of status quo? Will the increased burden of bureaucracy imposed by Sarbanes-Oxley encourage directors and senior management teams to retreat into a traditional zone of comfort? Obviously, the answers depend on many factors.

Certainly, numerous developments in corporate governance are possible. However, at XCEO, Inc., we foresee three credible scenarios, one of which is likely to occur.

Scenario A: SOX is helpful, but insufficient. In the first scenario, the stakeholder community continues to leverage their newfound strength by intensifying their focus on such issues as executive compensation and majority voting provisions for election of directors. Shareholders and other stakeholders consider SOX to be helpful; however, they think it insufficiently addresses other major stakeholder issues. Traditional boards continue to focus more sharply on compliance than on opportunity, but highly enlightened boards strengthen their efforts to distinguish their companies by leveraging good corporate governance and partnering with the CEO to accelerate the pace toward long-term shareholder value.

Scenario B: SOX becomes well entrenched. In the second scenario, SOX becomes well entrenched and is deemed exceptionally effective. Shareholders benefit from the rise in corporate earnings, due in part to restored confidence in the capital markets. Traditional boards breathe a sigh of relief and maintain a steady-as-we-go attitude. Conversely, as in the first scenario, highly enlightened boards strengthen their efforts to distinguish their companies by leveraging good corporate governance and partnering with the CEO to accelerate their pace toward long-term shareholder value.

Scenario C: SOX fails. In the third scenario, Corporate America is besieged by another set of major corporate meltdowns. Shareholders lose confidence in SOX and look for increased regulation to restore their confidence; all other major stakeholders rally to put more pressure on boards to change, causing traditional boards to recognize the need to take their corporate governance activities to another level. Traditional boards begin to value good corporate governance as a strategic imperative and long-term competitive advantage. Highly enlightened boards, as in the first two scenarios, strengthen their efforts to distinguish their companies by leveraging good corporate governance and partnering with the CEO to accelerate their pace toward long-term shareholder value.

In any scenario, leveraging good corporate governance is the key to building long-term shareholder value and earning broad-based stakeholder appreciation. An enlightened board makes a big difference in the performance of any corporation by consistently seeking regulatory compliance and the highest levels of corporate success over the long term.

The Realities of Enlightened Corporate Governance

Enlightened corporate governance is all about the pursuit of what is possible versus what is required. Good corporate governance should mean more than merely meeting the requirements of the job. Corporate boards and individual directors who merely maintain regulatory compliance are likely to satisfy the interests of short-term stakeholders and minimize their risks of corporate failure, but they also minimize the possibility of substantial long-term shareholder gain.

When corporate governance is enlightened, regulatory compliance becomes part of a pursuit of increasing value for long-term shareholders. Enlightened corporate boards and directors have strong convictions about their responsibilities and want to do more than what is required; they want to do what is possible to increase the value of the corporation. They are sincere in their work, and they are passionate about their responsibilities. They maintain the highest moral, ethical, and legal standards and exude confidence in their company. They strive to be, and expect to be, the benchmark for other companies. Enlightened boards and directors very much value as privileges the freedom and rights they have been granted to serve their shareholders.

An enlightened board is the direct result of the efforts of individual directors who work as a team toward a common set of objectives. In such a team, individuals have unique roles. Teamwork within the board does not mean that directors all agree on every issue or that they all must demonstrate their independence by having different views on every issue. In this case, teamwork means having a commitment to the success of the company.

A Look Forward

Looking forward, all stakeholders need to remain focused on corporate governance to make sure we hold the gains that have been achieved. Corporate boards must accelerate their pace toward excellent performance. Equally important, we must work to ensure that we do not become inundated by superfluous rules and regulations that make us feel better without adding value to the companies on which we depend.

A 2006 survey of more than 1,200 directors of Fortune 1000 companies revealed that the Sarbanes-Oxley Act has been more of an impediment than an aid to good corporate governance. Almost 60% of these directors strongly believed that SOX should be repealed or overhauled. Despite SOX's detailed focus on director independence, the representation of inside directors on boards has not changed in more than a decade, with inside directors holding an average of 2 board seats. Moreover, for the first time since 1990, seats held by outside directors actually decreased, with the average number per board declining from nine to eight.[ix] Nearly 75% of these Fortune 1000 directors reported that SOX made them more cautious directors, not better directors.

Enlightened corporate governance truly is a work in progress, affected by new pronouncements from around the globe. For example, 2005 legislation enacted in Norway will require large, publicly traded private companies to fill 40% of their board seats with women by 2008, a follow-up on previous legislation that already requires Norway's state-owned companies to do the same.[x,xi] Similar legislation in Sweden requires 25% of director seats be filled by women.[xii] Enlightened boards want to lead their corporations and serve their shareowners with conviction. They do not want or need to be led by pure government regulation.

Corporate Governance will be a topic of major concern for an extended period of time. In fact, at XCEO, Inc., we project that it will be embedded into the fabric of all walks of life. Directors are facing exciting opportunities to seize the lead towards instilling enlightenment into corporate life.

Notes

[i] Levitt, A. (1998). Corporate governance: Integrity in the information age. Remarks presented at Tulane University, New Orleans, Louisiana, March 12, 1998). Retrieved May 30, 2006, from http://www.sec.gov/news/speech/speecharchive/1998/spch206.txt.

[ii] Charkham, J. (1994). *Keeping good company: A study of corporate governance in five countries*, pp. 215-225. New York: Oxford University Press.

[iii] The Conference Board. (2005, October 10). U.S. institutional investors boost control of U.S. equity market assets. *News*. Retrieved July 31, 2006, from http://www.conference-board.org/utilities/pressPrinterFriendly.cfm?press_ID=2726.

[iv] Bivens, L. J., & Weller, C. E. (2004, September). Institutional shareholder concentration, corporate governance changes, and diverging fortunes of capital and labor. Paper presented at the conference, Pension Fund Capitalism and the Crisis of Old-Age Security in the United States, Center for Economic Policy Analysis (CEPA), New School University, New York.

[v] U.S. Securities and Exchange Commission. (2004, December 7). Registration under the Advisers Act of certain hedge fund advisers. [Release No. IA-2333; File No. S7-30-04]. (RIN 3235-AJ25). Washington, DC: Author. Retrieved July 31, 2006, from http://www.sec.gov/rules/final/ia-2333.htm.

[vi] Kane, T., Schaefer, B., & Fraser, A. A. (2004, May 13). Myths and realities: The false crisis of outsourcing. Backgrounder 1757. The *Heritage Foundation: Research: Economy.* Retrieved July 31, 2006, from http://www.heritage.org/Research/Economy/bg1757.cfm#_ftnref9.

[vii] U.S. Department of Labor, Bureau of Labor Statistics. (2003). *Occupational outlook handbook: Tomorrow's jobs.* Retrieved July 6, 2006, from http://www.bis.gov/oco/oco2003.htm.

[viii] Thurman, L. G. (1990). The board of directors: An exploratory study of the corporate governance process behind boardroom doors, p. 173. Unpublished doctoral dissertation, United States International University, San Diego, CA.

[ix] Korn/Ferry International. (2006). *Korn/Ferry 32nd annual board of directors study: Celebrating three decades of governance analysis.* Retrieved July 31, 2006, from http://www.kornferry.com/Library/Process. asp?P=Pubs_Detail&CID=1510&LID=1.

[x] Flynn, P. M., & Adams, S. M. (2004, September/October). Women on board. *BizEd Magazine, 34-39.* Retrieved July 31, 2006, from http://72.14.209.104/search?q=cache:8v-SKtQsZ4kJ:www.aacsb.edu/publications/archives/SepOct04/p34-39.pdf+legislation,+Sweden,+corporate+boards,+women,+directors&hl=en&gl=us&ct=clnk&cd=3&client=safari.

[xi] Dvorak, P. (2006, March 30). Breaking into the boardroom: Women gain seats as directors. CareerJournal.com. Retrieved July 31, 2006, from http://www.careerjournal.com/columnists/theorypractice/20060330-theorypractice.html.

[xii] Cross Border. (2006, July 19). Investors say no to legislation on female board membership. *IR Magazine.* Retrieved July 31, 2006, from http://www.thecrossbordergroup.com/DesktopModules/Lab_Issues/PressReleaseView.aspx?ItemID=19628.

Bibliography

Ackman, D. (2004, May 25). Spitzer vs. Grasso—For love or money. *Forbes.com*. Retrieved August 4, 2006, from www.forbes.com/

Ackman, D. (2004, September 8). Judge throws the book at Quattrone. *Forbes.com*. Retrieved May 27, 2006, from http://www.forbes.com/

Allen, W. T. (1992, November). Defining the role of outside directors in an age of global competition. *Director's Monthly, 16*(11), 1.

Allen, W. T. (1999, January). Free markets focus on corporate governance. *Directorship, 25*(1), 10.

Alliance for Nonprofit Management. (n.d.). What is strategic planning? Overview. Retrieved August 7, 2006, from http://www.allianceonline.org/FAQ/strategic_planning/what_is_strategic_planning.faq.

American Bar Association, Section of Business Law. (1994). *Corporate directors guide* (2nd ed.). Chicago: Author.

Ames, B. C. (1996). Leadership requires making this the priority. *Directors & Boards, 21*(1), 48-50.

Andrews, K. R. (1980). Directors' responsibility for corporate strategy. *Harvard Business Review, 58*(6), 30-42.

Annual Executive Pay Survey. (1995, April 15). *Business Week,* 37-57.

Annual Executive Pay Survey. (1996, April 14). *Business Week,* 23-36.

Annual Executive Pay Survey. (1997, April 21). *Business Week,* 32-42.

Annual Executive Pay Survey. (1998, April 20). *Business Week,* 62-70.

Armour, S. (2006, January 26). Enron woes reverberate through lives: Many saw retirement plans evaporate with stock price. *USA Today*, pp. 1B-2B.

245

Atkins, P. S. (2006). *Remarks before the Securities Regulation Institute.* Speech by the Securities and Exchange Commissioner, San Diego, California, January 19, 2006. Retrieved July 5, 2006, from http://www.sec.gov/news/speech/spch011906psa.htm.

Bacon, J. (1981). *Corporate directorship practices: The nominating committee and the director selection process.* New York: The Conference Board.

Bacon, J., & Brown, J. K. (1975). *Corporate directorship practices.* New York: The Conference Board.

Baker, N. C. (1993, March). E-managers feel eyes of the board upon them. *Environment Today, 4*(3), 1, 22.

Balkcom, J. E. (1994). The new board: Redrawing the lines. *Directors & Boards, 18*(3). 25-27.

Ball, D. G. (1994). Revolution in the board room. *St. John's Law Review, 247,* 22.

Barkema, H. G., Gomez-Mejia, L. (1998, April). Managerial compensation and firm performance: A general research framework. *Academy of Management Journal 41*(2), 135-145.

Bassett, L. C. (1998). Putting board evaluation to work. *The Corporate Board, 19*(109), 20.

Beam v. Stewart, Del., No. 501. [2003. 3/31/04].

Bearle, A. A., Jr., & Means, G. C. (1932). *The modern corporation and private property.* New York: Macmillan.

Beavers, J. T. (2003, October) Are boards control-literate? *Internal Auditor.* Retrieved May 27, 2006, from *LookSmart,* http://www. findarticles.com/

Bhagat, S., Black, B. S., & Blair, M. (2004). Relational investing and firm performance. *Journal of Financial Research, 27,* 1-30.

Big labor goes to bat in boardrooms. (2004, April 15). *BusinessWeekonline.* Retrieved May 17, 2006, from www.businessweek.com/

Bird, S. W. (1999, January). Marketplace revolution calls for entrepreneurs on boards. *Directorship, 25*(1), 1.

Bivens, L. J., & Weller, C. E. (2004, September). Institutional shareholder concentration, corporate governance changes, and diverging fortunes of capital and labor. Paper presented at the conference, Pension Fund Capitalism and the Crisis of Old-Age Security in the United States, Center for Economic Policy Analysis (CEPA), New School University, New York.

Black, B. S. (1998, March-April). Does shareholder activism improve company performance? *The Corporate Board, 19*(109), 1.

Blair, A. (1998, February 27). More bonuses and a model for the future. *Investors Chronicle, 123*(1567), 24.

Blair, M. M. (1994, Winter). CEO pay: Why it has become so controversial. *Brookings Review 12,* 22-27.

Blair, M. M. (1995). *Ownership and control: Rethinking corporate governance for the twenty-first century.* Washington, DC: The Brookings Institution.

Blair, M. M., & Uppal, G. (1993). *The deal decade handbook.* Washington, DC: The Brookings Institution.

Bommer, W. H., & Ellstrand, A. E. (1996). CEO successor choice: Its antecedents and influence on subsequent firm performance. *Group & Organization Management, 21*(1), 105-123.

Borokhovich, K. A., Parrino, R., & Trapani, T. (1996). Outside directors and CEO selection. *Journal of Financial and Quantitative Analysis, 31,* 377-397.

Boros, E. (1995). *Minority shareholders' remedies.* New York: Oxford University Press.

Bowen, W. G. (1994). *Inside the boardroom: Governance by directors and trustees.* New York: John Wiley.

Bradner, J. H. (1995). *The board members' guide: A beneficiary bestiary.* Winnetka, IL: Conversation Press.

Brancato, C. K. (1997). *Institutional investors and corporate governance: Best practices for increasing corporate value.* Chicago: Irwin Professional.

Brodern, P. (1985). *Outrageous misconduct: The asbestos industry on trial.* New York: Pantheon.

Brown, L. D., & Caylor, M. L. (2004). Corporate governance and firm performance. *Social Science Research Network.* Retrieved June 3, 2006, from http://papers.ssrn.com/sol3/papers.cfm?abstract_id=586423.

Brown, R. D. (1994). Corporate governance: The director as watchdog, juggler or fall guy. *Canadian Business Review, 21*(1), 39-41.

Bruce, H. J. (1997). Duty, honor, company. *Directors & Boards, 21*(2), 12-16.

Bryant, A. (1998, January 5). How the mighty have fallen and sometimes profited anyway. *New York Times,* p. D4.

Bureau of Labor Statistics. (2006). U.S. Department of Labor. http://www.bls.gov.

Burnett-Hall, R. (1994, March). Directors' liabilities: The environmental element. *Accountancy, 113*(1207), 130-131.

Burrough, B., & Helyar, J. (1990). *Barbarians at the gate.* New York: Harper & Row.

Byrne, J. A. (1994, April 25). That eye-popping executive pay: Is anybody worth this much? *Business Week, 3368,* 52.

Byrne, J. A. (1996, April 22). How high can CEO pay go? *Business Week,* 3472.

Byrne, J. A. (1996, November 25). The best and worst of boards. *Business Week.* Retrieved July 10, 2006, from http://www.businessweek.com/1996/48/b35031.htm.

Byrne, J. (1997, December 8). Directors in the hot seat: Activists are singling out individual board members who don't measure up. *Business Week,* 100.

Byrne, J. (1997, December 8). The best and worst boards: Our special report on corporate governance. *Business Week,* 90.

Byrnes, N., Henry, D., Thornton, E., & Dwyer, P. (2003, September 22). Reform: Who's making the grade. *Business Week Online.* Retrieved August 2, 2006, from http://www.businessweek.com/

Cadbury, A. (1990). *The Company Chairman.* Cambridge, England: FitzWilliam.

Cadbury, A. (1997, November-December). Summing up the governance reports. *The Corporate Board, 18*(107), 6. (Infotrac Article No. A20163324).

Cadbury Committee. (1992). *Cadbury Committee report: Financial aspects of corporate governance.* Basingstoke, England: Burgess Science.

Cannella, B., & Lubatkin, M. (1993). Succession as a sociopolitical process: Internal impediments to outsider selection. *Academy of Management Journal, 36*(4), 763-793.

Caremark International Inc. (1997, December). Securities class action alert. *Investors Research Bureau, 12*(12), 48.

Carr, E. H. (1967). *What is history?* New York: Random.

Carson, T. L. (2003). Self–interest and business ethics: Some lessons of the recent corporate scandals. *Journal of Business Ethics, 43*(4), 389-394.

Carver, J. (1996). *Three steps to fiduciary responsibility.* San Francisco: Jossey-Bass.

Carver, J. (1997). *Boards that make a difference: A new design for leadership in nonprofit and public organizations* (2nd ed.). San Francisco: Jossey-Bass.

Carver, J. (1997). *The chairperson's role as servant-leader to the board.* San Francisco: Jossey-Bass.

Carver, J., & Carver, M. M. (1996). *Basic principles of policy governance.* San Francisco: Jossey-Bass.

Carver, J., & Carver, M, M. (1996). *Your roles and responsibilities as a board member.* San Francisco: Jossey-Bass.

Carver, J., & Carver M. M. (1997). *Making diversity meaningful in the boardroom.* San Francisco: Jossey-Bass.

Carson, T. L. (2003). Self–Interest and Business Ethics: Some Lessons of the Recent Corporate Scandals. *Journal of Business Ethics, 43*(4), 389-394.

Cassis, Y. (1997). *Big business: The European experience in the twentieth century.* Oxford, England: Oxford University Press.

Catalyst. (2006). 2005 Catalyst census of women board directors of the Fortune 500: Ten years later. Author. Catalyst Publication Code D43. Retrieved July 21, 2006, from http://www.catalystwomen.org/files/full/2005%20WBD.pdf.

Catalyst. (2006, March 29). Catalyst census of women board directors of the Fortune 500. [Press release]. Author. Retrieved July 21, 2006, from http://www.catalystwomen. org/ pressroom/press_releases/3_29_06%20%20WBD%20release.pdf.

Censoplano & Zuppone, 2003.

Charan, R. (1991, September-October). How networks reshape organizations—For results. *Harvard Business Review, 91503*, 104.

Charan, R. (1998). *Boards at work: How corporate boards create competitive advantage.* San Francisco: Jossey-Bass.

Charan, R., & Useem, F. (2002). Why companies fail. *Fortune, 145*(11), 50-62.

Charkham, J. (1994). *Keeping good company: A study of corporate governance in five countries.* New York: Oxford University Press.

Chenok, Philip B. (1996, November). What's new with financial reporting. *Directorship, 23*(10), 12.

Chew, D. H. (Ed.). (1997). *Studies in international corporate finance and governance systems: A comparison of the U.S., Japan & Europe.* New York: Oxford University Press.

Citigroup, Inc. (2000, April 20). Citigroup successfully completes subsequent merger for Travelers Property Casualty Corp. *Citigroup Press Room.* Retrieved August 1, 2006, from http://citigroup.com/

Citizen Works. (2006, January 3). Report finds plenty of room for improvement in corporate governance. *The Corporate Reform Weekly, (5)*1, p. 2.

Clurman, R. M. (1993). *Who's in charge?* New York: Whittle.

Coardiz, D. (1993). Corporate hangmen. *Financial World, 162,* 24-28.

Coffee, J. (1981). No soul to damn, no body to kick: An un-scandalized inquiry into the problem of corporate punishment. *Michigan Law Review, 79,* 386.

Conference Board. (1999). *Board diversity in U.S. corporations.* New York: Author. (1230-99-RR).

Conference Board. (2005, October 10). U.S. institutional investors boost control of U.S. equity market assets. *The Conference Board: News.* Retrieved August 2, 2006, from http://www.conference-board.org/

Conger, J., Finegold, D., & Lawler, E., III. (1998). Appraising boardroom performance. *Harvard Business Review, 98102,* 136-140.

Connolly, J. (2005, September-October). Why some board members are paid more than others. *Corporate Board Member Magazine.* Retrieved August 3, 2006, from http://www. boardmember.com/

Convergent stakeholder theory. *Academy of Management Review, 24*(2) 206-221.

Corcoran, E. (1998, April 18). Netscape's CEO takes heat, not cash. *Washington Post*, p. D1.

Core, J. E., Holthausen, R. W., & Larcker, D. F. (1999). Corporate governance, chief executive compensation, and firm performance. *Journal of Financial Economics, 51,* 371-406.

Corporate governance: The view from the boardroom. (2004). *McKinsey Quarterly,* 2004. Available from McKinsey & Company, http://www.mckinsey.com/governance/

Coulson-Thomas, C. (1993). *Creating excellence in the boardroom: A guide to shaping directorial competence and board effectiveness.* New York: McGraw-Hill.

County Information Project. (n.d.). Houston county profile. Texas Association of Counties. Retrieved August 17, 2006, from http://www.txcip.org/tac/census/profile. php?FIPS=48225.

Cowan, A. (1993, June 12). Board room back scratching? *New York Times*, p. D1.

Crawford, C. J. (1999). *The reform of corporate governance: Major trends in the U.S. corporate board room.* Ann Arbor, MI: UMI.

Crawford, C. J. (2005). *Corporate rise: The x principles of extreme personal leadership.* Santa Clara, CA: XCEO, Inc.

Crawford, K. (2005, March 15). Ex-WorldCom CEO Ebbers guilty. *CNNMoney.com.* Retrieved May 17, 2006, from http://money.cnn.com/2005/03/15/news/newsmakers/ ebbers/index.htm.

Crawford, K. (2005, June 6). Lea Fastow ends prison term. *CNNMoney.com*. Retrieved May 26, 2006, from http://money.

Cross Border. (2006, July 19). Investors say no to legislation on female board membership. *IR Magazine*. Retrieved July 31, 2006, from http://www.thecrossbordergroup.com/DesktopModules/Lab_Issues/PressReleaseView.aspx?ItemID=19628.

Crystal, G. (1995). Nowhere to go but down. *Financial Executive, 11*:64.

Crystal, G. (2004, April 28). Cendent's 'new' Henry Silverman cuts pay twice. *Bloomberg.com*. Retrieved July 12, 2006, from http://quote.bloomberg.com/

Crystal, G. S. (1991, October 29). The compensation 500. *Financial World, 145,* 34-42.

Cunningham, L. A. (1998, July-August). Warren Buffet on the role of the board. *The Corporate Board, 19*(111), 6-10.

Daily, C. (1995). The relationship between board composition and leadership structure and bankruptcy reorganization outcomes. *Journal of Management, 21*(6), 1041. (Infotrac Article No. A17792501).

Daily, C. M., & Dalton, D. R. (1998). Does board composition affect corporate performance? No! *Directorship, 24*(7), 7-9.

Dalton, D., Daily, C., Ellstrand, A., & Johnson, J. (1998). Meta-analytic reviews of board composition, leadership structure, and financial performance. *Strategic Management Journal, 19,* 269-90.

Dalton, D. R., Todor, W. D., Spendolini, M. J., Fielding, G. J., & Porter, L. W. (1980). Organization structure and performance: A critical review. *Academy of Management Review, 5,* 49-64.

Darrow, B. (1995, April 24). A view from the biggest software maker. *Computer Reseller News*, p. 110.

Dash, E., & Labaton, S. (2006, May 23). A Fannie Mae settlement is reported. *New York Times*. Retrieved May 24, 2006, from http://www.nytimes.com/

Daum, J. H., Neff, T, & Norris, J. C. (2006). *Spencer Stuart 2006 board diversity report.* Retrieved July 21, 2006, from http://www.spencerstuart.com/research/articles/955/

David Hume Institute. (1995). *Corporate governance. Hume Papers on Public Policy, 3*(4). Edinburgh, Scotland: Edinburgh University Press.

David, P., Kochhar, R., & Levitas, E. (1998). The effect of institutional investors on the level and mix of CEO compensation. *Academy of Management Journal, 41*(2): 200-208.

Davidson, W. N., III, Nemec, C., Worrell, D. L., & Lin, J. (2002). *Journal of Management & Governance, 6*(4), 295-321.

Dawe, B., Hernandez, G. P., & Testaverde, C. J. (1996/1997, December-January). Officers' and directors' liability, Pt. 2. *International Commercial Litigation*, 15, 10-13.

Dayton, K. N. (1984). From the boardroom. Corporate governance: The other side of the coin. *Harvard Business Review, 84104,* 1-5.

deGruyter, W. (1994). *Institutional investors and corporate governance.* Berlin, Germany: WB-Druck Gmbh, Rieden.

Delaware court spurns claims in Stewart case. (2004, May 3). *Corporate Governance Report.*

Demb, A., & Neubauer, F. (1992). *The corporate board: Confronting the paradoxes.* Oxford, England: Oxford University Press.

Deutsch, C. H. (2003, January 26). The revolution that wasn't. *New York Times,* Sec. 3, p. 1.

Deutsch, C. H. (2003, February 23). Revolt of the shareholders: At annual meetings, anger will ratchet up a notch. *New York Times,* Sec. 3, p. 1.

Dimsdale, N., & Prevezer, M. (Eds.). (1994). *Capital markets and corporate governance.* New York: Oxford University Press.

Directors must go the distance. (1997, April). *Australian Accountant, 67*(3), 12.

Directors should be sizable shareholders. (1997, February 22). *Financial Post,* p. 26.

Directorship databank dividends. (1998, April). *Directorship, 24*(4), 13.

Dolan, T. C. (1996, September/October). Observations on governance. *Health-care Executive, 11*(5), 5.

Donaldson, G. (1995). A new tool for boards: The strategic audit. *Harvard Business Review, 73*(4). 99-107.

Dorf, P., & VanDeWalle, K. (2004, March 9). Splitting the roles of CEO and chairman of the board. *Corporate Board Member Magazine.* Retrieved June 2, 2006, from http://www.boardmember.com/network/index.pl?section=1086&article_id=11846&show=article.

Downing, P. (1997). Governing for stakeholders. *The Corporate Board, 18*(107), 13. (Infotrac Article No. A20163325).

Drucker, P. (1981). *Toward the next economics and other essays.* New York: Harper & Row.

DuPont names new biotechnology advisory panel members. (2004, July 19). Retrieved August 4, 2006, from http://www2.DuPont.com/Media_Center/en_US/news_releases/2004/nr07_19_04a.html.

Dvorak, P. (2006, March 30). Breaking into the boardroom: Women gain seats as directors. *CareerJournal.com.* Retrieved July 31, 2006, from http://www. careerjournal.com/columnists/theorypractice/20060330-theorypractice.html.

Eastman, L. J. (1995). *Succession planning: An annotated bibliography and summary of commonly reported organizational practices.* New York: Center for Creative Leadership.

Edison, C. H. (1986). Our past and present: Historical inquiry in education. *Journal of Thought, 21,* 13-27.

Elderson, F. (1997, February). Directors' and officers' liability, Pt. 3. *International Commercial Litigation, 16,* 25-27.

Ellig, B. R., & Minehan, M. (1998). *Future focus on HR in the 21st century.* New York: Society of Human Resources.

Elson, C. M. (1998, November). A director-professor speaks out. *Directorship, 24*(10), 1-16.

Elson, C. M. (1999, January). Does good governance create better corporate performance? *Directorship, 25*(1), 5-6.

Eltman, F. (2006, April 28). Guilty plea marks stunning fall for Kumar. *Examiner.com.* Retrieved May 26, 2006, from http: //www.examiner.com/

Enron fights for life after bid collapse. (2001, November 29). *BBC News.* Retrieved August 17, 2006, from http://news.bbc.co.uk/

Epstein, M. J. (1992). Corporate governance and the shareholders' revolt. *Management Accounting, 74*(2), 32-35.

Ex-WorldCom CFO Scott Sullivan gets 5 years. (2005, August 11). *FoxNews.com.* Retrieved May 17, 2006, from http://www.foxnews.com/

Fama, E. F., & Jensen, M. (1983). Separation of ownership and control. *Journal of Law and Economics 26,* 301-325.

Fan, P. J. (1985). Essays on vertical integration and corporate governance. Unpublished doctoral dissertation, Katz Graduate School of Business, University of Pittsburgh, Pennsylvania.

Fannie Mae agrees to put in new controls: Policies aimed at preventing faulty accounting. (2005, March 9). *Associated Press.* Retrieved June 4, 2006, from http://www.msnbc. msn.com/id/7137248/

Fastow and his wife plead guilty. (2004, January 14). *CNNMoney.com.* Retrieved November 10, 2005, from http://money.cnn.com/

Fein, D. B., & Roer, P. L. (2004). New NYSE and Nasdaq listing standards designed to enhance corporate governance at public companies. *GC New England Magazine* (First Quarter). [Reprint]. Retrieved August 5, 2006, from http://www.wiggin.com/db30/cgi-bin/pubs/New%20NYSE%20david%20patti.pdf.

Fink, J. (2005, June 21). John Rigas sentenced to 15 years in prison. *Buffalo Business First.* Retrieved May 27, 2006, from http://www.bizjournals.com/buffalo/

Fleming, M. J. (1994). Three Essays in corporate governance. Unpublished doctoral dissertation, Harvard University, Boston, Massachusetts.

Fleming, R. W. (1998). Shareholder vs. stakeholder value: A view from Toronto. *Directorship, 24*(8), 1-3.

Flume, R. (1998, February 9). Pension funds led corporate governance revolution; Not just for gadflies anymore, investor activism gets results. *Pensions and Investments, 26*(3), 19.

Flume, R. (1998, February 9). Shareholders keep directors feeling the heat. *Pensions and Investments, 26*(3), 19.

Flynn, J., Peterson, T., Miller, K. L., Echikson, W, & Edmondson, G. (1998, November 30). Boss under fire: European CEOs are scrambling to meet the demands of shareholders. *Business Week,* 52-54.

Flynn, P. M., & Adams, S. M. (2004, September/October). Women on board. *BizEd Magazine,* 34-39. Retrieved July 31, 2006, from http://72.14.209.104/ search?q=cache:8v-SKtQsZ4kJ:www.aacsb.edu/publications/archives/SepOct04/p34-39.pdf+legislation,+Sweden,,+corporate+boards,+women,+directors&hl=en&gl=us& ct=clnk&cd=3&client=safari.

Freeman, R. E. (1999). Divergent stakeholder theory. *Academy of Management Review, 24*(2), 233-236.

Freidheim, C. F. (1996). New world order in the boardroom. *Directors & Boards, 20*(4), 6-12.

Friedman, M. (1970, September 13). The social responsibility of business is to increase its profits. *New York Times Magazine.*

Friedman, S.D., & Singh, H. (1989). CEO succession and stockholder reaction: The influence of organizational context and event analysis. *Academy of Management Journal, 32,* 718-744.

Fukoa, M. (1995). *Financial integration, corporate governance, and the performance of multinational companies.* Washington, DC: The Brookings Institution.

Gall, M. D, Borg, W. R., & Gall, J. P. (1996). *Educational research: An introduction.* White Plains, NY: Longman.

Gallagher, T. J. (1995, May-June). A vice-president for corporate governance? *The Corporate Board, 16*(92), 16.

Garen, J. E. (1994). Executive compensation and principal-agent theory. *Journal of Political Economy, 102*(6), 1198.

Gembrowski, S. (1996, April 12). Institutional investors take larger control of companies. *San Diego Daily Transcript.*

Gething, M. (1996). Do we really need criminal and civil penalties for contraventions of directors' duties? *Australian Business Law Review, 24*(5), 375-390.

Goforth, C. (1994). Proxy reform as a means of increasing shareholder participation in corporate governance: Too little, but not too late. *American University Law Review, 43,* 379-465.

Golden, B. R., & Zajac, E. J. (2001). When will boards influence strategy? *Strategic Management Journal, 22,* 1087-1111.

Gomez-Mejia, L. R. (1994). Executive compensation: A reassessment and a future research agenda. In K. M. Rowland & G. R. Ferris (Eds.), *Research in Personnel and Human Resources Management, 12,* 161-222.

Gomez-Mejia, L. R., & Wiseman, R. (1997). Reframing executive compensation: An assessment and outlook. *Journal of Management 23*(3): 291-374.

Goodstein, J. & Boeker, W. (1991). Turbulence at the top: A new perspective on governance structure changes and strategic change. *Academy of Management Journal, 34*(2), 306-330.

Gordon, J. N. (1994). Institutions as relational investors: A new look at cumulative voting. *Columbia Law Review, 94,* 124-181.

Gordon, L. A., & Pound, J. (1993, January 11). Active investing in the U.S. equity market: Past performance and future prospects. Paper presented to the Board. Retrieved January 13, 2004, from http://www.governancematters.com/

Greeno, J. L. (1993). The director as environmental steward. *Directors & Boards, 18*(1), 17-22.

Gugler, K. (Ed.). (2001). *Corporate governance and economic performance.* Oxford, England: Oxford University Press.

Guy, J. W. (1994). *How to invest someone else's money.* New York: Irwin Professional.

Hamill, John. (1996). In pursuit of boardroom diversity. *Boston Business Journal, 16*(18), 26.

Hammer, M. (1997). *Beyond the end of management.* New York: Gibson.

Hammer, M., & Champy, J. (1993). *Re-engineering the corporation: A manifesto for business revolution.* New York: HarperBusiness.

Handy, C. (1990). *The age of unreason.* Boston: Harvard Business School Press.

Handy, C. (1996). *The gods of management.* New York: Oxford University Press.

Handy, C. (1997). *Finding sense in uncertainty.* New York: Gibson.

Hangstefer, J. B. (1997). *Creating and sustaining company growth: An entrepreneurial perspective for established companies.* Waltham, MA: Burton-Merrill.

Hartocollis, A. (2006, May 13). Ex-Tyco chief to settle tax evasion charges. *New York Times.* Retrieved May 17, 2006, from http://www.nytimes.com/

Hawley, J. P., Williams, A. T., & Miller, J. U. (1994, Fall). Getting the herd to run: Shareholder activism at the California Employees' Retirement System. *Business and the Contemporary World, 11,* 12.

Heidrick, R. L. (1996). Good corporate directors don't grow on trees--Here's how to plan for succession. *Directorship, 22*(6), 12-15.

Henwood, D. (1997). *Wall Street.* New York: Verso.

Hilsenrath, J. E. (1998, October 26). Evolution not revolution: Corporate governance is not being transformed by Asia's crisis nearly as quickly as some had expected: Maybe investors have themselves to blame. *The Asian Wall Street Journal,* p. S4.

Holstein, W. J. (2004, April 25). Office space: Armchair M.B.A.; Smoothing the way to a new C.E.O. *New York Times.*

Houle, C. O. (1989). *Governing boards: Their nature and nurture.* San Francisco: Jossey-Bass.

How leaders meet top challenges. (1997, June). *Association Management, 49*(6), 134-136.

How one woman manages in world of male directors. (1997, November 25). *Wall Street Journal,* pp. B1, B7.

Howe, F. (1995). *Welcome to the board: Your guide to effective participation.* San Francisco: Jossey-Bass.

HP replaces CEO. (2005, February 9). *WebProNews.* Retrieved June 8, 2006, from http://www.webpronews.com/

Hwang, S. (1993, August 23). Fired Tambrands CEO was unusually close to a consulting firm. *Wall Street Journal,* p. A1.

Hymowitz, C., & Lublin, J. (2004, April 20). McDonald's CEO tragedy holds lessons. *Wall Street Journal, Dow Jones.*

Ingrassia, P. (1994, November 23). Memo to board: Management isn't always wrong. *Wall Street Journal,* p. A14.

Interdependence, stock ownership key to corporate governance. (2003, January 6). *Corporate Governance Report.*

Internal Revenue Service. (1993, December 20). Disallowance of deductions for employee remuneration in excess of $1,000,000. Federal Register (58 FR66310, EE-61-93). Washington, DC: Government Printing Office.

Investment Responsibility Research Center. (2002). Board practices, board pay. Available from http://www.irrc.org/

It's tough keeping track of all those do's and don'ts. (1997, October). *Director's Alert, 1*(10), 8-9.

Iwata, E. (2004, March 16). To split or not to split? *USA Today.* Retrieved June 4, 2006, from http://www.usatoday.com/

Jackson, T., & Lewis, W. (1995, June 19). Call to pay U.S. directors in stock. *Financial Times,* p. 3.

Jacobs, M. T. (1991). *Short-term America: The causes and cures of our business myopia.* Boston: Harvard Business School Press.

Jakiwczyk, R. A. (1996). Essays on corporate governance and control. Unpublished doctoral dissertation, Harvard University, Boston, Massachusetts.

Jensen, M., & Meckling, W. (1976). Theory of the firm: Managerial behaviour, agency costs and ownership structure, *Journal of Financial Economics, 3,* 305-360.

Jensen, M. C. (1991). Corporate control and the politics of finance. *Journal of Applied Corporate Finance, 4*(2), 22-30.

Jensen, M. C. (1993). The modern industrial revolution, exit, and the failure of internal control systems. *Journal of Finance, 48*(3), 831-880.

Jensen, M. C. (2000). *A theory of the firm: Governance, residual claims, and organizational forms.* Cambridge, MA: Harvard University Press.

Jensen, M. C., & Murphy, K. J. (1990). CEO incentives: It's not how much you pay, but how. *Harvard Business Review, 90308,* 17.

Jensen, M. C., & Murphy, K. J. (1990). Performance pay and top-management incentives. *Journal of Political Economy, 98*(2), 225-64.

Johnson, C. (2005, July 13). Ebbers gets 25-year sentence for role in WorldCom fraud. *Washingtonpost.com.* Retrieved May 17, 2006, from http://www.washingtonpost.com/

Johnson, D. W. (1996). Globalizing your board. *Directors & Boards, 20*(2), 37-40.

Kane, T., Schaefer, B., & Fraser, A. A. (2004, May 13). Myths and realities: The false crisis of outsourcing. Backgrounder 1757. The *Heritage Foundation: Research: Economy.* Retrieved July 31, 2006, from http://www.heritage.org/Research/Economy/bg1757.cfm#_ftnref9.

Kangas, E. A. (1997, July). 20th anniversary reflections: A new order of things. *Chief Executive, 125,* 32-34.

Kaufman, D. H. (Ed.). (1995). *Japanese corporate governance: A comparative study of systems in Japan and the United States.* New York: The Pacific Institute/The Asia Institute.

Kavanagh, D. (1997). UK court keeps duty of care hurdle high. *International Financial Law Review, 16*(8), 31-32.

Kay, I. T. (1992). *Value at the top: Solution to the executive compensation crisis.* New York: HarperBusiness.

Kay, I. T. (1998). *CEO pay and shareholder value: Helping the U.S. win the global economic war*. New York: St. Lucie Press.

Keasey, K., Thompson, S., & Wright, M. (Eds.). (1997). *Corporate governance: Economic, management, and financial issues*. Oxford, England: Oxford University Press.

Keasey, K., & Wright, M. (Eds.). (1997). *Corporate governance: Responsibilities, risks and remuneration*. New York: John Wiley.

Kelley, K. (1997). *The new biology of business*. New York: Gibson.

Kensinger, J. W., & Martin, J. D. (1996). *Relationship investing: What active institutional investors want from management*. Morristown, NJ: Financial Executives Research Foundation.

Kerr, J., & Bettis, R. A. (1987). Boards of directors, top management compensation, and shareholder returns. *Academy of Management Journal, 30*, 645-664.

Kester, W. C. (1991). *Japanese takeovers: The global contest for corporate control*. Boston: Harvard Business School Press.

Key witnesses in the Enron trial. (2006, May 17). *Washingtonpost.com*. Retrieved May 17, 2006, from http://www.washingtonpost.com/

Kirwin, J. (2004, June 7). EC to set criteria for independent directors. Published by BNA, Inc.

Knepper, W., & Bailey, D. (1985). *Liability of corporate officers and directors*. Charlottesville, VA: Michie.

Knowles, R. G. (1995, February 20). Lawyer urges tough corporate pollution governance. *National Underwriter, 99*(8), 7-8.

Kopinksi, T. C. (2005). Independent board chair proposals get mixed reception. In 2005 postseason report: *Corporate governance at a crossroads*. Rockville, Maryland: Institutional Shareholder Services.

Koretz, G. (1997, November 24.) A boardroom gender gap: Women say they get short shrift. *Business Week, 32*.

Korn, Lester B. (1983, March-April). Board composition and governance: 1973-1982. *The Corporate Board, 9*(49), 20.

Korn/Ferry International. (1996). 23rd annual board of directors study. Board meeting in session. New York: Author.

Korn/Ferry International. (1997). 24th annual board of directors study. Board meeting in session. New York: Author.

Korn/Ferry International. (1998). *Evaluating the board of directors*. Board meeting in session. New York: Author.

Korn/Ferry International. (2006). Korn/Ferry 32nd annual board of directors study: Celebrating three decades of governance analysis. Retrieved July 31, 2006, from http://www.kornferry.com/Library/Process.asp?P=Pubs_Detail&CID=1510&LID=1.

Kotz, R. F. (1998). Technology company boards: In search of a new model. *Directors & Boards, 22*(3), 26-28.

Kozlowski, L. D. (1995). The vitals of accountability. *Directors & Boards, 20*(1), 9-12.

Krantz, M. (2005, February 11). Ousting CEOs often boosts stock price. *USA Today*.

Lambert, R. (1997, September 15). Corporate control. *Financial Times*, p. 22.

Latinos on board. (1998, May 2). *Wall Street Journal*, p. B1.

Lear, R. (1995, December). The hair-shirt director. *Chief Executive*, 12.

Leemputte, P. J., & Benda, P. (1998). High-velocity approach places a premium on opportunities. *Executive Agenda*, 27.

Leone, M. (1996, January). Why utility board membership is changing. *Electrical World*, *210*(1), 62.

Levine, G. (2005, June 20). Adelphia founder John Rigas sentenced to 15 years. *Forbes. com*. Retrieved May 27, 2006, from http://www.forbes.com/facesinthenews/2005/06/20/0620autofacescan10.html.

Levitt, A. (1998). Corporate governance: Integrity in the information age. Remarks presented at Tulane University, New Orleans, Lousiana, March 12, 1998). Retrieved May 30, 2006, from http://www.sec.gov/news/speech/speecharchive/1998/spch206.txt.

Levitt, A. (1998, July-August). The SEC looks at governance. *The Corporate Board*, *19*(111), 1-5.

Lewis, M. (1992, Summer). Give directors restricted stock. *Directors and Boards*, 16.

Lightfoot, R. W., & Kester, C. W. (1992). *Note on corporate governance systems: The United States, Germany, and Japan*. Harvard Business School case no. 292-012. Boston: Harvard Business School Press.

Lipton, M., & Lorsch, J. W. (1992). A modest proposal for improved corporate governance. *The Business Lawyer*, *48*(11), 59.

Listen up. (1996, November 26). *Business Week*. Retrieved November 20, 2000, from www.businessweek.com/

Lohr, S. (1992, April 12). Pulling down the corporate clubhouse. *New York Times*, p. B1.

Longstreth, B. (1990). Takeovers, corporate governance, and stock ownership: Some disquieting trends. *Journal of Portfolio Management*, 54-59.

Loomis, C. J. (2006, June 25). Warren Buffet gives away his fortune. *CNNMoney.com*. Retrieved May 17, 2006, from http://money.cnn.com/

Lorsch, J. W. (1995). Empowering the board. *Harvard Business Review, 95107,* 107-117.

Lorsch, J. W., & Graff, S. (1996). Corporate governance. In_*International encyclopedia of business and management* (IEBM Series, Vol. 1, pp. 772-782). New York: Routledge.

Lorsch, J. W., & MacIver, E. A. (1989). *Pawns and potentates: The reality of America's corporate boards*. Boston: Harvard Business School Press.

Lorsch, J. W., & MacIver, E. A. (1991). Corporate governance and investment time horizons. Unpublished paper, Harvard Business School, Boston, Massachusetts.

Lowenstein, L. (1988). *What's wrong with Wall Street?* Reading, MA: Addison Wesley.

Lublin, J. S. (1991, June 6). More chief executives are being forced out by tougher boards. *Wall Street Journal*, p. A1.

Lublin, J. S. (1992). Shareholders campaign to dilute power of chief executives by splitting top jobs. *Wall Street Journal*, p. B1.

Lublin, June 24, 1997.

Lublin, J. S. (1997, July 3). Investors urge older directors to step down. *Wall Street Journal* (E. E.), p. B1.

Lublin, J. S. (1998, April 15). CalPERS trustees adopt standards for governance. *Wall Street Journal*, p. B2.

Lublin, J. S. (1998, December 4). Major Disney investor scraps calling for greater board independence. *Wall Street Journal*, p. B6.

Lublin, J. S. (2003, July 22). Boardrooms under renovation. *Wall Street Journal*.

Lublin, J. S., & Calian, S. (1998, November 23). Activist pension funds create alliance across Atlantic to press lackluster firms. *Wall Street Journal*, p. A4.

Lucier, C., Schuyt, R., & Tse, E. (2005, Summer). CEO succession 2005: The world's most prominent temp workers. *Strategy+Business, 39*. Reprint No. 05204.

Lucier, C., Spiegel, E., & Schuyt, R. (2005, June 24). Why CEOs fall: The causes and consequences of turnover at the top. Booz Allen Hamilton Report Issue.

Lutton, L. (1997, September 29). Indiana's home Bancorp hangs keep out sign on board. *American Banker, 162*(187), 8.

MacAvoy, P. W. & Millstein, I. M. (2003). The recurrent crisis in corporate governance. New York: Palgrave Macmillan.

MacLeod, H. (1995, August 23). Company directors balance perks and suits. *Journal of Commerce and Commercial, 405*(28544), p. 1A.

Magnet, M. (1992). Directors, wake up! *Fortune* (June 15): 85-92.

Mahoney, W. F. (1993). *The active shareholder: Exercising your rights, increasing your profits, and minimizing your risks.* New York: John Wiley.

March, J. G., & Olsen, J. P. (1989). *Rediscovering institutions: The organizational basis of politics.* New York: Free Press.

Marcus, B. (1992, October). How directors mind the store at Home Depot. *Directorship, 42*(10), 1.

Markoff, J. (1997, October 6). Microsoft is the latest target of Nader's consumer crusade. *New York Times,* pp. D1, D10.

Mastellone, C., Monteiro N., & Piers, M. (1997, March). Directors' and officers' liability, Pt. 4. *International Commercial Litigation, 17,* 14-17.

Maw, N. G. (1994). *Maw on corporate governance.* Aldershot, New York: Dartmouth.

McCullagh, D. (2000, January 10). AOL, Time Warner to merge. *Lycos Wired News.* Retrieved August 1, 2006, from http://www.wired.com/

McKinsey & Company. (n.d.). Governance beyond the board: Interview with Paul Coombes. *Managing in Turbulent Times.* Retrieved July 18, 2006, from http://www.mckinsey.com/ideas/MITT/govbeyondboard/

McKinsey & Company. (2002). *Global Investor Opinion Survey: Key Findings.* New York: Author. Retrieved July 27, 2006, from http://www.mckinsey.com/

Meyer, P. (1997). *CEO pay: A comprehensive look.* Scottsdale, Arizona: American Compensation Association.

Millstein, I. (1993, November). Advising a CEO on boardroom relations. *American Lawyer,* 87.

Millstein, I. (1993, November). Globalizing governance guidelines: Proposed new standards from OECD. *Directorship, 23*(10), 1.

Millstein, I. (1998). *Corporate governance: Improving competitiveness and access to capital in global markets.* New York: Organization for Economic Cooperation and Development (OECD).

Monks, R. (1992, April 3). *Letter to Exxon shareholder: 1992 Exxon proxy statement.* New Jersey: Author.

Monks, R. (1995, Spring). Shareholders and director selection. *Directors and Boards,* 10.

Monks, R. A. G. (1996). The American corporation at the end of the twentieth century: An outline of ownership based governance. Speech given at Cambridge University, July, 1996. Retrieved May 27, 2006, from http://www.lens-library.com/info/cambridge.html.

Monks, R., & Minow, N. (1995). *Corporate governance.* Cambridge, MA: Blackwell.

Monks, R., & Minow, N. (1996). *Watching the watchers: Corporate governance for the 21st century.* Cambridge, MA: Blackwell.

Morgenson, G. (2004, April 20). Cendent chief takes pay cut. *New York Times.* Retrieved July 12, 2006, from http://www.nytimes.com.

NAACP takes directors to task. (1997, February). *Directors Alert, 1*(9), 2.

Nadler, D. A., Behan, B. A., & Nadler, M. B. (Eds.). (2005). *Building better boards: A blueprint for effective governance.* San Francisco: Jossey-Bass.

Nadler, P. (1995, October 24). Question of making board take the long-term view proves hard to pin down. *American Banker, 160*(205), 7.

National Association of Corporate Directors. (1993). *Report of the NACD blue ribbon commission on executive compensation guidelines for corporate directors.* Washington, DC: Author.

National Association of Corporate Directors. (1996). *Putting board evaluation to work.* Washington, DC: Author.

National Association of Corporate Directors. (1996). *Report of the NACD blue ribbon commission on executive compensation guidelines for corporate directors.* Washington, DC: Author.

Neidert, D. (1996, May-June). 19th Century Boards Operating in a 21st Century world. *Nonprofit World, 14*(3), 17-19.

New expectations for directors. (1996, November 26). *Business Week.* Retrieved from: http://www.businessweek.com.

New York Stock Exchange. (1990). *New York Stock Exchange fact book.* New York: Author.

New York Stock Exchange. (1992). *New York Stock Exchange fact book.* New York: Author.

Nobles, M. E. (2006, March 27). Houston, we have a comeback: Nonprofits crawling out of Enron hole. *NonProfit Times.* Retrieved August 18, 2006, from http://www.nptimes.com/

Norton, T. J. (1942). *The Constitution of the United States: Its sources and its applications.* New York: World Press.

Novak, M. (1996). *The future of the corporation.* Washington, DC: AEI Press.

Nussbaum, C. G., & Cummings, T. B. (2005, August 17). Decision in Walt Disney shareholder derivative suit criticizes but protects compensation decision of directors under business judgment rule. *Nixon Peabody LLD Corporate Responsibility Alert.* Retrieved July 12, 2005, from http://www.nixonpeabody.com/publications_detail3. asp?Type=P&PAID=&ID=1080.

Ocasio, W. (1999). Institutionalized action and corporate governance: The reliance on rules of CEO succession. *Administrative Science Quarterly, 44,* 384-416.

O'Hara, T. (2006, July 27). SEC rules tightened on pay disclosure. *WashingtonPost.com.* Retrieved August 5, 2006, from http://washingtonpost.com/

Oliver, R. (n.d.). The push towards greater independence for boards of directors doesn't relieve the board's important role in formation of corporate strategy. *Corporate Governance.*

O'Reilly, C. A., III, & Chatman, J. (1986). Organizational commitment and psychological attachment: The effects of compliance, identification, and internalization on prosocial behavior. *Journal of Applied Psychology, 71,* 492-499.

Orlikoff, J. (1998). Seven practices of super boards. *Association Management, 50*(1), 52.

Orlikoff, J. E., & Totten, M. K. (1997, January). Board job descriptions. *Trustee, 50*(1), 15-24.

Pasha, S. (2006, July 5). Enron founder Ken Lay dies. *CNNMoney.com.* Retrieved August 1, 2006, from http://money.cnn.com/

Pennings, J. M. (1980). *Interlocking directorates: Origins and consequences of connections among organizations' boards of directors.* San Francisco: Jossey-Bass.

Pereira, P., & O'Heir, J. (1996, September 2). Ingram taps Stead to lead global push: Beats 17 others for CEO. *Computer Reseller News,* p. 164.

Pew Research Center for the People & the Press. (2002, February 25). The new investor class. [Table.] *Business Week.* Retrieved August 18, 2002, from http://www.businessweek. com/

Pic, J. J. (1995). *Europe's diverse corporate boards: How they differ from each other and the U.S.* San Francisco: Spencer Stuart Executive Search Consultants.

Plender, J. (1997). *A stake in the future: The stake holding solution.* London: Nicholas Brealey.

Plender, J. (1996, February 1). Investors eager to call the tune. *Financial Times,* p. 35.

Porter, M. (1992, June). *Capital choices: Changing the way America invests in industry.* Research report to the Council on Competitiveness, Boston, Massachusetts.

Porter, M. E. (1996). What is Strategy? *Harvard Business Review 96608,* 61-78.

Pound, J. (1995). The promise of the governed corporation. *Harvard Business Review, 73*(2), 89-98.

Power of corporate boards. (1997, September 29). *Business Week,* 10.

Pozen, R. C. (1994). Institutional investors: The reluctant activists. *Harvard Business Review,* 94111, 140-149.

President's Corporate Fraud Task Force. (2002). United States Department of Justice, Office of the Deputy Attorney General, Corporate Fraud Task Force. Retrieved May 20, 2006, from http://www.usdoj.gov/dag/cftf/

Putting board evaluation to work. (1998, March-April). *The Corporate Board, 19*(109), 22.

Quinn, R., & Lees, P. (1984). Attraction and harassment: Dynamics of sexual politics. *Organizational Dynamics, 13*(3), 13-46.

Ratner, D. L. (1978). *Institutional investors. Teaching materials.* Mineola, NY: The Foundation Press.

Rechner, P. L. (1986). Corporate governance, shareholder wealth, and financial performance: A four-wave longitudinal assessment. Unpublished doctoral dissertation, Indiana University.

Rechner, P. L., & Dalton, D. R. (1991). CEO duality and organizational performance: A longitudinal analysis. *Strategic Management Journal, 12*, 120, 155-160.

Reinganum, J. F. (1985). Innovation and industry evolution. *Quarterly Journal of Economics, 100*, 81-99.

Reingold, J., Borrus, A., & Hammonds, K. H. (1997, May 12). Even executives are wincing at executive pay: Many say it's too high, though they're not as mad as the public. *Business Week*, 3526; 40.

Reingold, J., Melcher, R., & McWilliams, G. (1998, April 20). Executive pay: Stock options plus a bull market made a mockery of many attempts to link pay to performance. *Business Week, 3574*, 2.

Rezaee, Z., Szendi, J. Z., & Aggarwal, R. (1995). Corporate governance and accountability for environmental concerns. *Managerial Auditing Journal, 10*(8), 27-33.

Rhoads, C. (1995, August 9). New breed of directors is tougher, harder to keep. *American Banker*, 8.

Rich, J. (1998). Find a way to grow. *Perspectives, 8*(2), 6. Sibson and Company.

Roberts, H., & Owen, L. L. P. (2004, December 3). Not as independent as you thought? *HRO Alert*. Retrieved July 18, 2006, from http://www.hro.com/

Robinson, F., & Chou Pauze, C. (1997, September). What is a board's liability for not adopting a compliance program? *Health-care Financial Management, 51*(9), 64. (Infotrac Article No. A20076545).

Romero, S. (2006, January 25). Hard times haunt Enron's ex-workers: Few find jobs of equal stature years after company's collapse. *New York Times* (Late Edition), p. C1.

Rovet, E. (1993, October). Making sense of due diligence. *CA Magazine, 126*(9), 55-57.

Russell Reynolds Associates. (1998a, March). *1997-1998 board compensation survey: A companion volume to the 1997-1998 board practices survey*. New York: Author.

Russell Reynolds Associates. (1998b, March). *1997-1998 board practices survey: The structure and compensation of boards of directors at S&P 1500 companies*. New York: Author.

Saidel, J. R. (1991). Resource interdependence: The relationship between state agencies and nonprofit organizations. *Public Administration Review 51*, 543-53.

Salmon, W. (1993). Crisis prevention: How to gear up your board. *Harvard Business Review, 93106*, 69.

Sarnoff, N. (2003, August 22). Granite soliciting bidders for now-famous Enron building. *Houston Business Journal.* Retrieved August 17, 2006, from http://www.bizjoiurnals. com/houston/

Sassalos, S. C. (1994). Three essays in corporate governance and control. Unpublished doctoral dissertation, University of California, Berkeley.

Schroeder, M. (2003, July). Corporate reform: The first year: Cleaner living, no easy riches; Critics say Sarbanes-Oxley law hobbles stocks, chills risk taking, but upshot is far less dramatic. *Wall Street Journal* (E. E.).

SEC proposes disclosure rules on directors' nominations. (2003, September 1). *Corporate Governance Report.*

Sevick, M., & Tufano, P. (1997). Board structure and fee-setting in the U.S. mutual fund industry. *Journal of Financial Economics, 46*(3), 321.

Shiller, R. J. (1992). *Who's minding the store? The report of the Twentieth Century Fund Task Force on market speculation and corporate governance.* New York: The Twentieth Century Fund Press.

Shleifer, A., & Vishny, R. (1986). Large shareholders and corporate control. *Journal of Political Economy, 94, 461-488.*

Sifonis, J. G., & Goldberg, B. (1996). *Corporation on a tightrope balancing leadership, governance, and technology in an age of complexity.* Oxford, England: Oxford University Press.

Significant data for directors 1999: Board policies and governance trends. (1999, January). *Directorship, 1*(1), 3.

Slywotzky, A. J. (1996). *Value migration: How to think several moves ahead of the competition.* Boston: Harvard Business School Press.

Smale to leave GM after turnaround. (1999, November 3). *Cincinnati Post.* Retrieved from http://news.cincypost.com/

Smale will stay on GM board beyond age 70. (1997, December 22). *Wall Street Journal,* pp. B1, B11.

Smith, A. (1937). *The wealth of nations.* New York: Random House.

Smith, P. (1997, April). Company directors and environmental offenses. *Management Accounting, 75*(4), 46-47.

Solomon, D. (2003, October 3). SEC faces criticism of board-of-director proposal. *Wall Street Journal,* p. C5.

Solomon, D. (2004, April 4). Loophole limits independence. *Wall Street Journal,* p. C1.

Sommer, A. A., Jr. (1991). *Whom should the corporation serve? The Berle-Dodd debate revisited sixty years later.* Delaware: J. Corp.

Sorensen, O. (1997). Board size, composition, and maintenance. *The Corporate Board, 18*(107), 32.

Spencer Stuart Executive Search Consultants. (1994). *Board trends and practices at major American corporations. 1994 Board Index.* San Francisco: Author.

Spencer Stuart Executive Search Consultants. (1996). *Board trends and practices at major American corporations. 1996 Board Index.* San Francisco: Author.

Spencer Stuart Executive Search Consultants. (1997). *Board trends and practices at S&P 500 corporations. 1997 Board Index.* San Francisco: Author.

Spencer Stuart Executive Search Consultants. (1997). *Technology boards of directors: 1997 survey by Spencer Stuart's Global High-Technology Practice.* San Francisco: Author.

Spencer Stuart Executive Search Consultants. (1998). *Board trends and practices at S&P 500 corporations. 1998 Board Index.* San Francisco: Author.

Spencer Stuart Executive Search Consultants. (2004). Spencer Stuart board index, 2004. Retrieved August 3, 2006, from http://content.spencerstuart.com/sswebsite/pdf/lib/SSBI-2004.pdf.

Spencer Stuart Executive Search Consultants. (2006). 2006 board diversity report. San Francisco: Author. Retrieved August 2, 2006, from http://content.spencerstuart.com/sswebsite/pdf/lib/Board_Diversity_Report_2006.pdf.

Sproull, N. L. (1995). *Handbook of research methods: A guide for practitioners and students in the social sciences.* Metuchen, New Jersey: Scarecrow Press.

Stapledon, G. P. (1996). *Institutional shareholders and corporate governance.* Oxford, England: Clarendon Press.

Stern, P. G. (1996). The power and the process. *Directors & Boards, 21*(1), 113.

Stewart, T. (1993). The king is dead. *Fortune, 34,* 40.

Sundaramurthy, C., & Rechner, P. (1997, March). Conflicting shareholder interests: An empirical analysis of fair price provisions. *Business and Society, 36,*(1), 73.

Survey: CEO compensation jumps 30% in 2004. (2005, October 31). *USATODAY.com.* Retrieved May 26, 2006, from http://www.usatoday.com/

Swanson, A. (1992). *Building a better board: A guide to effective leadership.* Rockville, MD: Fund Raising Institute.

Technology company boards: In search of the differences. (1998). *Directors & Boards, 22*(3), 29-31.

Teslik, S. (1993, August). The governance of Oozcskblnya. *CII Central Newsletter for the Council of Institutional Investors, 6,* 8.

Thain, D. H., & Leighton, D. S. R. (1994). Effective director dissent. *Business Quarterly, 58*(4), 34-48.

Thurman, L. G. (1990). The board of directors: An exploratory study of the corporate governance process behind boardroom doors. Unpublished doctoral dissertation, United States International University, San Diego, CA.

TIAA-CREF. (1993, September). *Policy statement on corporate governance.* New York: Author.

TIAA-CREF. (2003, January 1). TIAA-CREF supports SEC proxy disclosure proposal: Introduction and background. *TIAA-CREF Web Center/Siteline.* Retrieved May 25, 2006, from http://www.tiaa-cref.org/siteline/

Tichy, N. M., & Cohen, E. (1997). *The leadership engine: How winning companies build leaders at every level.* New York: HarperBusiness.

Tosi, H. L., Werner, S., Katz, J. P., & Gomez-Mejia, L. R. (2000). How much does performance matter? A meta-analysis of CEO pay studies. *Journal of Management, 26,* 301-339.

Townley, P. (1993). Accountable, but to whom? *Across the Board, 30*(8), 11-12.

Tricker, R. I. (1994). *International corporate governance: Text, readings and cases.* New York: Prentice Hall.

Under pressure. (1995, October). *CA Magazine, 99*(1071), 41. (Infotrac Article No. A17706010).

U.S. Department of Justice. (2004, July 8). Former Enron chairman and chief executive officer Kenneth L. Lay charged with conspiracy, fraud, false statements. [Press Release]. Washington, DC: Author. Retrieved August 17, 2006, from http://www.usdoj.gov/

U.S. Department of Labor, Bureau of Labor Statistics. (2003). *Occupational outlook handbook: Tomorrow's jobs.* Retrieved July 6, 2006, from http://www.bis.gov/oco/oco2003.htm.

U.S. Securities and Exchange Commission. (2004, January 14). SEC settles civil fraud charges filed against Andrew S. Fastow, former Enron chief financial officer. Litigation Release No. 18543.

U.S. Securities and Exchange Commission. (2004, December 7). Registration under the Advisers Act of certain hedge fund advisers. [Release No. IA-2333; File No. S7-30-04]. (RIN 3235-AJ25). Washington, DC: Author. Retrieved July 31, 2006, from http://www.sec.gov/rules/final/ia-2333.htm.

Vance, S. (1983). *Corporate leadership, boards, directors, and strategy.* New York: McGraw Hill.

Varallo, G., & Dreisbach, D. A. (1996). *Fundamentals of corporate governance: A guide for directors and corporate counsel.* Chicago: American Bar Association.

Veasey, E. N. (2004). Musings From the center of the corporate universe. Remarks made at Section of Business Law Luncheon, American Bar Association Annual Meeting, August 9, 2004, Atlanta, Georgia.

Veasey, E. N. (2004, November). Juxtaposing best practices and Delaware corporate jurisprudence—part II. *The Metropolitan Corporate Counsel,* p. 46.

Verstegen R., L., & Buchholtz, A. K. (2001). Trust, risk, and shareholder decision-making: An investor perspective on corporate governance. *Business Ethics Quarterly. 11*: 177-193.

Vickers, M., McNamee, M., Coy, P. Henry, D., Thornton, E., & Der Hovanesian, M. (2002, February 25). The betrayed investor. *Business Week.* Retrieved August 18, 2006, from http://www.businessweek.com/

Vogel, D. (1998). *Lobbying the corporation.* New York: Basic.

Wall Street project (1997, Sept). *Directors Alert, 1*(9).

Walsh & Seward, l990.

Ward, R. D. (1997). *21st century corporate board.* New York: John Wiley.

Warner, J., Watts, R., & Wruck, K. (1988). Stock prices and top management. *Journal of Financial Economics, 20,* 431-460.

Warner, M. (1996). Corporate governance. *International encyclopedia of business and management*, (IEBM Series, Vol. 1, 777.) New York: Routledge.

Wayne, L. (1993, February 3). Assuaging investor discontent. *New York Times*, p. D1.

Wealthy crusaders combat CEO pay. (1999, February). *Directors Alert, 3*(2), 2.

Weidenbaum, M. (1994). *The evolving corporate board.* St. Louis, MO: Washington University Center for the Study of American Business.

Wharton, C.R., Lorsch, J.W., & Hanson, L. (1991, November-December). Advice and dissent: Rating the corporate governance compact. *Harvard Business Review, 91603,* 139.

What the best boards do. (1996, November 26). *Business Week.* Retrieved from http://www.businessweek.com/

White, B. (2004, May 26). Grasso, Sptizer take it personal. *WashingtonPost.com.* Retrieved August 5, 2006, from http://www.washingtonpost.com.

Whiting, B. G. (1990). *Knights and knaves of corporate boardrooms.* Buffalo, NY: Bearly.

Whiting, R. (2004, January 19). Ellison now only CEO. *Information Week.* Retrieved June 4, 2006, from http://www.informationweek.com/

Why corporate governance today? (1995, August 14). *California Public Employees' Retirement System, 1.*

Wiersema, M., & Bantel, K. Top management team turnover as an adaptation mechanism: The role of the environment. *Strategic Management Journal, 14,* 485–504.

Williams, H. M., Shapiro, I. S. (1979). *Power and accountability: The changing role of the corporate board of directors.* New York: Carnegie-Mellon University Press.

Williams, K. (1995, February). Environmental issues take top priority. *Management Accounting, 76*(8), 18.

Winners and losers in Enron's demise. (2001, November 29). *Fox News.* Retrieved August 18, 2006, from http://www.foxnews.com.

Women at the top: A scorecard. (1998, November 23). *Business Week, 3605,* 83.

Wray, C. (2005, February). Prosecuting corporate crimes. *eJournal USA.* Retrieved May 26, 2006, from http://usinfo.state.gov/journals/ites/0205/ijee/wray.htm.

Zuppone, 2003.

Index

The letter *f* or *n* following a page number denotes a figure or note on that page.